Praise for *Fury*

"A frank, personal dissection of anger and its cultural implications."
—*The Dallas Morning News*

"Another raw, memorable chronicle of emotional recovery . . . an intimate, lyrical portrait of a young woman's discovery of love and understanding."
—*Booklist*

"Zailckas deconstructs the meaning of anger to make it less intimidating."
—Associated Press

"Fastidiously researched and a compelling read about an emotion few people, even fewer women, care to acknowledge or discuss."
—entertainmentrealm.com

"[Zailckas's] sharp sense of self-deprication, while comically dark, passes far beyond the boundaries of humor into a terrain of frank, and often brutal, self-assessment. Throughout, Zailckas is keenly aware of her inability to cope with anger. . . . A harrowing tale of one woman's journey into the depths of her own psychosis."
—*Kirkus Reviews*

"An intriguing and often heartbreaking follow-up on uncovering—and embracing—her anger. Zailckas is at her most blisteringly honest when she's trying to wrap her head around her complex and often-strained relationship with her mother."
—*Publishers Weekly*

Selected Praise for *Smashed*

"A mortifyingly credible story." —Janet Maslin, *The New York Times*

"Poised and elegiac . . . *Smashed* goes down with a slow, genteel burn."
—Dwight Garner, *The New York Times Book Review*

"This may be one of the best accounts of addiction, let along the college experience, or even what it means to be an average teenage girl in America. . . . While *Smashed* boasts important insight and information, this fine young writer's greatest gift is her gripping, vivid storytelling. A." —*Entertainment Weekly*

"The story's power lies not in Zailckas's crises but in her candor. Focusing less on the shock value of her experience than on how sadly common it is among her peers, she relays every detail of her desperation with subtle wit and refreshing insight. With so many troubled teens becoming authors lately, bookstores are flooded with boozy bios by former girls gone wild. This one rises to the top."
—*People*

"Even with all the studies on the topic, *Smashed* seems to offer the best examination of the relationship between women and alcohol in a clear and brilliant way. Zailckas's honest voice and journalistic eye for detail lift the veil off this lifestyle and show what a universal experience it can be for some women." —Associated Press

"Haunting . . . [Zailckas is] a talented new writer—and well worth watching and encouraging." —*The Dallas Morning News*

"Brilliant and horrifying." —*The Baltimore Sun*

PENGUIN BOOKS

FURY

Koren Zailckas's memoir *Smashed: Story of a Drunken Girlhood* appeared on ten national bestseller lists and spent twenty weeks on the *New York Times* bestseller list. She lives in Brooklyn, New York, with her husband and daughter.

KOREN ZAILCKAS

True Tales of a Good Girl Gone Ballistic

Fury

PENGUIN BOOKS

PENGUIN BOOKS
Published by the Penguin Group
Penguin Group (USA) Inc., 375 Hudson Street, New York, New York 10014, U.S.A. · Penguin Group
(Canada), 90 Eglinton Avenue East, Suite 700, Toronto, Ontario, Canada M4P 2Y3 (a division of Pearson
Penguin Canada Inc.) · Penguin Books Ltd, 80 Strand, London WC2R 0RL, England · Penguin Ireland,
25 St. Stephen's Green, Dublin 2, Ireland (a division of Penguin Books Ltd) · Penguin Books Australia Ltd,
250 Camberwell Road, Camberwell, Victoria 3124, Australia (a division of Pearson Australia Group
Pty Ltd) · Penguin Books India Pvt Ltd, 11 Community Centre, Panchsheel Park, New Delhi – 110 017,
India · Penguin Group (NZ), 67 Apollo Drive, Rosedale, Auckland 0632, New Zealand (a division of
Pearson New Zealand Ltd) · Penguin Books (South Africa) (Pty) Ltd, 24 Sturdee Avenue, Rosebank,
Johannesburg 2196, South Africa

Penguin Books Ltd, Registered Offices: 80 Strand, London WC2R 0RL, England

First published in the United States of America by Viking Penguin,
a member of Penguin Group (USA) Inc. 2010
Published with a new introduction and additional back matter in Penguin Books 2012

10 9 8 7 6 5 4 3 2 1

Grateful acknowledgment is made for permission to reprint excerpts from the following copyrighted works:
"Mine enemy is growing old" from *The Poems of Emily Dickinson*, Thomas H. Johnson, ed., Cambridge,
Mass.: The Belknap Press of Harvard University Press. Copyright © 1951, 1955, 1979, 1983 by the President
and Fellows of Harvard College. Reprinted by permission of the publishers and the Trustees of Amherst
College.
   Diary by Chuck Palahniuk. Copyright © 2003 by Chuck Palahniuk. Used by permission of Doubleday,
a division of Random House, Inc.
   Seneca: Volume I, Loeb Classical Library Volume 214, translated by John W. Basore, Cambridge, Mass.:
Harvard University Press. Copyright © 1928 by the President and Fellows of Harvard College. Reprinted by
permission of the publishers and the Trustees of the Loeb Classical Library. Loeb Classical Library® is a
registered trademark of the President and Fellows of Harvard College.
   A Field Guide to Getting Lost by Rebecca Solnit. Copyright © Rebecca Solnit, 2005. Used by permission
of Viking Penguin, a member of Penguin Group (USA) Inc.

THE LIBRARY OF CONGRESS HAS CATALOGED THE HARDCOVER EDITION AS FOLLOWS:
Zailckas, Koren.
   Fury : a memoir / Koren Zailckas.
      p. cm.
   Continues: Smashed. New York : Viking, 2005.
   ISBN 978-0-670-02230-4 (hc.)
   ISBN 978-0-14-312037-7 (pbk.)
   1. Zailckas, Koren. 2. Anger—Case studies. 3. Zailckas, Koren—Relations
with men. 4. Separation (Psychology)—Case studies. 5. Zailckas, Koren—
Family. 6. Young women—United States--Biography. 7. Buddhism—Miscellanea.
   I. Zailckas, Koren. Smashed. II. Title.
B F575.A5Z35 2010
   818'.603—dc22
[B]   2010005319

Printed in the United States of America
Designed by Carla Bolte • Set in Warnock Light

*Penguin is committed to publishing works of quality and integrity. In that spirit, we are proud to offer this book
to our readers; however, the story, the experiences, and the words are the author's alone.*

ALWAYS LEARNING   PEARSON

Anger as soon as fed is dead—
Tis starving makes it fat.

—EMILY DICKINSON, "Mine Enemy Is Growing Old"

CONTENTS

One bleary-eyed morning when I was twenty-three, I awoke with ashtray breath, a headache that felt more like a grade-III concussion, and a sneaking suspicion that I'd humiliated myself the evening before. As far as weekends go, this was no aberration. I'd spent nearly every Sunday morning—dating as far back as high school graduation—with a dizzying blood alcohol content and the same liver-curling feel of guilt. HANGOVERS, read the novelty T-shirt balled up on my bedroom floor, THE ANNOYING PERIODS BETWEEN IN-EBRIATION. I remedied my delicate condition by closing the blinds, chasing three aspirin with a cup of stale coffee, and repeating an oft-pledged vow to quit drinking completely. Only this time a stunning thing happened. Those first feeble days of abstinence quickly became whole boozeless years. At last I made good on that hasty, nausea-induced promise.

When I wrote my first memoir, *Smashed,* I was living in a ratty studio apartment in Alphabet City that I'm positive was never intended to be a halfway house for recovering binge-drinkers. If anything, the building was a monument to depravity, having enjoyed previous lives as an illegal nightclub, a stash house for mannite (a substance used to cut cocaine and heroin), and the makeshift studio where the Bad Brains and the Beastie Boys laid down their early recordings.

On a typical night, the surrounding neighborhood was a playground for the drunk and disorderly. Four stories below, dive-bar patrons squatted to pee between parked cars. One story above, my

NYU-student-neighbors could be found in the throes of another midterm party, their empty Pabst cans keeling down the fire escape. The nagging bass line of their stereo didn't let up until TV infomercials gave way to the 5 A.M. news.

Even so, I cleaned up my act from that unlikely locale. For the first time ever I was serious about sobriety. I suspected teenage boozing had stunted me. Socially and emotionally, I still felt fourteen— incidentally, the age when I'd had my first drink. A decade later, I still hadn't the foggiest clue how to express romantic interest short of slurring sweet nothings in some poor boy's ear. I didn't know how to bond with a friend unless I was holding her hair while she chundered on a street curb. I was unclear what to do with my hands at a party unless I was holding a drink (if not two). I wanted to 'fess up, grow up, wise up, and mature to my chronological age. So as a rowdy party swirled around me, I found myself seduced by the calm at the eye of the storm, reflecting honestly on the way alcohol had shaped my entry to adulthood.

In those early days of sobriety, a lot of recollections scudded back to me, but most chilling was the memory of waking up from a blackout in my childhood bed and discovering, with a cold bolt of horror, that I was wearing a hospital gown. I was sixteen at the time, and that razor-close call was one of the seminal moments in my less-than-happy adolescence. To quote my father (himself quoting the ER doctor), just a few more slugs of vodka and I might have died right there on the rickety dock that was the scene of our underage party.

As shocking and terrible as that teenage stomach pumping should have been, I managed not to think on that ordeal much in the years that followed. Back in my drinking days, a slew of defense mechanisms kept me from revisiting the awkward family breakfast the morning after the grave event: my mother had bawled, my father had been hauntingly silent, and I had senselessly tried to hide the hospital ID bracelet on my wrist. Although I rarely thought of the incident in my drinking days, I became fixated on it in abstinence.

With a horror that was seven years delayed, I tried to come to terms with that first blackout and all it foretold about my fate as a drinker.

I've only ever been able to make sense of anything by typing written words on a page. Where personal matters are concerned, there's simply a shorter distance between my brain and my keyboard than there is between my brain and my bumbling tongue. Maybe that's because I grew up in a family that welcomed neither emotion nor autonomy. My mother was attentive, but also engulfing—the kind of Italian matriarch who insisted on styling my hair until I left for college and dominating other aspects of my life long after. In childhood, I'd learned that honesty was a virtue best reserved for a locked diary. Confessional writing was cathartic, but the blank page was also one of few places where I could trust my own feelings, desires, and perceptions. Only in writing could my emotional responses safely vary from my mother's reactions. Only by drinking could I drown out the insecurities I'd internalized from her and shirk the ambitions she had in mind for me.

So, in an effort to fully explore the circumstances surrounding my near alcohol poisoning, I wrote about it. But that passage alone failed to explain the full basis and backdrop of my drinking. It didn't even touch on the drinking culture on American college campuses. It didn't account for why girls like me were drinking so much younger and so much more than the many generations of women who'd come before us—a 40 percent increase in binge drinking since 1979, according to the *Journal of the American Academy of Child and Adolescent Psychology.*

To bridge the gap, I continued to write a blue streak. In four short months, I had penned my whole sorry drunkalogue, beginning with my first drink and ending with my very last. I named the book *Smashed.* And driven by a sense of righteous indignation—I didn't agree with news-magazine articles that suggested girls like myself were boozing harder because we were so "liberated," "girl-powered," "sassy," et cetera—I published it. In a stroke of the surreal, the book became an oft-quoted, oft-studied, oft-shared-between-friends and ultracontroversial bestseller.

These days, I'm often asked to weigh in on drink-related issues. Parents want advice for preventing preteen raids on their liquor cabinets, colleges want to know how to keep their campuses free of barf bits and Mardi Gras beads. But I've never fancied myself some kind of recovery guru. Not only do I lack the domineering streak it takes to tell people how they ought to live, but in the years following *Smashed*, I wasn't exactly the portrait of all things smugly self-actualized. Sober? Yes. But even fully reformed, I remained only halfway happy. Years of escapist-style drinking left me feeling dispossessed and unexpectedly vulnerable to a backlog of raw emotions that for so long I'd muted with binge drinking. At first, the success of *Smashed* only exacerbated my instability. Having aired some of my most private misgivings on a national scale, I craved invisibility and withdrew from even my longtime friends. Whatever praise writing earned me only made me feel smaller, and the criticism hurt disproportionately. For purposes of survival, I lulled myself into a robotic existence in which I felt neither full pain nor maximum pleasure.

Don't get me wrong, life wasn't exactly a steaming dog pile. During this same period, I managed to kick binge drinking sans rehab and without admissions of "powerlessness," a success that some of the clinicians who I met while touring for *Smashed* attributed to my not having the "addiction gene."

Free psych assessments are to memoirists what swag is to movie stars, and in addition to the regular groups of young women and mothers who turned up at my book signings, I also tended to draw drug counselors, youth ministers, psychologists, psychiatrists, social workers, and counselors. All of these knowledgeable and compassionate people offered their insights about my hard-drinking past.

"You're lucky," remarked the counselor from the Utah rehabilitation center. "You don't seem to have the addiction gene."

So what *did* I have?

To quote the family therapist at the Connecticut library: "Probably a trauma in childhood or a period of long-term stress. Something that led you to self-soothe and manifest abuse."

This well-meaning woman bent on diagnosing me, and anyone else who brought up questions about early childhood, was met with my deer-in-headlights stare. There were places I wasn't yet ready to venture. When *Smashed* first came out, I made it a point to limit discussions about my family. Ma and Pa Zailckas did not feature prominently in my first memoir. And whenever reviewers cited my "absent and negligent" parents as the cause of my underage drinking, I was quick to e-mail the section editor, hitting him with one of the many sound-bites I'd fashioned about my "ever-present, if not omnipresent, mother" or the way "I had a will to drink, so I found a way to drink." Was my family life cozy? Hardly. But whatever was wrong didn't seem to have a tidy label, and my parents weren't solely to blame. I couldn't say, for instance, I was raised by drug addicts, or schizophrenics, or lupine animals. I knew only that my family felt insular, almost hermetically sealed. The environment at home often fluctuated between incomprehensible rage and an icy indifference that felt like punishment, but I wasn't ready to connect that to my drinking. Despite my private misgivings about some of the choices they'd made, I was fiercely protective of my parents. Criticism of my mother, in particular, riddled me with anxiety. After *Smashed,* TV producers often angled to interview my parents, but I tried my fiercest to keep them separate from most things related to my writing. Exhume my childhood in print? Never. Instead of looking backward, I tried to focus my attention on sobriety.

The first two years of staying sober found me young and embarrassed. I didn't crave alcohol. Walking home through Manhattan on a warm spring evening, I don't ever remember a liquor store calling out to me, at least not in the manner of other guilty pleasures, i.e., soft-serve ice cream, a twelve-dollar bunch of bodega lilacs, or the ruffled sundress spotlit in a boutique window. Still, I was not wholly comfortable with the label non-drinker. Whenever I met up with friends at a bar, or a book party, or a music venue, I worried (irrationally) that all eyes were on the glass of ice water in my hand and feared the (mostly unrealized) moment when a stranger might call on me to explain why I wasn't drinking something harder.

For all the social anxiety of those early years, they were happier and less complicated than the ones that were to follow. In my third year A.D. (after drinking), my emotions boomed, all at once, at high volume. Suddenly I was hit with feelings that my brain was inexperienced at processing and memories that had long ago been muffled by the white noise of binges and blackouts. I'd known, from the time I wrote *Smashed*, that drinking had been the way I numbed out resentment, anxiety, shame, injury, or, conversely, expressed them without inhibition. But even sober, I had little understanding about where these disturbing emotions came from and no clue how to communicate them to the people around me. On good days, the uproar made it difficult to concentrate. On bad ones, I wanted to curl up in the fetal position and weep until reinforcements arrived.

Because my internal world felt scrambled, I spent my fourth year of abstinence on a single-minded hunt for control. Suddenly, it was not enough to have given up alcohol. That was bantam weight. I also swore off meat, dairy, sugar, TV, caffeine, spontaneity, cynicism, and fun. That was the year, twenty-six, when I spent New Year's Eve at a dead-silent group meditation. Only when the clock struck twelve and the New York streets roared with the sound of party poppers and spit-whistling did it occur to me that renunciation and self-denial had become my new addiction.

In my fifth year of sobriety, I set out to write the book you now hold in your hands. In retrospect I see that it began as a manifestation of my defense mechanisms. It was a way of getting close to a subject that frightened me without investing too much of my own emotion in it. I didn't initially set out to write another memoir. Ludicrously, I thought I was writing a journalistic book of essays exploring "American anger" and, later, "female anger." Although I didn't realize it at the time, writing about other people's rage was my way of unconsciously denying the emotion that I found shameful, obscene, and dangerous. By passing it off on the outside world, I could explore the taboo from a safer distance. I persuaded myself that women everywhere have difficulty accessing their anger because an age-old double standard decrees it isn't ladylike or feminine.

And while I remain convinced that many young women grapple with their anger the way that I have, it wasn't until I focused the lens of my study on my own damaged psyche that I started to find the clues I needed to unlock my troubles and find an identity I could be at peace with. I'd poisoned myself with repressed anger, and when drinking was no longer the pressure valve I could release when I was about to explode, I was forced to handle, head on, the toxic sludge that had been building in me.

I experiment with many courses of treatment in the pages that follow. I meditate Zen-monkishly, swig homeopathic remedies, and "vent" in the controlled environment of an anger management retreat. But ultimately, nothing helped me more than talk therapy. A therapist helped me uncover and understand my defense mechanisms, plus she taught me the language that I needed to address conflict and express hurt directly (prior to therapy, that had seemed like Swahili). Initially, conversations about long-harbored resentments felt terrible, but confiding how I felt enabled me to make peace with my past and helped me gather the perspective and grace that I'd need to weather the next difficult conversation. Although romance was never the point, therapy also revealed why I was compulsively drawn to ill-timed relationships and ill-suited partners. It helped me identify my dirty habits—behaviors like expecting men to read my mind and deludedly thinking that I could read theirs— that screwed up relationships with even compatible men and spawned the codependency that led to disappointment.

To this day, I still don't know whether men are more comfortable with their fury than women. Not only is that an unanswerable question, but halfway through my research, I fell in love, had my heart broken, and had to briefly move back to my girlhood home. Metaphorically speaking, I found myself smack dab in the place I've been avoiding all of my life: a kind of emotional North Korea that involved my family, my mother, and my childhood. There, I finally realized the source of my writer's block. The book I sought to write wasn't working because I was actually writing about my own deep-seated issues. I came to the topic because, as an adult, I needed to figure out what I had not learned as a girl: how to express disagreement, how to fight with people, how to be human, flawed, honest. In order to have the life I wanted I finally had to feel the full range of my human emotions.

Fury is a self-referential book because the writing process led me to as many revelations as the kindhearted and perceptive people I met along the way. Ultimately, I wrote this book in the form of a memoir because I hoped it might help others who seesaw, for reasons unknown to them, between compliance and resentment, between stuffing their anger and raging blindly. I only hope this publication might create what *Smashed* once did: a band of people brought together by a shared experience. Sometimes mining the personal helps us unearth the cultural. Sometimes remembering is the only way we can begin to forget.

PROLOGUE *Giving Up the Ghost*

A story without emotion is no story at all. The writer in me knew this. But at twenty-seven, I found myself struggling with an unacknowledged anger-management hitch: Strong emotion wasn't destroying my life so much as my heart-palpitating fear of it.

"Cholerophobic." That's what one shrink called my abnormal and unwarranted fear of getting angry, my persistent state of vanilla-beige. A Web site advertising a "trusted," "effective" treatment for this anger disorder defined it with a salesman's flourish:

> *Cholerophobia is a defense mechanism created by the unconscious mind. At some point in the cholerophobe's past, there was an event linking anger to emotional trauma. Avoiding the emotion means living in fear, missing out on life experiences big and small and living a life that is only a shadow of what it might be.*

I read this with a sharp pinch of despair, knowing that my anger disorder was once reinforced by drinking, an addiction that also prevented me from fully participating in my life. The pages that follow are an account of the continued aftermath of my stunted adolescence. Here is the fallout from the years spent drowning emotion with drink instead of recognizing my feelings, exploring them, and, in doing so, reclaiming my family's particular power to obliterate or redeem me. I didn't set out to write a sequel to *Smashed*, but I have lived without an awareness of my past, and every life crisis dredged up the unexamined aspects of a much older story.

If you hear the echoes of a kid's complaint in these pages it's because this book was born of childhood emotions that never found an exit hatch during the years they might have been less mortifying and marginally more appropriate. Had these feelings come to light then, my blow-ups might have been pertinent, confiding, spontaneous, fleeting. Here, however, my festered anger is frequently accompanied by stupidity, insanity, obscenity. Honesty forces me to cringe and acknowledge these "ire" works instead of making myself more presentable. The truth is: Starved for anger's release, I first howled primitively. Rage-o-phobe turned fury fiend—moderation never really was my thing.

I need to thank my family for vetting this account. In reading this book and its various drafts, they've been privy to the kinds of conversations that usually pass only between a person and her therapist. I'm awed by their bravery and grateful to them for respecting my desire to explore my emotions in this context, for understanding that I can't go on describing myself exclusively in their language and anecdotes. It's like going through life performing a sham accent and dressing in someone else's clothes.

My mother is a powerful presence in my life, and from my childhood I've taken her word on what she occasionally and not always unkindly called my "difficult" disposition. "Born angry." That's what she always said of me. As proof, she describes my colicky infancy. No proffered comfort ever soothed me as a baby, she says, not her arms, a pacifier, or the Moses basket that my handy dad roped from a ceiling beam. Likewise, she's quick to remind me of my preschool years, when fear of separation, fear of strangers, fear of my own stumpy shadow tightened my dimpled arms, nooselike, around her neck.

Lacking my own memories of these early years, I always thought it would be rude to refute the ones that she had to offer. My parents seemed like the archivists of my early history, and I believed what they told me because I thought I had no means to contradict them. My memory doesn't switch on until later in my toddler years, when a fleck of chili pepper settles on my tongue by mistake. And even that first recollection brings to mind emotional Niagaras in line with what they described. I remember stinging outrage, then humiliated panic.

When I acknowledged feeling, I found a way to address the incongruity I always sensed. My folks may remember more from my days in the cradle, but I alone know what I felt as a kid. I was not born ticked off so much as simply born human and, in forbidding myself a full range of human emotions, a more malignant fury took shape. "A bad girl has never been born," wrote Virginia Satir, the famed family therapist. "Only persons with potentials are born. Something in that human being has to be denied, projected, ignored or distorted for her to become some kind of bad, sick, stupid or crazy girl or woman."

Throughout this account, I refer to an unrealized book. This isn't a literary device so much as an honest record of events. The book I was trying to write when I undertook this subject four years ago died on the delivery table for the same reason this record now exists: I set out to write an objective book about modern remedies for anger and I ended up with an achingly personal account of why I went looking for remedies in the first place.

From the first word, this has been an uncanny project. I wrote this book in real time, transcribing many events even as they continued to play themselves out. As the story developed, my progress began to undo my previous work. When I began telling this account, I was hiding behind the same defense mechanisms this story helped me define and forced me to part with. Many times over, writing about anger forced me to break apart my ego, my identity. Within my motivations, I found my memories. Within my memories, my emotions. Within my emotions, my kerneled essence.

I often wonder whether a biological imperative first led me to set these words down. My desire to start a family ignited some pre-occupation with my natural-born one, a drive that is paralleled in nature. When, for example, a female sea turtle (or a salmon) reaches adulthood and finds herself ready to lay, she migrates back to the exact nesting ground where she was born, sometimes swimming thousands of miles to get there. The homing instinct serves an evolutionary purpose. Something worked in that spot. The conditions surrounding her birth and her earliest youth—the tides, the temperature—were good enough to sustain life. She was born, after all, and she survived. She's still here.

During the years described here, I reached a point where my own continued sanity depended on revisiting some dreaded childhood terrain in order to figure out what about the way I was raised didn't work and, also, what did. Flailing in work and disappointed in my relationships, I could either look hard at the unspeakable emotions I'd felt as a kid or they'd continue to blind me to the present moment. All things considered, I was still healthy and young, I had the time to explore and the energy to create, and I couldn't turn away from the chance to figure out how to speak with spontaneity and love with veracity.

For me, longing led me back to my past. I have one man to thank in particular. By rejecting me, he spurred me to root out the difficult emotions I'd buried in the blanched expanse of my youth. There I found not just anger but also gratitude—not only for him, but also for my slippery sister, my gentle father, my impassioned mother, and, most tender days, for my life as it is.

I couldn't connect with humanity until I stopped fighting my own. Here, at last, I surrender to it.

ONE   *Incitement*
───

Lost really has two disparate meanings. Losing things is about the
familiar falling away, getting lost is about the unfamiliar appearing.

—REBECCA SOLNIT, *A Field Guide to Getting Lost*

1

The captain has illuminated the fasten-seat-belt sign. The sky is flashing gray through the tiny, oval windows and the jet engines shiver with turbulence.

For the moment, I'm too distraught to give much notice to anything beyond the TV in the seat back in front of me. I've pinned my gaze to the stupefying channel called "flight map." On the screen, a cartoon plane charts my course over the Atlantic. Each passing hour nudges me farther away from the man and the isle I can't understand, not for all the puddings and mushy peas nor the pages I've thumbed in *British History for Dummies.*

Luggage rattles in the overhead compartments, but I barely notice. The raucous self-abuse in my head is loud too. I'm recounting, martyrly, any vaguely nasty comment anyone's ever directed my way. I'm trying to figure out precisely which character flaw might be responsible for my latest life failure when the gentleman beside me seeks to offer another:

"Girl," he tells me, "you might be the quietest person I ever seen. Cardboard boxes make more noise than you."

Now, I am not a creature who is given to sudden fits of candor. Not in my spoken life, anyway. But because he seems like somebody who's faced some tribulations, I say something like, "I don't mean to be rude, but a man just broke up with me in the worst way, at the worst possible time, and under the worst circumstances in my limited experience. So you'll have to excuse me if I don't feel like talking." I lower my seat back an inch and return my gaze to the screen's flyspeck plane. I go back to doing my best impression of a lobotomized sloth, blanking out with a fleece blanket draped over my chest and a blue-black fog swaddling my brain.

But the old man doesn't seem to have heard me. He describes the sights he saw in London. He tells me about the engagements keeping him from joining his wife on a later flight. He pulls a plastic photo sleeve from his wallet and tries to enchant me with the ordinary miracles of his giggling grandsons.

If I had an ounce of attention for anything outside of my own suffering, I would have cracked a neighborly smile by now. But in this black hole, no human warmth can reach me. I can only think how closely this conversation resembles those I'll encounter over the next month at my parents' house—a place I'm limping back to like a buck-shot deer, not because I expect to find any empathy there, but because subletters still occupy my apartment in New York and, given the cruel facts surrounding my breakup, the prospect of staying in Brighton had seemed even more deranged than this frantic retreat.

Tears crawl down my cheeks, and I fire back, "Look, it's nothing personal. The man I uprooted my life for just told me, Fact: He does not think he loves me. Evidence: He does not want to marry me. Bottom line: He just can't keep me around. And, in the wake of it all, I'd prefer to just sit here quietly. I don't want to chitchat about London tower. I don't want to discuss the immense savings of buying booze duty-free."

For a moment, the cabin seems to fall silent. The flight attendant, belted into her foldaway seat, looks up with a sour expression. Even the turbulence seems to stop. The baby in the next aisle awakens with a howl.

Sopping with shame over my sudden lack of patience and manners, I start to pant. My throat feels constricted. I wrench my hood over my frizzled head in a lame attempt to conceal my absurdity.

The man's eyes are exacting behind the gunmetal frames of his glasses. Sixty-five, maybe, he smells of vinegar, cigarettes, and ruined leather. Handing me the chocolate-chip cookie from his tray (I'd earlier refused the in-flight lunch), he says, "Well, it don't do no good piling famine on top a heartache. For chrissake, eat something."

Buddhists opine that a truly benevolent person doesn't have a single enemy. But as the plane arrows down into Halifax (where I'll connect to my hometown of Boston), I begin to wonder if the opposite also holds true. A truly aggressive person must perceive no one but adversaries. How else could I have spoiled this sweet granddad's flight, mistaking his concern for mistreatment?

———

What compelled me to move to England in the first place? A more self-possessed person might have explored this question before she brown-boxed the contents of her apartment in Manhattan. Before she sublet the only home she knew in exchange for a rented room that grew dank at night when the garden snails slipped inside to consort beneath her bed.

But at twenty-seven, I was not that person. The facts of my life still seemed largely beyond my control. I felt steered (or rather, flung) through the world not by intention or foresight, but by some uncontrollable force (my own subconscious, which I knew as "fate"). The question—Why did I move to England?—hits me only in hindsight, as I sit heartbroken on a homeward-bound plane.

The short answer is easy: I moved to Brighton for love, or at least the possibility of it.

More specifically: I moved there for a singer-songwriter, the front man for an indie-rock outfit called BrakesBrakesBrakes. A guy who spent four out of seven days touring Stockholm or Istanbul or Cologne with his band and the other three averting my gaze with what seemed to me like withholding or indifference. (Let's call him the Lark. After a breakup, it's less painful to refer to a person by euphemism, and my man shared the bird's talents for both singing and flight.)

I'd also planned to devote my summer abroad to the book of essays I'm writing about American remedies for rage. But with the months ticking down until my deadline, I've hit an impasse. I hardly know how to account for the yawning dread I feel every time I sit down to write. Years ago, when I'd written my first memoir, my chief problem was getting my stubby fingers to type fast enough to keep up with the words that dashed like ticker tape through my mind. Now, a fat cloud rolls over my brain every afternoon when I sit down to work. There's nothing but scudding tumbleweeds between my ears. Most days, a blank Word document stares me down and wins.

A thornier question—and another I'm working through only in retrospect—is, Did I really *need* to leave England when I did?

My flatmate in Brighton tried to persuade me to stay. She said, "It feels as though you're letting the Lark run you off. You're letting him dictate the terms. It seems like you're giving him exactly what he wants."

But by that time I'd already booked my plane ticket. Besides, I'd insisted that leaving was my decision. "Brighton was always a mistake," I said. I claimed I wasn't happy. I hated pubs and despised mince. I was sick of saying "toilet" when I meant "ladies' room," "swimming costume" when I meant "bathing suit," and "proper wanker" when I meant "fucking asshole." I hadn't seen the sun in a month. I was appalled by the verbal tics creeping into my vocabulary. I was walking around saying things like "curious, that," and "this pudding is gorgeous." I told my flatmate I wanted to go back home to bright ignorance and ridiculous optimism, where people blessed me when I sneezed and told me to "have a great day" even though they didn't mean it.

The morning after the fight even the Lark had told me to stay. But my bratty response, in between tossing T-shirts and mud-caked Wellingtons into a yawning suitcase, had been: "Stay for what? To play the slot machines at the pier? To lie on the beach in the pissing rain? So I can stroll around town and bump into *you*?"

Withdrawal is the way we've weathered fights in my family, maybe because my folks were married in the 1970s, when couples were first warned to excuse themselves, "take a break," and postpone fights until they'd achieved a "calmed" state of "self-control."

As Aristotle said, "Anger seems to listen to argument to some extent, but to mishear it, as do hasty servants who run out before they have heard the whole of what one says, and then muddle the order." It appears also that we Zailckases heard only the former part of the advice about stepping away from an argument. Whenever there's conflict at home, my younger sister chain-smokes and drowns out the annoyance with a CD Walkman, her headphones hissing sneering choruses. My father retreats to the highball glass, the ice maker, and the liquor cabinet, in that order. When we were kids, when we'd pissed my mother off she would climb into her car and go out for long drives that typically ended at off-price department stores. (Today, she crawls into bed for an evasive nap.) Ironically, I've adopted her first method, one I'd found traumatic as a girl. In the irrational or intuitive ways of a child, I often worried she wouldn't come back.

In the heat of conflict, my family takes ample "breaks" but rarely returns to address the beef directly. Our version of "cooling off" is best summed up by my sister, who prefers to "deal with" anger "alone." Per protocol, we ignore each other for the rest of the day and never refer to the god-awful mess.

Leaving England was just one more example of this. After my fight with the Lark there seemed like little to do but rise from bed, kill the stereo, and heave-ho myself out the bedroom window.

Our backyard in Brighton was an ongoing project. Bulbs awaited planting in egg cartons. Garden tools hid in the grass. Barbed roses twisted up behind the elemental things: a gooseberry bush, trailing rosemary, dwarf sage, mint, silver thyme.

All night I stayed curled in that quaint English garden, brimming in equal parts with hatred and ache. A crescent moon sniggered. A pious stray cat samboed across the stone wall. The seagull's wretched caws matched the ones stymied in my clenched throat. Come sunup, I'd decided to go home.

———

In Halifax, I approach the immigration desk, blank-eyed, rumpled, and lost to the world, looking every bit like what those government types call a "suspicious character."

The immigration officer is an effeminate man in his twenties with a sweet upturned nose and a thin padding of what mothers call "baby fat." "So what brings you to Canada?" he asks, as his delicate hands tilt my passport from side to side, making its hologram dance.

"Just connecting," I say. "Flying to New England from the olde one."

"And how long have you been in the UK?" he asks. "Are you traveling today on business or pleasure?"

"I wouldn't exactly call it pleasure," I say. In another bout of verbal projectile vomit I tell him I moved to Britain a month ago for a boyfriend who'd just called it quits.

Whatever professionalism the boy's been clinging to melts. "Oh, honey!" he cries. "That did *not* happen!"

Sadly, sweet pea, it did.

His podium shivers as his wet stamp hits the pages of my passport. Handing it back, he gives me a consoling smile. "Get home safe, honey," he says. "Hugs to you."

———

With no free seats in the departure lounge, I sink onto the carpet beneath a row of pay phones. A new emotion's beginning to badger me. Guilt, the heavyset child, is tugging on my coattails. Guilt's arrival is no coincidence, but a clever diversion. I'm so preoccupied with the tyke's persistent prodding that I don't even notice when anger—an emotion I imagine as a man with dog's teeth and a raven-black pompadour—stops whispering provocations in my ear. Maybe I'm repressing anger by indulging guilt in its place. Or perhaps this substitution is a human response. From my research, I remember from B. M. Fridhandler and J. R. Averill's 1982 study: "The typical episode of anger does not end abruptly. Anger merges into, or becomes mingled with, some other affective state."

Or maybe I'm simply more comfortable with guilt than I am with rage. I was raised Catholic, and guilt has been a part of my life since the first time I'd entered a confessional, dropped to my bony eight-year-old knees, and morbidly announced, "Bless me father, I've sinned." The response had been, "And what sins are you guilty of, child?" My answers: sneaking jelly beans; wasting milk when there are children starving in Africa; speaking out of turn; not smiling enough; not holding my sister's hand because she had a wart; giving my mother a migraine.

Two decades later I'm still well acquainted with guilt's crippling weight. I know what to do with the feeling (it prefers to be coddled). And I've got a wealth of sins to keep the pudgy imp entertained.

Earlier this summer, when I read Harriet Lerner's *The Dance of Anger*, I identified with an affliction the psychotherapist calls the "nice lady syndrome."

> Although "nice ladies" are not very good at feeling angry, we may be great at feeling guilty. As with depression or feeling hurt, we may cultivate guilt in order to blot out the awareness of our own anger. Anger and guilt are just about incompatible.

I cultivated such an appetite for guilt that neither the Catholicism of my childhood nor my recent agnosticism served it up in large enough portions.

About a year before I met the Lark, my growing enthusiasm for yoga had led to an interest in Buddhism. In the past, whenever I had heard the word "karma," I'd attached to it the translation "you reap what you sow." But in yoga, where I had my first brushes with Sanskrit, I learned that karma merely means "action." Negative karma was the result of the foul things we did, said, and thought. Plus the accumulation of *all* the miserable things we'd done, said, and thought in *all* of our miserable past lives.

In my flawed understanding of Buddhist karma, it seemed like Catholic sin on steroids. I transposed "past lives" with "original sin." "Confession" became "purification." "Pray" became "meditate." "Miracle" became "blessing." And the concept of "rebirth" came to stand in for "hell."

Even Buddhist rebirth seemed to be described with precision that seemed Alighierian. Like the *Inferno*, Buddhist texts seemed to tell me I'd be reincarnated as whatever best punished my blackest crime. I'd assume the form of a demon (if I'd been envious), a hungry ghost (if I'd lacked impulse control), an animal (if I'd been ignorant, lazy, and prejudiced). And if, simply for the sake of argument, I was an angry person, I'd go to hell in a hatchback, or, as Geshe Kelsang Gyatso claimed in his *Introduction to Buddhism*, I'd be reborn into a place "ravaged by war and disease, or where there is continuous conflict."

Of course, the guilt I brought to Buddhism was a misinterpretation or, as the Buddhists would say, a "delusion" of my own tortured mind. Later down the line, I'd learn Tibetans don't even have a word that translates into our English "guilt." For the time being, allow me to say that I'd taken to my interpretation of Buddhism smittenly, like Narcissus to water.

———

Why do matters of Buddhism come to mind this evening in the Halifax airport? Because I've decided that this whole experience with the Lark must be bad karma coming home to roost. I'm haunted, in particular, by a passage by Geshe Kelsang Gyatso: "Another powerful method for overcoming anger and the wish to retaliate is to see all undesirable situations as a reflection of our own faults and shortcomings. If someone insults us, for instance, we can remember the teachings on karma and think, 'I would not be suffering this harm now if I had not insulted someone similarly in the past.'"

Yes sir, guilt is far easier for me to tap into than rage. I'm convinced that the events of the past two days are the result of some diabolic relationship karma. *Maybe*, I think, *I hurt a past boyfriend more than I realized or more than he'd ever let on.* My eyes sting. I stand, swallowing and staring at the pay phone's numbers. Eventually, I take the receiver off of its metal perch and force a coin into the slot. With a bruised heart and an apology in my teeth, I listen to it ring.

I don't call the Lark, as some might guess, but rather my boyfriend before him. Had this man (still a friend) picked up I would have told him how sorry I was if I'd ever belittled him. Or frightened him. Or made him feel inconsequential. If I'd hurt him. If I'd complicated his life. If I hadn't provided a decent explanation or given him a satisfying good-bye.

Denied an outlet, guilt weighs heavily on my shoulders. An overindulged child, it pulls my hair and cups my ears with its hands. It goads me on with its little heels.

Across the terminal, I imagine Anger watching us behind a copy of the *Halifax Herald*. I don't have to make eye contact with him. I'm well acquainted with his tics—his high whimper, the way he scratches his ear with his nails and licks his warm chops with flourish.

TWO *Anger Ignored*

The weather today is an increasing trend toward denial.

—CHUCK PALAHNIUK, *Diary: A Novel*

2
_____

A curious thing happens in the dying light outside Logan Airport, where my father picks me up. I spot his car first (a dried-blood-red sedan). Then his dog (a nippy, black shelter mutt, whining in the open passenger window). Finally, I see Papa Zailckas himself, rounding the car and moving toward me with washed-out worry on his face. He's a teddy bear of a man with round cheeks, button-nosed features, and a deep summer tan. He's wearing the uniform of his forced retirement (Henley shirt, aged loafers, carpenter jeans) and cultivating some new agriculture on his face, something approximating a goatee. I know in a cerebral way that I'm both happy and grateful to see him, yet when he leans forward to hug me, my skin creeps. I feel myself hardening over, giving in to irrational annoyance.

This is an odd reaction indeed. Particularly because I've grown close to my father in recent years. In some ways he's assumed the role of a mother and sister to me. My own mother works eighteen-hour shifts as a "visual merchandiser," designing department store displays, and my newly married twenty-two-year-old sister lives on her husband's marine base, where she is either largely out of touch or out of cell phone range. In the absence of female company, my father's become the person with whom I trade recipes and CDs. When I visit, we go to yoga classes together. We must make a laughable picture. Sitting side by side on matching nonslip mats, our brown eyes slitted, our hands upturned on our knees, our Lithuanian cheeks distended as we hum *om* and exotic words like *namaste*.

I'm not sure what makes me bristle. Maybe the past few days have left me resenting not only the Lark but also men in general. Or maybe I feel like my dear dad is too glad to have me home to distract him from his empty nest, regardless of the circumstances. There's the old man ignoring the gloom in my face. He's going on about how much fun we're going to have doing yoga on the deck and driving out to the Cape on the weekends and trying his new recipe for summer peach salad.

There's also a chance that I feel embarrassed for confiding so much in him. After my fight with the Lark there was a sprawling exchange of instant messages in which I'd first asked my dad if he had room for me at home while my New York subletters finished out their lease. I saved a small snippet of this typed conversation, because, even in the midst of a depressive episode, I found the whole thing vaguely amusing:

RZailckas: I can't believe that little shit. It sounds like drugs to me.

KZailckas: I've never seen the Lark taking drugs.

RZailckas: Maybe it was . . . what's that drug what's his name's son had a problem with?

KZailckas: He doesn't take crystal meth.

RZailckas: That's it. Crystal meth. Hold on, I'm Googling the warning signs for crystal meth.

KZailckas: I feel like all this came right out of the blue.

KZailckas: Like a meteor just dropped on my head.

RZailckas: Here we go . . . "Loss of appetite and weight loss."

KZailckas: He definitely didn't want me to stay here in Brighton.

RZailckas: "Aggression. Dilated pupils. Rapid speech."

RZailckas: "Over-confidence. Changes in dress, friends and slang.

Drug paraphernalia like light bulbs and glass straws, known as 'lollies' and 'popeye.'"
RZailckas: How did he act this morning?
KZailckas: Remorseful, also kind of shell-shocked, mortified.
RZailckas: Have you slept yet?
KZailckas: Not a wink.
KZailckas: I'm still in survival mode. I'm not even tired.

Turns out, my ill temper isn't father-specific. We've barely hit the Mass Pike when the little black mutt with a wrinkled brow and big, commiserative eyes tries to curl into my lap. Now, I should note that I like dogs, and when I visit my parents, I usually let the hot-breathed critters curl up in my bed three at a time. But something in the beast makes me recoil, and I shove the dog away with such fierce revulsion that I see my father wince in profile, and the car swerves a little in its lane.

The strength of my reaction surprises even me. But for the next three months this violent reaction will happen every time some gentle sap (beast or brethren) tries to cheer or, worse yet, console me.

———

My parents' house is more or less as I remember it. A rustic retreat, with fruit in the trees and potpourri on the stove. Its windows are open to the orchestra of late summer. The familiarity of the place should comfort me. But I'm averse to solace and all of its condescension ("you're better off this way," "you deserve so much better," "the slouch isn't fit to shine your shoes"). Homecoming feels like vinegar in the wound. It's a reminder of my failures: failure of foresight; failure to survive abroad; failure to love and be loved.

Curling into my childhood bed feels like a regression. All my life I've avoided relying on others or, even more, asking for help. I've thought of myself as self-contained, self-supporting, freewheeling, nonaligned. I'd give anything to be back in New York, where I might crumple without anyone seeing.

———

Later that night, in "my" bedroom, I'm staring at the contents of my unzipped suitcase when my mother comes in.

She's fresh from a nap and pajamaed in loose linen pants, her rust-colored hair pulled into a ponytail. Even in her middle fifties, she has bright, almost girlish features. Her heart-shaped face is as smooth and fair as anything in your china cabinet. She sinks onto the bed and goes about patting the small blond dog that's camou-flaged in the quilts. She talks for a minute about how lucky I was to see the Lark's true colors when I did. Her words are astringent, her assessment unsparing.

"I know you feel bad," she says with a certain sad shyness in her voice, suggesting she might share my experience. I vaguely remem-ber a story my uncle told me about how, in her early twenties, a philandering boyfriend had left my smitten mom and married someone else.

"As time goes on, you'll feel better. But I won't lie to you. This will always hurt," she says.

There's a certain shock, a shiver, when it becomes clear that a confidante is reenacting some past ordeal. I sense I am filling the role of my mother thirty years ago. It isn't her fault. I'm ripe for projec-tion. My vacant disposition is like a blank movie screen.

"Would you go back to him?" Mom asks. "If he told you he was sorry? If he came back saying he had changed?"

I know the politically expedient answer. "No," I say. "Not a chance."

"Good girl," she says, scratching the dog round its collar. "That's my smart girl. That's very good."

3

———

During my earliest weeks at my folks' house I try to journal in a wire-bound notebook. Its size: roughly that of a cigarette pack. Its cover: glum gray, the color of mental confusion. I begin this diary because people keep telling me how important it is to "emote," "vent," "write down my feelings," and "get it all out." There's a lot of talk during this time about "healing." Lots of prescriptions for "good mental health."

Try as I might to use the notebook for this purpose, I can't seem to write more than lists of books I'm reading, snippets of letters that arrive in the mail, newspaper headlines, and occasional, free-floating quotations.

In retrospect, I think the notebook's undemonstrative nature owes something to animus. I'd written *Smashed* not because I was ambitious (I had the get-up-and-go of a sack of Yukon Gold potatoes) and not because writing down my feelings was cathartic (it felt more like playing one's own neurosurgeon sans anesthesia). No. I'd made a habit—and eventually a profession—of memoir because I hail from one of those families where shows of emotion are discouraged. Talk of "feelings" is implicitly banned on the basis that it makes people uncomfortable. Later, I'll think I resented being advised, in self-help speak, by my loved ones to "journal" when all I wanted was someone—a friend, a relative, a Good Samaritan hotline—who might give me the permission to talk. I take it as an act of defiance that I didn't emote into that gray book. But the little record constructed there does give a rough outline that helps me account, day by day, for the better part of two glassy-eyed weeks.

On Saturday, July 28, Alyssa, a friend who is studying homeopathy, calls from Boulder to say she's express-mailed me "emotional remedies." Four bottles will arrive at my folks' house in two days' time. They will be labeled: "Natrum Muriaticum" (for grief), "Lachesis" (for jealousy), "Lycopodium" (for fear, particularly fear of failure), and "Staphysagria" (for suppressed rage). I should mix the bottles according to her printed instructions, ingest the remedy for whatever emotion seems to be overwhelming me, and never take the same potion two days in a row. The routine might make me feel worse in the beginning, Alyssa warns. But in time, the remedies will make my psyche fight the grief I'm feeling "the way my immune system would attack a cold."

Although I've studied Eastern philosophies like yoga and Buddhism, I've always thought of my interest in them as more academic than anything else. In real life, there's a limit to my patience with anything that smacks of metaphysics. I've squirmed at the mention of "mind expansion" or "warm healing energy." I've dismissed things like acupressure as quackery. I don't like drum circles, public nudity, or strangers touching my feet.

It's a testimony to my hopelessness that I agree to try Alyssa's remedies. I'm desperate to glom onto whatever relief homeopathy might bring me, even if it ends up being (as I suspect) a placebo effect. By nightfall, I've express ordered *Homeopathy: An A to Z Home Handbook* from an online bookstore. A few days later, I'm jotting down remedies I suspect I need. In my little gray diary I find brief descriptions of two I considered ordering:

Sepia (Ink of the cuttlefish): People who need sepia are irritable or angry when contradicted. They are averse to family and averse to consolation. They are averse to company even as they fear being alone. They are hysterical. They fear insanity. They may be overwhelmingly apathetic.

Aurum (Gold): Aurum is for people with an exaggerated sense of duty. Such an individual may be under the delusion that she has failed. She has strong feelings of guilt, severe depression and fits of anger. She may desire death or crave suicidal intervention.

On Sunday, July 29, I awake to the respective buzzing and beeping of my American and British cell phones. Upon inspection, both are lit with matching text messages from the Lark (which I dissect ad nauseam in my notebook). *I need to know you are safe somewhere,* the Lark's texted. *Please let me know.*

I wonder, *Which is aching: his heart or his conscience?*

I spend the morning trying to place the lines of poetry these messages bring to mind. While driving that afternoon, I realize I am hearing an echo of Theognis to his lover:

> *We aren't shutting you out of the revel, and we aren't inviting you, either.*
>   *For you're a pain when you're present, and beloved when you're away.*

Pulling over to jot the lines into my notebook, I wonder whether the Lark can only care for me in my absence. I wonder if I can only despise him in his.

————

On Monday, July 30, I run out of whatever willpower has kept me from responding to the Lark's text message, and I sit down to compose a fine-tuned e-mail (edited here for length):

I received your text message. . . . I guess it won't hurt to tell you that I'm back in the States, tapping this message between the on-again-off-again blinking of an electrical outage. I ask you: why can't I escape these rotten rainstorms?

As for the other night, we sure had 'A Modern Midnight Conversation.' [A reference to our favorite Hogarth.] As devastating as it was to hear some of the things you had to say, more than anything, I wish you didn't have to get quite so far over-the-edge before you felt you could tell them to me. [He had been drinking heavily that night. We'd earlier gone to see a band at a venue on Gloucester Place.]

Because alongside whatever small condolences you had to offer, that archimage, that alcoholic voodoo, also made you say some things that were pretty barbed and inhumane. And I know that's not you. You've always been one of the most empathetic people I know. You're usually so generous in word and action.

Try my damndest, I can't work up any real haggishness for you. . . . I'm here for you always and any old time. Ring me up if you ever need an ear, okay? Pierce my pocket with a text message. Tap me out an e-mail. I miss talking to you, notwithstanding. You're in my dreams, despite.

On Tuesday, July 31, I awake after a series of nightmares. I dreamed that I am in grade school. I walk up to the math teacher and tell him that I've found a formula for everything. For inner peace, for empathy, for making things right. He shakes his head no, saying the formula in my hand doesn't work. He tells me: *You forgot to carry the one.* I dreamed that I find a knife in my bed. I dreamed of an auditorium full of strangers (you, readers?) all laughing and pointing at me.

Checking my e-mail that morning, I find the following (abridged) reply from the Lark:

I said some awful things that night for which I'm really, cringingly ashamed. I think I was trying to get you to hate me. Thank you for seeing through my idiocy. . . . I care about you so much. These past few days have been some of the hardest. I can only say I was trying to do my best for you, to end things without lying to you or leading you on. I hope you understand. You really are amazing. . . . I feel an emptiness that will take some time to fill.

On Wednesday, August 1, Alyssa's package arrives with a thump on the doorstep. Carving it open (and ignoring for the moment how good it feels to gash something with a sharp knife), I remove what looks like four empty vessels from a puddle of packing peanuts. Holding each of the brown bottles up to my bedside lamp, I finally spot something the size of a grain of sand rolling around inside each one.

I unfold a note that I find in the box. Alyssa says homeopathy treats "like with like." Thus, Nat-Mur is liquefied grief. And Staphysagria is bottled, bottled-up rage. I can't decide which remedy to mix and take first. At the moment, all I feel is lethargy, and my thoughtful friend hasn't sent along a remedy for that.

Also in her note, Alyssa directs me to the work of legendary family therapist Virginia Satir. A male friend recently introduced her to Satir's books and brought her to meet the director of Boulder's Peoplemaking institute, where counselors employ Satir's method and teach her work. "It's magical stuff," she tells me. "It seems to really transform people. Satir thought the family is a microcosm. Once you've healed the family, you know how to heal the world."

That afternoon, my sister calls to say she's been fired from her job at a women's shelter.

"Why?" I ask.

Because her boss instructed her to stay late. And she'd told him no, she'd stayed late two weeks in a row. He said that if she didn't stay, she might as well go and clean out her desk.

"And how did you respond?" I ask.

"I basically laid down and died while he berated me and told me what a worthless employee I was! I wish I could have told him what I really think! I would have loved to call him a balding, fascist prick, to tell him that he ran that place like a Nazi death camp!" She sounds breathless. Her voice is booming like a brass instrument.

"How do you do that?" I ask her.

"What?"

"Get angry like that? Go ballistic? Have a shit fit, or whatever you call it?"

"It's easy," she says.

"Teach me."

I tell her it's an instrument of survival. Without it, I'm a sitting duck out here.

"Well, when the Lark was fighting with you the night you broke up . . ."

"Yes?"

"What was the first thought that occurred to you?"

"I thought, 'You're right. I'm horrible. I can hardly bear to look at myself.' I thought, 'Everything you've ever said about me is true.'"

"Wow," she says. "That's really fucked up. I don't know what to do with that."

4
___

In Buddhism, there's a popular piece of advice that says that when a man insults you, think on the subject. If his criticism doesn't apply, you should ignore the abuse. But on the flip side, if the good man has you pegged, you should thank him for calling attention to your failings and set about the business of improving yourself.

Nearly every religion devotes some attention to anger. In their book *Anger: The Struggle for Emotional Control in America's History*, Peter N. and Carol Zisowitz Stearns assert that Christianity and Judaism take "a middle position on the subject of anger." In further reading I found more proof that although Christianity generally considers anger a sin, it also allows for a loophole called "righteous indignation" or "justified anger," which William Leslie Davidson describes as "the right to abhor, and to give expression to our abhorrence of, injury and injustice, cruelty, impiety, and wrong." Judaism also contends that anger at the sight of a wrongdoing is holy. According to the Torah, "A wrathful man stirs up discord, but he that is slow to anger appeases strife." The emotion is misguided only if it kindles temper, which supposedly gives way to recklessness.

The Stearnses suggest there is "considerable praise for anger in Islam." But the Qur'an says power resides not in the ability to strike someone else but in the ability to stay cool under pressure. "Most hated to Allah is a person who is fiercely hostile and quarrelsome."

For the Stearnses, Buddhism is the only religion that prohibits anger absolutely. Although their conclusion isn't quite right, it's easy to see how they came to it. "Anger," the Buddha said, "is a poison and an obstacle to enlightenment." And Geshe Kelsang Gyatso, founder of Buddhism's New Kadampa Tradition, writes in his book

How to Solve Our Human Problems, "[A]nger is everyone's principal enemy. . . . Anger never helps us. . . . All anger ever does is . . . bring nothing but unhappiness."

Given Buddhism's supposed anti-anger stance, I find it particularly funny that I've recently gravitated to it. No doubt it appeals to my inner cholerophobe. I like the specificity with which Buddhist teachers seem to speak about rage. In psychological books, I've mostly found vague and conflicting definitions of the emotion, such as "anger is a negative phenomenological feeling state" or "anger is the emotion into which most others tend to pass." Christa Reiser writes, "Often, there is no explicit definition of anger." Buddhism, on the other hand, really seems to pin anger down to a dissection plate. Geshe Kelsang Gyatso defines anger as a product of a "deluded mind that focuses on an animate or inanimate object, feels it to be unattractive, exaggerates its bad qualities and wishes to harm it."

That harm didn't even have to mean wishing you could wipe the snippy scowl off somebody's face. It could simply mean wanting to criticize him. It could mean envisioning—just for a second—a scenario where he dies alone, penniless, forgotten, and riddled with regret so that he might know just what "emptiness" is.

By August 2, I am deep into the habit of exaggerating the Lark's bad qualities. "He's just sociopathic," I hear myself tell a friend on the phone. "Con artists have more empathy. Wild animals have more self-control." And so I decide to try *tonglen*—a practice in Tibetan Buddhism that is also known as "sending and taking."

"Tonglen practice helps cultivate fearlessness," I'd once read in a book by the Buddhist nun Pema Chodron. "When you do this practice for some time, you begin to realize that fear has to do with wanting to protect your heart: you feel that something is going to harm your heart, and therefore you protect it."

Tonglen is a meditation and an oft-prescribed remedy for anger. To perform it, you are supposed to sit comfortably. Close your eyes. Envision your enemy. Then, with every inhale, you imagine relieving him of some of his fear, his frustration and contentiousness. With every exhale, you pretend you're sending him well-being, confidence, love, piece of mind.

The Dalai Lama claims to do *tonglen* every day, giving special attention to the Chinese officials who torture and murder Tibetans. "I visualize them," he says. "I draw their ignorance, prejudice, hatred, and pride into myself."

The point of the meditation isn't to change the world so much as to change your perspective. The Dalai Lama goes on to add, "You cannot actually give away your happiness and take other's suffering on yourself. But the practice will certainly increase your compassion."

Buddhistly speaking, compassion is the Holy Grail. It's the no-fail antidote to rage.

———

I decide to sit, pretzel-legged, on my bedroom floor. I nest one hand into the palm of the other the way I've read about in meditation books, and let my thumb tips lightly kiss. I try to tune out the sounds of the afternoon: a dog barking, a garden hose hitting the hydrangea bush, a honeybee ambushing my window screen. I try to forget the hour: noon in Boston, 5:00 P.M. in Brighton. Slitting my eyes, I relax them until the world softly blurs. I breathe in and feel my lungs shiver. There's a flicker of panic in my chest. Something about this makes me feel vulnerable.

A knock sounds at my bedroom door. It's my father, with some transparent excuse for checking in on me. He just wants to tell me that he's going next door to borrow a garden tool. Or to ask me if I intend to use the car. Or to tell me that there's hot water on the stove on the off chance that I want some tea. I mumble a small barbed reply and, hearing the door close behind him, go back to the dirty business of *tonglen*.

Through my closed eyes, I try to envision the Lark. For some reason, the night after the Kent Music Festival comes to mind first. In the early morning hours I'd awoken to the light of a desk lamp, the sound of a jazz record doing the whirling dervish, and the Lark staring out the bedside window.

With a wince, I picture him as I saw him that morning. His eyes are heavy with some tense and conflicted emotion. His brow furrowed, there are soft lines around his eyes. It's painful and absurd to visualize him in such intricate detail. I see his concise freckled nose and the sandy stubble that peppers his cheek. In memory, I watch his lips part slightly, as though he is about to recite whatever resolution is taking shape in this head. My breath cracks in my chest. What had he been doing awake at that hour? I see the pen between his fingers. Beneath it is the curling green notebook where he jots ideas for song lyrics.

Remembering *tonglen*, I try to imagine the book is filled with his troubles and hang-ups; his current anxieties and past traumas; the reasons why he held his heart so close to him, like an animal guarding its fresh kill. I picture myself prying the book from his hands. With every inhale, I imagine tearing a page from the spine and balling it up in my fist.

———

With *tonglen* calming me, it's easy to remember the better parts of our time together. I remember the way the Lark had entered my life like, well, an alien landing. He'd materialized all at once, like someone beamed across a vast distance and time, foreign in every way but somehow recognizable.

One stifling June day in 2006, an e-mail arrived in my electronic mailbox. How to describe something that changes everything? Delivered by a social networking site, in many ways it was a plea for advice. In two days, the Lark had written, he was flying to Nashville to record his band's second album. That said, he had written the lyrics of only two of its songs. He'd procrastinated. He was panicked. He asked me what I thought he should do.

The Lark's words were vibrant and confessional and tender. Later, when I asked him why he'd contacted a total stranger, let alone divulged so much information to her, he'd seemed to blank out, as though failing to see why it might seem unnatural. When I'd pressed, he had tried to jog his memory aloud. "I wrote you because you were fit?" he'd joked. "Because you were on our mailing list even though we'd only played New York once? Because you were looking for someone to teach you to play drums and I thought I'd volunteer? I remember you liked loads of really great music. Your profile was hilarious."

I'd had an equally unnatural flutter of déjà vu the moment I'd read the Lark's opening words. Given the trouble my own career was giving me, I surely identified with the pressure he was under. But there was something deeper in the Lark's message that appealed to me. His easy expression of his feelings tapped into my own. Had he approached me with these questions in person, I might have seized up in the face of such human fallibility, which echoed my own and would have put me on guard. But the Lark had found my emotions through their only known entrance and exit way: written words.

Borrow, I'd typed back.

Lift something from bathroom graffiti, or newspaper headlines, or the marginalia that you find in secondhand books. It's just storytelling, right? And something tells me you, mister, are quite the storyteller. At any rate, beg, borrow, steal, churn it out. I'm not the least bit worried about you.

———

One year after this first correspondence, *tonglen* also forces my thoughts back to the Lark's lovely face. He comes to me in a procession of images.

At my front door for the first time—when he'd arrived in New York for the sole purpose of seeing me. His eyes had been at once relieved, curious, frightened, and overjoyed, and his arms had been laden with small, tender presents for me (an etching he'd made, a copy of Laurie Lee's *Cider with Rosie*, a tiny brooch in the shape of a sparrow). I see him on the tip of Roosevelt Island, among the brilliant glare of the skyscrapers and the dumb hovering of Circle Line cruises, where he later claimed he'd first wanted to kiss me. Then, without warning, these images give way to another one. The Lark sitting in my bedroom window on the night of our fight in Brighton, smoking a cigarette to its freckled filter, his slim legs crossed at the knees and a hostile aura hanging around him.

———

Our fight was sparked when the Lark failed to respond to my casual mention of staying in Brighton on a more permanent basis, taking over the lease on my flat when my flatmate moved to Hong Kong in the fall. Reflexively, I'd filled the silence with talk of my work.

I told the Lark about a quote I had read by a therapist called Celia Halas, who'd said women express anger far less frequently than men. "In fact, men generally feel quite comfortable with anger, express it freely," Halas had written. "Women are generally afraid to express their anger. They've been taught that to do so is unladylike. They fear the reaction they will get if their rage breaks forth."

I told the Lark the girlfriends I'd made in Brighton agreed on this point. In Britain's class-obsessed culture, my new friends had told me they were reluctant to let loose and get fully savage because they didn't want to be viewed as masculine or "chavy" (the limey equivalent of trailer park trash).

The Lark turned to face me head-on. His cigarette was poised at his lower lip. He felt just the opposite. In all the relationships he knew, it was the women who did the tirading while their men humored and appeased them. I can't remember exactly the way the Lark framed his argument, but it mirrored that of Herb Goldberg, the clinical psychologist who wrote *The Hazards of Being Male*: "I've found that . . . the male is very blocked in his expression of anger toward women. It is 'unmanly' to acknowledge openly his vulnerability or his anger. Frequently it ties in with the fear of being a bully, and consequently his anger over the situation emerges only indirectly."

I'd responded with a meaningless, idiot noise. I'd said, "I see your point. In British culture, I find women a little more domineering and men slightly more . . . docile." I chose my words carefully. We both seemed to be aware that some fuse was slowly burning down its wick.

Trying to pull an about-face and politely exit the topic, I said, "Maybe mine is just an American perspective. I'm thinking of that cowboy culture that still informs the U.S. Back home, an angry outburst reaffirms a man's masculinity. But angry American women? I don't know. I just think rage undermines their femininity. Angry chicks are still perceived as unladylike, unmaternal, unsophisticated, unattractive—"

The Lark shouted at the top of his practiced lungs: "How many cowboys do *YOU* know?! How much time have *YOU* spent in Texas?!"

I muttered something about Houston, Dallas, Austin, Lubbock. I own Merle Haggard records and real cowboy boots. I hadn't been trying to wind him up. Though in hindsight, it's easy to see why these comments made him thrash.

The Lark snorted. "I've been all over Texas!" he shouted. "Cowboys are *courteous*! They're *hospitable*! If you need anything at all, they go out of their way to help!"

A riptide had opened up in this conversation, probably on account of the very late hour. Just when I'd begun to feel like I'd finally dog-paddled my way back to some safe shore, a subcurrent dragged me back into the row. And now, bogged down by the details of an irrelevant tangent, we were miles from the argument's original theme.

The Lark opened his mouth. He shouted so loudly it made all my little bud vases rattle. He'd known ex-girlfriends who had hit him when they fought. This, when he'd never raised—never even considered raising—a finger to them. "And *you* think women are *bad* at anger?! Where did you get that?! Why would you want to perpetuate it?! What *kind of person* does that fucking make *you*?!"

My ears were ringing. My head fell into my hands. "What *kind of person* does that make me?!" I screamed back. I was choke-breathed and shedding convulsive tears. But I sensed even these came off like provocation. Only moments earlier I'd been quoting an article about how women's tears are just as often an assertion of anger.

I'd stormed off to the bathroom and balanced myself on the edge of the tub, sobbing into the bath mat. I decided, while contemplating a bloom of mold on the soap dish, to say whatever I needed to in order to patch things up. I couldn't bear to send the Lark back to his flat this way. My anxiety wouldn't allow me a moment's sleep if I curled up in bed beside him, but I thought it would be even worse to wake up alone, feeling despised and disposed of.

A few weeks earlier, I'd learned that this almost pathological "need to be liked" was the mark of a Spike 3 personality profile, according to the Minnesota Multiphasic Personality Inventory—a character evaluation that's guaranteed to depress you faster than an online IQ test. Although I'd taken it strictly out of curiosity, I was, shall we say, uncomfortable in "confrontive situations" that involved getting angry or asserting myself. I'd been known on occasion to be "Pollyannish and conventional," which sweetness I'd sometimes used to gloss over my "unusual behavior." Intimacy wasn't second nature to me, although I supposed I could be both overly "dependent" and (this made me laugh) "seductive, without being conscious of it, as a way of minimizing hostility." My childhood, as I remembered it, was not all tree-climbing, rope-skipping glee. What I best remembered was a hard knot of dread that stayed with me until I discovered alcohol at fourteen. I had at least one parent who might qualify, in my mind, as "evaluative" and "rejecting." The last part of the Spike 3's description, which also happened to be the worst part, fit me like a pair of well-worn sneakers: When I did express anger, it came in "impulsive" or "inappropriate" forms. This, because it was so "poorly integrated."

After ten minutes in my flat's bathroom, I'd behaved in a very Spike 3 fashion, choosing to skip over the remainder of my fight with the Lark and jump ahead to putting it behind us.

I reentered the bedroom feeling steadier. More composed. The

Lark was still sitting in the window, inspecting the cigarette between his thumb and forefinger and drinking from a jam jar filled with stale red wine he'd found in the kitchen. I told him I was sorry. Sorry that he'd experienced that kind of ugliness. And sorry that our conversation awakened those old feelings of betrayal. You *do* know, I ask him, that *I'd* never hurt you that way?

Silence.

Time slowed. Muted gush played on the stereo. The song was a naïve little pop song, hushed and lo-fi.

I persevered. I promised the Lark I'd never hurt him in the ways that those women had. I'd never be so careless with his heart.

The Lark, in profile, still didn't answer.

"I only ask, in return, that you're not careless with mine. Deal?"

The Lark's eyes slowly moved from his cigarette to me. In them, I thought I saw either revulsion or terror.

"Does that mean 'no deal'?" I asked, with a small, trusting laugh. "Does that mean you *intend* to hurt me? That you *mean* to break my heart?"

"I don't know. I mean, I don't think so," sighed the Lark.

To borrow from Sappho and Archilochos: His response gnawed a hole in my vitals. It pierced me through the bones and snatched the lungs right out of my chest. I bargained. I groveled like a dog on a chain. I buried my face in my hands. Puked, inwardly. Turned a disconcerting shade of reddish purple.

———

Anna Karenina first said hate begins where love leaves off.

At my parents' house, I reach the part of *tonglen* where I'm supposed to send the Lark all the love, acceptance, and contentment that I desire for myself. But I can't seem to do it. I know, in a detached way, that I ought to send him: a loving partner, even if she isn't me; happy children, even if they aren't mine; a future that glitters like the Chrysler Building, even if there's no place for me in it. But I can't wish him well without me.

In an instant, my perspective has changed, as though someone's loaded it with a new tray of slides. Where I might have seen the Lark cupping an orange monarch in his palm (we'd once gone to the butterfly exhibit at the natural history museum), I see him hogging the bed as he had after our fight. His feet twitch. His teeth grind softly. I'm offended by his serenity, that even in the midst of our breakup he can slow his mind to the crawling tempo of sleep. Instead of seeing the Lark's shy radiance the first time he'd kissed me outside a community garden on East Twelfth Street, I see him in our last moments together, shifting his weight as I tried to find his coat. *Like a horse*, I'd thought then. *Stamping his feet at the race gate. Waiting for the announcer to shout "And they're off!"*

My deep, meditative breaths turn frantic and jagged. I abandon my *tonglen* and get up from the floor. I won't ever attempt this again.

THREE *Anger Turned Inward*

Depression is anger without enthusiasm.

—UNKNOWN

5
_____

In the past, I've always avoided emotional talk on the grounds that my feelings seem far too oppressive and snarled for me to differentiate. In the past, anyone who asked me how I felt was treated to a puzzled and puzzling response: "I don't know." A dubious answer, but I wasn't shirking. I was so deaf to my emotional clatter that the question stumped me bitterly.

Now, homeopathy makes me pin my emotions to a single word. I consider a row of brown bottles lined up on the kitchen windowsill and find myself in an uncomfortable position where I can't default on the question: *What am I feeling?*

To choose the right remedy, I have to take a daily inventory of what I am feeling and suss out the predominant emotion: fear of writing; despondency over the Lark (I won't call it "grief" no matter what Alyssa says, as I know nobody's died); annoyance over my father's concerned supervision; submission to the big characters of my mother and sister, who report back from work with hot diatribes about their days.

Every morning, I obediently set out to parse whether I feel fearful or depressed, pessimistic or just plain pissed off. I eye the labels ("Nat-Mur"; "Lach"; "Staph"; "Lyc") as if time is of the essence. It's hardly bomb disposal and yet that's precisely the meticulous gravity I bring to the task.

Most days that August, I take Natrum Muriaticum or Lycopodium. Alyssa claims they will cure my "despair" and "fear of the future," respectively.

I still don't feel any conscious anger at the Lark, although I occasionally wonder if I could be rip shit without being aware of it. Could anger be in me after all, darting around unseen like a small, red fish beneath the surface of my catatonic murk?

If I *am*—both secretly angry and desperate to avoid the feeling—it would make sense to hide from the emotion in my parents' house. The Zailckases balk at any hint of rage. When I look back on my early childhood, I struggle to remember any conversations in which my parents revealed the deeper sources of their emotions with me or encouraged me to tell them about my own.

My parents' feelings always seemed veiled behind mixed messages. My young mother, then a toothpick-waisted brunette in her late twenties, was always rubbing her temples to mask the anger she tried to pass off as a headache. She claimed "nothing's the matter" as tears cascaded down her rouged cheeks or as she shouted with far more venom than a spilled glass of juice seemed to call for. As a kid, it all led me to suspect she was angry with me for a deeper, more mysterious offense. My father is mostly absent from these memories, gone for weeks and occasionally months at a time on business trips. When at home, he blamed all his fury on the stresses of work; he exploded over everyday annoyances like the way someone had loaded the dishwasher. Later, a journal from my early teenage years asks, "How is it that my father can pretend to be so blind to the big issues and so relentless about the small ones?"

As a small child, before my sister was born, whenever I turned my anger on my mom and dad my backside often met the end of a hairbrush. I also was variously bribed through tantrums with sheets of butterfly stickers, banished to my room, denied some long-awaited privilege, or yelled at in return. Whenever I expressed anger at someone outside of our little triad, my mother, although mortified and reprimanding, did not act like the end was quite so nigh as she did when I resisted her. In public, when I shot someone a dirty look or raised my voice above a protesting whimper, my coiffed mom would smile through her teeth and pull me aside by the skin on my arm, warning me not to "wear my heart on my sleeve."

As a kid, I knew the warning meant I shouldn't show my feelings openly or clue anyone in to my internal state. As an adult, when curiosity sent me tracing the roots of the expression, I found out that it's a reference to the Middle Ages, when a man would wear his lover's ribbon or handkerchief on his sleeve, thereby publicly announcing their involvement. The phrase was first recorded in Shakespeare's *Othello*, where it draws a negative connotation. At the part where treacherous Iago hatches a plan to feign openness in an attempt to dupe Roderigo, he says, "I will wear my heart upon my sleeve, for daws to peck at." I'm sure my mother didn't want me to be emotionally forthcoming for fear that other people would use my feelings to wound or manipulate me, but that's exactly what I'd always felt she was doing whenever she reached for the phrase.

As I approached adolescence, my mother seemed to monitor me incessantly, as if explicitly trying to prevent me from showing any hint of teenage anger or angst. On one afternoon in particular, a disagreement with her drove me into my closet with the cordless telephone, which seemed like the only place I could vent my frustrations to a friend without her listening in. Only I had underestimated her talent for eavesdropping. She chose that exact moment (coincidentally, she said) to scrub the shower in the adjacent bathroom, the only place in the house where she could (and did) overhear my mouthy teenage ranting. Later, she used what she heard as grounds for revoking my phone privileges. I'd most likely called her a bitch.

She said she read entries I wrote about her in my diary, the only place it seemed safe to lend words to emotions, because I purposely left them out for her to see. The way I remember it, she dug up and read the journals I squirreled away under my mattress. Today, in one of the journals that survived, I find a line that seems telling. In a description of my mother my sixteen-year-old hand had written: "Like a watched pot, she expects I won't boil."

It's difficult to say which of us evoked the other's crazy behavior. Was I cagey with my anger because my mother seemed so desperate to squelch it? Or was my mother invasive because I guarded my feelings so closely? I could tell she felt equally frustrated by our stand-off. I remember feeling a stab of guilt when I caught her bent over the bestselling *Reviving Ophelia*, studying it with the same worried concentration someone might give the instruction manual of an appliance that's gone inexplicably bust. A crueler thought, which trailed behind that emotion like a comet's tail, likely said something like: *Look inside yourself. Give your own emotions as much scrutiny. Fix yourself before you try to overhaul me.*

———

My parents' heritage might have contributed to their attitudes about anger. According to Carol Tavris: "When Anglo-Americans are angry, they tend to proceed in stages from small steps to larger ones: First, they hint around. . . . Then they talk to neighbors and friends. . . . If they get no results, they may talk directly and calmly, to [the person with whom they have the problem]. Next they will express their anger directly to [that person]. Eventually, if they are angry enough, they will take the matter to the courts."

But my Sicilian mother has mob revenge in her blood, and my father hails from the kind of Lithuanian stock that, with a Balt's knack for the melodramatic, casts pagan curses whenever they're inflamed. Historically, Lithuanian invectives include: "May you hang yourself from a dead branch!" "May your tongue no longer fit in your mouth!" "May the spring's first thunder kill you!"

On both sides of my family tree are ancestors with a preternatural talent for rage. However, immigration to the States made them self-conscious and ashamed of the rabid tempers that drew attention to their status as foreigners. They taught their children and grandchildren to disguise (but not accept and talk out) their anger. Whenever most Zailckases are angry, we follow a unique series of steps: a methodology of avoidance passed down for generations.

First, we do nothing. We stew, brood, stick out our lower lips, and chafe inwardly. This period of moping can last weeks, months, years, even decades. The most talented sulkers in our clan carry grudges to their cremation urns.

If our rage overcomes our brooding, the second step in the series is shit fit, complete with tantrums, mortal threats, and the disowning of friends and family.

The third step is denial. When confronted after our shows of rage, we assume an expression of scaly silence, dazed disinterest, or child-eyed ignorance. This is not always a question of playacting. As a Zailckas, one's well-honed defense mechanisms might actually convince her that she truly doesn't remember the incident. If our foe forces the topic, we flee. Those of us who struggle with the conviction needed to pull off step number three take further action to remain unapproachable. We seclude ourselves, self-medicate, self-punish, and/or drink alcoholically.

The final step in the series is transference. Denying a conflict and avoiding the feelings of anger it evokes leaves us with an unsettled feeling. What do we do with the bitter taste lingering in our mouths? We spit it out at a new target. We let the coworker, the love interest, or the new next-door neighbor stand in for the person who's truly wronged us. This step happens largely beyond our consciousness. We mishear and misinterpret the bewildered folks who have the misfortune to interact with us; we squint until they begin to look like our old adversaries; and shoehorn past conflicts into this fresh context. And, of course, whenever this new tension gets too taut to stand, we refer back to the beginning of the series and repeat steps one through four until nearly everyone has been bullied, bulldozed, or pushed far away. We repeat until the world confirms our ugliest suspicions.

6

I continue to take my homeopathic remedies throughout the dead-locked month of August. I don't really believe in them, but I'm still hoping for relief. I'm waiting for the remedies to make me feel better, or perhaps I'm attempting to use them the way I'd do with Western medicine. I wait for each tablespoon I slurp down to lift me up, blank me out, pry me from the iron grip of my mood.

I've long forgotten the words in Alyssa's note. Homeopathy, she'd written, will not mask anger's symptoms: "These remedies will not dispel your emotions. They'll bring about learning when you are ready for it."

But so far I haven't learned much from my split with the Lark. It's not for lack of scrutiny. All day, every day, my mind turns over the facts of the summer, examining it from every angle before violently purging myself of all thoughts of the affair the way an exasperated child might throw some uncooperative object to the floor with both hands. Then, I can't resist picking the story back up and allowing the missing information to unhinge me again.

I stumble through the days, as if disoriented by a bright glare. I shield myself from sunshine, conversation, the smell of food on the barbeque, the bubbly sounds of pop music or laughter. Hours seem to pass at the pace of whole years.

Freud famously thought a healthy person was characterized by her ability to love and her ability to work. For the month of August, I can't do either. I begin to think of myself as a failed adult, a failing writer. I'm a stunted twenty-seven-year-old in coffee-stained shorts and the same T-shirt I've worn to bed countless nights in a row, turbid, absent, and socially weird, pretending she doesn't hear the hushed, noble tones of her family's attempts to diagnose her.

One friend says it's post-traumatic stress.

My sister insists it's bipolar disorder, a family predisposition rearing its afflicted head.

My mother tells me her best friend isn't surprised when she hears the news of my breakup. "Jane said she never really thought you'd find your match with a British rock musician, knowing everything you represent." (By what I "represent," I assume she means what a newspaper profile once called "the face of teenage binge drinking," or at least its reformed counterpart.)

———

Whenever someone insists that I must be mad at the Lark, I stolidly maintain that I'm not.

The English word "angry" isn't nuanced enough to describe the deranged jumble of pangs in my chest. All day long, my so-called feelings on the matter collide: Shock needles outrage; humiliation blindly nuzzles self-pity; regret falls lustily into depression's arms.

Neither is my demeanor that of a woman enraged. To see me slumped, glassy-eyed, holding a sandwich someone has cut for me into four "manageable" pieces, a person might tell you I look much more like a woman subdued.

7

When it comes to human emotions, I've become very picky about wording.

One afternoon, I find a word in my reading that pegs me far better than the English "angry." The word comes from Ifaluk—the language of an atoll by the same name located all the way in Micronesia. I spot it in the writings of Catherine Lutz, an anthropologist who lived for a year on the island of only 430 inhabitants. The word is *song*.

Fitting, maybe, because a musician first stirred the feeling in me. Ironic, perhaps, because—even as my ability to pay attention to books is slowly beginning to return to me—music still grates against some vulnerable, pathetic, pink part of my soul. Every note feels like a provocation. Every song, be it a ballad or banger, feels like a backhanded slap. I'd once heard Tom Wolfe say that music is the only art form that cuts straight to our central nervous systems, without our brain's input. It's possible that music stirs up feelings my brain would rather explain away. Maybe that's why I've begun to shy away from records and avoid the radio, moving around in a dense aura of silence.

In Ifaluk *song* means the kind of "righteous indignation" or "justifiable anger" caused by a breach of social rules. The island's inhabitants don't just approve of the emotion on a moral level, they also see it as a social duty: a person is doing a disservice to both the offender and her community if she sits by and tacitly does nothing while someone behaves like an antisocial brute.

Linguists say *song* is less aggressive than anger and less likely to spur an offensive attack. A person who feels *song* might gently mock or reprimand her transgressor, but she also withdraws, refuses to eat, and mopes around like a graying ape. According to Anna Wierzbicka, the violence caused by *song* is "directed toward oneself rather than toward the guilty person."

Even though a person in *song* turns her fury inward, she still intends it to have an outward effect. The goal is to clue the offending person in to his no-no and prompt him to see its consequences. Very often, people in *song* go as far as attempting suicide to prove their point. For that reason, the normal Ifaluk reaction to *song* is *metagu*—or remorse mingled with concern about the self-harm the angry ninny might do.

At my parents' house, my behavior has *song* written all over it. It's real and spreading through me like a slow rot. Forget about time "healing all wounds"; each new day only finds me gaunter, redder in the eyes, and far more likely to drool in public.

But, beneath my gloom, I quietly believe my struggle is noble. I have a childlike (and certainly childish) belief that it can somehow influence the Lark, even if he isn't there to witness it. I'm not proud to admit this, but at my most despairing moments I envision my love groveling for forgiveness like a thief at a cross. When I refuse a meal, it's with a flash of loathing. When I light a cigarette, it's with a hot twitch of malice. Whenever I take a stab at conversation, I often realize I am speaking to and for the Lark's benefit, almost as though he is standing on the sidelines listening and, I hope, assuming the blame.

———

I'm not the only one in my family with a distinct talent for *song*.

My father, at least when it comes to his frustrations with me, also relies on shows of dejection. That's not to say that my old man doesn't get angry with me, only that he thinks I'm too fragile to cope with what he's convinced is his torrential temper.

I *know* when I've pissed the man off. Those are the instances when he seems to wrestle the cork from a wine bottle early. I might hear him vent his frustrations with me in whispered shouts at my mother. He collapses in front of his bedroom's TV, swaddled in a mien of wounded sensitivity. How boyish he always seems to me then. He'll lie with his head cradled in the crook of his elbow. His hair is gently cowlicked. The violet reflection of sports highlights play out over his face with a flicker.

Seeing him that way usually wrings a bucket-size portion of *metagu* out of me. In the past, my guilt on such evenings has been protective and very nearly maternal. Unemployment combined with empty-nest syndrome has transformed my once formidable father into someone subdued and easily hurt.

But ever since my fight with the Lark, I've grown short-tempered with Dad's downhearted face. Suddenly, I'm nettled by his moping discontent. I'm unmoved by the tentative quality in his eyes. I snub him during weekdays when we find ourselves home together, stepping on each other's toes and intruding on each other's malaise.

"The things we despise in others are the things we most despise in ourselves," a yoga teacher once said while she rearranged my hips into a posture that felt like dislocation. At the time the statement sounded too neat and tidy to contain any real human truth. In retrospect, I reach for this concept in an effort to describe why I'm so hard on my father—a man who is emotionally afflicted in the same ways I am.

But, in the absence of an abusive third party, we can't both play the part of victim. How can we *both* walk around looking utterly oppressed by the landscape, by the late afternoon hour, by the tribulations of life on this put-upon planet? Wasn't it only a matter of time before one person's *song* had to yield to the other's?

(Today I think just the opposite. Our *song* fed each other's. Virginia Satir thought low self-esteem is contagious in families. Michele Baldwin, one of Satir's former colleagues, writes, "Often [two spouses struggling with low self-esteem] disregard [their] inner feelings, and any stress tends to augment their feelings of low self-esteem. Children growing up in that environment usually have low self-worth.)

Through the doorway of his office, I watch him and see all the traits that I ache to cut out of myself. He seems too hungry for affection, too eager to win the approval of others. He seems too sentimental, too thin-skinned, too vulnerable to criticism and attached to his loneliness, but, perhaps most of all, he's too reluctant to stand up for himself. I see all of my own weaknesses, specifically the ones that I imagine drove the Lark away. I judge my Papa Z. until the thoughts make me feel wicked and crippled with a bad conscience. Most of the day I keep to myself. I give my irritation a very wide berth.

As the weeks go on, Dad and I confront each other in our stilted, backhanded ways. I find myself jabbing him about inconsequentialities: his driving, his router's erratic WiFi connection, and the way the bored barking of his dim-witted dogs ruins my concentration for work.

For his part, Dad's reactions are brutal and misdirected. When I rail against his driving, he revs his engine, flexes his horn, thrusts his middle finger out the window, and denounces the roads' arrays of idiots, assholes, and ethnics. After I mouth off about my difficulties getting online, he phones the router's technical support department and chews them out for being "outsourced idiots" with no hope of solving his problem. He even goes as far as calling his wriggly rescue dog a "pain in the ass." These are choice words for the animal that rides shotgun, who sleeps in his bed, under his sheets, between him and his wife.

Two years later, on the streets of New York, I see a girl of no more than five engaged in a howling argument with a pleading man I can't help but assume is her father. They're positioned at one end of a crosswalk, their noise competing with the steady grind of traffic. The girl holds an old-fashioned horse-on-a-stick between her tiny, clawed fingers. She's sobbing beneath her shelf of mahogany bangs. "I would rather be anywhere than be here with you!" she yowls with a disarmingly raw and almost adult resonance. I'm moved by the clarity of her fury, which is trusting, direct, and, dare I say, courageous in its little resolve. *How much more forthright than any anger I've ever exchanged with my father,* I think while I take a step toward traffic.

8
___

Failing to squelch my daily squabbles with my father or settle on a solution for my feelings about the Lark, I resign myself to a course of Staphysagria—the remedy that Alyssa prescribes for anger.

It's still difficult to believe that the tablespoon I slug back every morning contains any real substance besides H_2O. To give you an idea of just how diluted one dose is: The "remedy"—which is no larger than a grain of sand—must be thinned with eight tablespoons of water and a few drops of ethyl alcohol, and then shaken vigorously (to "potentize" it). But it doesn't end there. Alyssa says I have to add just a small dash of that dilution to eight ounces of water and belt no more than a tablespoon a day of the second mixture.

Homeopaths believe a remedy is stronger the more it is diluted, but I'm not convinced there's any real agent in the bottles to begin with. I might as well swallow a salt grain, or a dust mite, or a watered-down mouse turd. For a supposed science, homeopathy seems to require too much magic, too many closed-eyes leaps of faith.

My second reservation has to do with the sweeping applications of the remedies themselves. One popular homeopathy Web site claims Staph is a remedy for "the person whose poor self-image derives from a past hurt that is followed by suppressed anger." Evidently, it's also helpful for a person who "feels a need to please everyone" and those who have a "fear of how they appear to others," as well as those who have been "sexually abused in the past or have been abandoned emotionally by their parents." Staph is also the suggested course of treatment for painful intercourse, urinary tract infections, headaches, itching eyes, pimples, and tobacco cravings. It's for teething infants and for postpartum mothers who experienced invasive treatments like Caesarean sections or episiotomies. Staph can be mixed with water and used as a natural bug repellent. It can be applied to the scalp to get rid of lice. Given all the various applications, I'm surprised it doesn't double as a drain opener, a natural sweetener, and maybe even an alternative fuel.

In spite of myself, I'm curious. In one article I learn that patients who need Staph generally seem sweet and gentle but have low self-esteem, a rather pathetic need to be liked, and difficulty standing up for themselves. They are easily bullied. They often write poetry. They tend to weep during consultations. In chronic cases, a Staph patient might actually be so estranged from her anger that she claims she never gets angry. In a book called *Homeopathic Psychology*, I learn that "[most people who need Staphysagria] have a certain mellowness or sweetness that belies the time-bomb anger ticking away beneath the surface of their consciousness. . . . The source of [their] suppressed anger is usually found in their childhood. [Their] parents were often restrictive and authoritarian, and as young children, [they] learned that it was not safe to express [their] displeasure; that only led to stricter punishment."

If any remedy seems custom-built for me, Staph is the one. Another homeopathy Web site tells me that Staph might be appropriate for someone who has "a smoldering resentment." She has outbursts only when her anger is in the late stages and is finally too great to be suppressed. In those cases she has an instinctive tendency to throw things; her emotions make her tremble; she immediately feels guilty and ashamed. *Homeopathic Psychology* claims "the commonest cause of the [Staph patient's] resentment is rejection by a loved one, usually a partner, especially when it is done in an aggressive, hurtful way."

In *Homeopathic Psychology* I also find a vague and mystical sentence about Staph: "After the remedy is taken there is often a brief 'explosion' as anger that was kept in check pours forth (it is wise to warn the patient so that plans can be made for him to be in a place where the anger can be vented harmlessly), followed by a genuine calm which may last indefinitely." Pray tell? I'm used to taking medicine that affects my body, not medicine that impacts my world.

One afternoon, on the computer in the public library, I find more information about the above phenomenon, which homeopaths called "healing aggravation."

"With the right homeopathic remedy," one doctor of Oriental sciences claims, "the universe will create the situations that you most need . . . to move you further along on your spiritual and emotional path. [It will confront you] with even more invasive themes so that [you can] unpeel another layer of [your] fear or anger and finally let it go for good."

The doctor goes on to tell the story of one of his patients, a woman who came to his homeopathy practice hoping to treat a vaginal infection that repeatedly returned after it had been treated with conventional medication. During her consultation, the homeopath also discovered the woman had a persistent fear of invasion, specifically of crimes like rape and robbery. According to the homeopath, her mother "always invaded [her] personal space as an infant and small child, and [her] older brother did the same, and [she] had a history of date rape in college." After giving her an in-depth questionnaire, the homeopath prescribed a remedy that matched her symptoms. The day after taking it, the woman takes a nap in her car, which is parked outside of a large shopping center. There, she awakes to the sight of a man's hand reaching through her open car window in an attempt to open the front door. The woman (who was, by that time, understandably traumatized and jittery) arrives home later that same evening to discover that ants have invaded her kitchen.

I think of that woman later that night, when I take my Staph for the very first time. I picture her phobia like a hardened pit in the middlemost part of her body, lodged there all her life. I see her: fearful while she waters her plants, fearful in traffic, fearful in board meetings, petrified while she greets her husband, washes her face, turns out the bedside light, and makes pained, diffident love. For a moment I entertain the idea that it might be just as bad to spend my whole life running from my unfelt emotions as it would be to endure a few months where they jar me from sleep, creep through my house's foundation, intrude on me, and become manifest.

"When we are progressing spiritually," the same doctor writes, "the first thing to happen is often the opposite of what we wanted to happen. . . . Homeopathy is based on the theory of resonance, so it makes sense that when you change your resonant field by taking a homeopathic remedy, the resonant field around you and thus the behavior of those around you will also change to accommodate your shift in energy."

9

Immediately after I take my first dose of Staph, I hear from the Lark. His e-mail comes through at 7:00 my time (midnight, his).

Prior to its sudden intrusion in my in-box, my evening, and my mood, I am experiencing a peculiar sensation of calm. I am reclined on a chair in my father's home office, experiencing the summer dusk like a shawl draped around my shoulders. The air is thick with humidity and domestic smells: sweat, cut fruit, wet dog, smoke from the backyard barbecue. I am dressed in proper clothes for the first time in weeks and softly sweating while I toy with an old film camera and listen to a folk song play out in my head.

Maybe, upon seeing it, I let out a yawp. Something like "You've got to be kidding me!" Or, most likely, "Fuck you!" Because my mother, who has been roaming the hallway with a batch of clean laundry, drops her basket and comes to read over my shoulder.

My doted-on dope has typed:

Koren, I haven't written for so long because I fear that when I do, I needle your heart a bit more, and I don't want to cause you any more pain. But I still want to hear from you, so I have been a bit stuck. It has just gotten sunny for the first time this summer, and reminds me that you never really saw much sun here. Are your memories awful? I hope not. Mine aren't.

The mystifying missive concludes with a few footnotes about his work life:

I have decided to buy a mini piano. We have played a couple of festivals in the past two weeks, both of which, I'm told, went well.

It ends with a request to "please write soon and tell me how you are."

"Ugh!" My mother clucks. "How condescending! As if you're just *so lost* without him! Don't reply. If I were you, I'd never speak to him again. Cut him off. Cut him loose. That's my two cents. Buh-bye buddy! Good riddance!"

After she leaves, I sit still for a few moments. Then I go downstairs and fill a dinner plate. For the first time in weeks, I eat with canine hunger. I fork down bulgur wheat and green beans. I inhale two beady ears of corn, a thick burger, ice cream with cut strawberries. Then, gasping, I take my distended stomach to bed and fall into a deep, sickened sleep.

———

Two days pass before I write back to the Lark. The delay is not an act of pride or willpower. Sickness is the only thing that keeps me from responding. For two god-awful days I vomit and shudder with migraines.

It's a condition that I've never before experienced and one I want to blame on healing aggravation. The Staph remedy seems to be inducing the same symptoms that one homeopathy Web site says it is often used to treat: sensations like "stupefying headache," "bursting pain in eyeballs," and, no joke, "brain feels squeezed."

Alyssa tells me she'll talk to her mentor about my adverse reaction, but, in the meantime, she urges me not to give up on homeopathy altogether. To hear her tell it, Staph is inciting an affliction that is already there. It's unleashing some old energy that I carried around on my back like a hermit crab's shell. If I can ride this out and really experience the pain and discomfort, she says, I'll be wiser and healthier for it.

As for the Lark's e-mail, it left me with a peculiar mix of outrage and exhilaration. *He misses me*, I think with a pleased little whoop. That thought is followed by a stingier one. Namely: *Where does the Lark get off writing, sending text messages, checking in on me as though we're still involved? What entitles him to know how I am and what I'm doing? Why should I divulge everything to someone who offers nothing of himself?*

These are the thoughts that I mean to express in reply, but in the end my e-mail goes through more revisions than a congressional bill. With every revision, I find myself cutting out more invectives. Just as often, I soften it to the consistency of something that's been mechanically chewed. *A Spike 3 disposition is seductive as a way of minimizing hostility.* My final draft is coquettish. My words stare back at me like contestants in a children's beauty pageant, too eager to wear the tacky garb I've dressed them in. They wink, twirl, sway their boyish hips.

I send the damning document anyway. *A Staph patient has a profound need to be liked.* There's no endearing way to put this. I just can't stand to be rejected again. I decide I'd rather be affected and vaguely needy than be honest, messy, and loathed.

I begin elfishly: "You infinite spazz, of course I'm glad to hear from you." From there I move on to amorous admission: "I'd be lying if I said I wasn't suffering from a bit of phantom limb syndrome. Some part of me still wakes up every morning, expecting to find you just a yawn and a stretch-of-an-arm away." Next, I stall. I stray to news about family, gossip about friends, and a brief update on my book-in-the-works (lying to say it's going well).

It isn't until the thirteenth paragraph that I finally let my aggression peek through. Even then, I'm vacillating and conflicted.

When it comes to—how do you put it? "Needling my heart"? You're not. Not in hearing from you, numb nut. I'm not even needled by the fact that you changed your mind about what we had going. To reiterate, the only thing that drew a little blood was the selfish (sorry) and weeniely way you went about telling me. Again, I am loath to call you a weenie, but you're older than any man I've ever dated before. And I haven't heard someone above the age of twenty sing the "I wanted to make you think I was an asshole" tune. Everyone else accounts for their emotions, acknowledges them, owns them and delivers them decently.

Such irony. Such hypocrisy. Today, I hold my thick head in my hands.

I start conjuring something called "the assertion of an ought." That's a term I found in the writing of a professor named Joseph de Rivera, who heads a peace studies program. He said, "Whenever we are angry, we somehow believe that we can influence the object of our anger. We assume that the other person is responsible for his actions and ought to behave differently."

I feel myself channeling what social psychologist Carol Tavris calls fury's "policing function." In *Anger: The Misunderstood Emotion*, she writes, "Anger is a sign that someone has broken [one of our culture's unspoken rules]. It announces that someone is not behaving as (you think) she or he *ought*."

Suddenly I'm not just an overreactive ex-girlfriend but a vigilante upholding the rules of common decency. I'm remembering the way Tavris talks about psychologist James Averill; he said, she writes, "that, for most of Western history, it has been up to individuals to see to it that their rights were respected and justice seen to; in the absence of a formal judiciary, anger operates as a personal one." I've learned that in situations when a court trial would be melodramatic, fury helps restore fair treatment.

I begin to hit my stride in the next paragraph. I tell the Lark:

Any real—what were your exact words? "Pain you might have caused me"? Was in the things that you said, silly man. Not just the things you said about my book (may I gently remind you that you haven't read a page of it), but also in the ones you had to say about me: the part about being a waste of time, but nice to have on your arm, although on the whole not worth keeping around just to . . . It's not worth finishing. It would look even more ridiculous in print. I've more than accepted the fact that you didn't feel for me what I felt for you. No one who loved anyone, even in a platonic way, would have said things that were quite so injurious—things that cut straight for her most tender parts.

But the very moment my anger is visible through my prose, I go sprinting as if to cover it with a raincoat:

That's the last I'm going to mention this though. Because I do want to be your friend. And because I understand what a late-night conversation it was.

Now you see it:

I only mention it now because after that bit about needling me, I feel like I need to reiterate: anything you feel like you're withholding from me is not a cause for pining, not if it means enduring what I saw the other night.

Now you don't:

I'm glad work is going well for you though. And I really have actively wondered about you, vaguely worried about you, missed the sound of you, the weight of you, regretted so many things I never said.

The whole thing amounts to a 1,600-word rebuttal to a 150-word note. All evidence to the contrary, I maintain that I'm not angry. The most I can do is admit to feeling hurt.

I conclude the letter with a plain-faced disclosure of grief:

Christ, as for the question of memories, I can't answer it right now. Not the fact that this ended, but the way in which it ended tarnished so many memories I would've liked to keep.

10

It feels good to evince some emotion, after a long month of keeping it to myself.

In Brighton, where I'd always secretly felt as though I'd intruded on the Lark's routine, I'd taken pains to stay deferential and agreeable. "If you prefer" became my catchall response. Along with more ingratiating slogans like: "Sure." "Whatever you think." "You don't have to go out of your way." "I can find it on my own." "I can go it alone." "I'm a big girl." "I'm flexible." "I'm easy." As the month passed, the effort involved in policing everything I thought I couldn't say had made me withdrawn in a manner that might've easily passed for someone snobbily disinterested or mute in a way that might have seemed as though I was giving the Lark the cold shoulder.

After I press the "send" button on my e-mail, I find myself imagining how the Lark might have felt in the face of that typical Zailckas aloofness: wresting conversation out of it; listening as his inquiries were returned with distracted, single words; feeling increasingly judged in the ensuing silence; feeling his resentments throb and rise like mercury in an old glass thermometer.

How strange, I start to think, *that I could only express some anger once I was safely outside the confines of our relationship.*

How, I wonder, *did I come by the idea that relationships should be as peaceful as a Sunday school picnic?*

————

Because I can't yet accept that my reluctance to fight with the Lark is a personal defect, I spend a day trying to figure out whether other Americans go to lengths to avoid anger in their romantic relationships, a conceit that Carol and Peter Stearns, the authors of *Anger: The Struggle for Emotional Control in American History*, say is left over from Victorian America. According to William Vernon Harris, *Anger* is the only book that attempts to chart American attitudes about anger over time.

In *Anger*, I learn that anger didn't rate high on a moralist's list of no-nos in colonial America. At that time, wrath still ranked among Christianity's seven deadly sins, but losing one's temper was small potatoes compared with so-called depravities like lust or pride. In a time when privacy was hard to come by—families were large, houses small, with few interior walls—anger helped create boundaries and eke out some personal space.

On the domestic front, newly married couples in colonial times weren't warned against raising their voices. Anger was only a predicament if it provoked violence, like when a husband or master went all Ike Turner on his servants or wife.

The Stearnses say there was even a Homeric appreciation for

anger as it pertained to passion. In stories like William Alcott's *The Young Husband*, published in 1840, they found it wasn't out of the ordinary to hear a hotheaded husband described as "spirited and quick tempered, as great, lovinghearted men always are."

I learn that the idea that love and anger shouldn't mingle first took hold during the Industrial Revolution. That was when Americans began to view home as a sanctuary from the noise, injury, and competition of the factory, and when family began to assume a role that Christopher Lasch called "a haven in a heartless world." That was when the idea emerged that couples must curb their anger, lest it compromise their chance at cozy domesticity.

I read quotes from Frederick Saunders's 1874 book, *About Women, Love and Marriage*, and think there is something to the way he describes home as "not simply a place to live in" but as a "sacred enclosure—the hallowed retreat of the virtues and the affections." I write notes to myself about how people began to accept home as a place akin to "innocence and Eden."

When my reading in *Anger* brings me to the Victorian era, I recognize something of myself in the austere bastards, with their ideas about "companionate marriage." It was the Victorians who first decided husbands and wives ought to be as loyal to one another as wounded war buddies, and that marriage should be the one place on earth where a person felt understood, encouraged, and psychically nourished. Just like me, the Victorians desperately wanted to believe that emotional openness was possible between two people, but—also like me—they were inclined to bury their heads in the sand when it came to confronting their rage.

The Victorians thought even one spat could cut true love off at the knees. In Orson Fowler's 1841 book, *Fowler on Matrimony*, the phrenologist suggested little more than "[a] single tart remark, or unkind tone of voice" could spell splitsville for a young couple. He went on to write, "[S]o extremely tender is the plant of connubial love, that small things embitter its fruits."

Ladies' magazines of the time attached deadly consequences to fights between spouses. Erma Leland's story "The First Quarrel," first published in *Peterson's Magazine* in 1875, describes a young wife whose nagging causes her husband to go out walking in the woods, where he is toppled by a falling pine and knocked into a coma. In Mary H. Paron's story "The Adopted Daughter," a wife's anger at her husband causes her to literally burst a blood vessel: "It was the demon of an ill regulated temper that possessed her. . . . [T]he white foam gathered on her lip, the veins stood out rigid and swollen over her forehead. . . . [S]he strove to move forward, and fell headlong to the floor, the blood gushing from her nose and mouth." In these stories, anger in marriage was literally a fatal mistake. It was not an emotion that might occasionally but innocuously surface between two people who shared everything from a bank account to a bed.

I grow a little squeamish when I realize how much time the Victorians devoted to a couple's "first quarrel," which they described as an event of apocalyptic proportions. In his 1852 marriage manual *Bridal Greetings*, Reverend Daniel Wise said of a couple's first fight: "Let that be avoided, and that hateful demon, discord, will never find a place at the domestic hearth. Let it have its existence, no matter . . . how brief its duration, and the demon will feel himself invited and will take his place, an odious, but an abiding guest, at the fireside." The author went on to caution wives, "Never quarrel . . . it is death to happiness." And to give husbands advice that's still repeated today: "If you become angry with her . . . she will never forget it."

Everyone knows the Victorians were a repressed bunch, but I learn there might be remnants of Victorian thinking in our modern culture too. Psychologist Brenda Shoshanna, author of *The Anger Diet*, advises readers in an article called "How to Stop the Fighting in Your Relationship" to "choose to be happy rather than right," "realize the price [they] are paying" for continued conflicts, and see how being "determined to win a battle" makes a relationship "doomed to failure."

The death of happiness.

The pettiness impeding a relationship's growth.

I hate to admit it, but these had always been my fears as well. It seems bizarre that, ten months into our relationship, the Lark and I still hadn't had our first fight—and even that one was in the throes of a breakup.

The more I think about it, the more I realize I only ever had one argument of note in my past relationships, and that fight was always the crescendo, the beginning of the end, an argument that proved the Victorians right.

I'd always told myself that this was because I wasn't the kind of person who values conflict in her relationships. I wasn't one to confuse pain with pleasure, injury with intimacy, theatrics with passion. I didn't live by those words of Nicharchos: "Now if you don't hate me, beloved, don't love me." Academically speaking, I'd always been intrigued by Sappho's assertion that desire is a mixture of affection and contempt. But where my own romantic life was concerned, I'd always gotten by, rather easily, without what lurid women's magazines call "the fire." Given the choice between screaming turmoil and screaming boredom, I'd always picked the latter.

At what point in my twenties did I make the command decision to skip the bittersweet nectar of eros and settle for the bland porridge of familiarity? Possibly around the time I quit drinking myself into repeated alcoholic blackouts. My boyfriends before the Lark were all as stoical as the queen's guards. They'd been patient, committed, and dispassionate, and I'd had to really debase myself to extract any emotion, either grin or grimace, from them.

11

Another thing happens after I start taking the anger remedy Staph.

One evening, after dinner, the phone rings. At the time, I'm standing over the kitchen sink, frowning, flicking stray seeds from a wedge of watermelon and thinking how lovely it would be if everyone went to bed and left me alone with my new, secret nighttime routine—the one where I wander through the moonlit woods like a teenager, fearing fisher cats (wild, weasel-like creatures that some New England natives claim can kill and eat a deer), slapping mosquitoes from my shoulders, and chain-smoking from a pack of light cigarettes.

My mother sighs and reaches to remove the screaming phone from its cradle. I know from her salty smile that my sister is on the other end of the line. And I know, just know from the way her expression shifts, that my sister is pregnant. For two years it seemed as though my sister urgently wished for a child. Curiously, that was as long as her relationship with our own mother had been strained, and just about as long as my relationship with Mom had been on the mend, following the publication of my book.

I trail my mother into the seldom-entered living room, where she slowly lowers herself into an armchair so prudishly unused it's barely seen a backside. Mom's been too absorbed in the conversation to even flick on a lamp. By the light of the hallway, I see her finger her lips and nod into the portable phone that she supports with one tense, upraised shoulder. She sits frozen and leaning forward on her haunches. She is literally on the edge of her seat.

I sink onto a patch of hardwood floor in the corner and listen while I let my eyes roll over the dimly lit room. Its Victorian vibe is always more frightening in the dark. Vines twist up the wallpaper. Doilies spread themselves, like cobwebs, over the dark furniture. An eerie family of dolls peers out from behind its glass case. They look the way my sister and I did in all our childhood photos: overdressed, uncomfortable, our mouths drawn down to nothing, and our big eyes startled beneath our blunt bangs.

My mother looks through me while she speaks into the receiver. "All this seems like an awful lot to take on so soon," she tells my sister. "But if you think you can manage it . . . Well then, I'm happy for you." The grandfather clock chimes, and her voice goes up a register to disguise her sudden swell of tears. "How far along did you say you are? Uh huh. Uh huh." Mournful tenderness overtakes her bristling surprise. "I know. Well, take it easy. Get to bed early tonight. Yes, take your vitamins."

The phone never gets passed my way. I see my mother jab the "off" button with her thumb. I look up and notice that my father has appeared in the hallway.

Outside, wolves wail.

A TV babbles in a far-off room.

———

I assure them that all this is news to me too. This, in spite of the fact that it's become my gig to know more about my sister than the two of them, whom she starkly keeps in the dark about her comings and goings.

In the past two years my fair-haired sibling has become uncommunicative, dare I say, cagey. She'd say she's never deceived anyone. She sees her fibs as minimizations. The stealthy schoolgirl once told me she lies through omission. She doesn't tell you anything.

But I'm not one to criticize. When I was in college there were a great many things that I kept from my family: drink-induced binges, blackouts—personal disasters they didn't know about until I showed them a draft of my first book. But it seems my sister has pumped up the volume on my adolescent secrecy. When she was twenty, there were a few months where none of us knew where in Miami she lived. Although my parents paid her tuition and helped with her bills, she was elusive and difficult to reach by phone. No one knew her live-in boyfriend's full name or could pin them to a mailing address.

For all her bravado in the outside world, she's always been fiercely guarded when it comes to our family.

To me, her secrecy just seems like the newest in a series of coping techniques. She hasn't always moved through the world sneering or laughing devilishly, flashing the barbell in her punctured tongue as she does. Her black makeup hasn't always been clotted in her eyes' outer corners. It's only recently that she disguises her delicate, white throat behind an armor plate's worth of steel jewelry. She hasn't always been bound up in chains, dog tags, wrist cuffs, hoop earrings, and stout, gothic crosses.

But from the time she was five, she's been hiding. She'd learned to shut herself in the finished basement of our house, watching the same VHS tapes (mostly Disney movies and G-rated sitcoms) over and over again. She spent so many hours underground, engrossed in her little escapism, that my parents nicknamed her "the Mole." When she went away to college it didn't surprise me that she selected film as her major. All her life it's been more acceptable to study actors' displays of emotion than it is to reveal her own.

The psychotherapist Virginia Satir calls the way we hide our feelings from others as well as from ourselves our "communication stances." It seems pretty clear to me that my sister is what Satir called a family's "distractor" (other psychologists have identified a similar role, which they call "the adjuster"). She seems to handle family stress by focusing my family's attention elsewhere, away from the context of our problems and away from our feelings.

Over the course of the past two years, my sister has begun to resemble the description that addiction author Claudia Black attributes to the distractor/adjuster: She seems "detached," "noninvested," "less visible within our family structure," and "oblivious to the conflicts and emotions at home." She misses some holidays. She skipped out on my grandmother's funeral and my cousin's wedding. She doesn't always acknowledge our birthdays. During the worst times, she leaves her voice-mail box full, not allowing any of us to leave her a phone message.

When she's present, she oozes chaos and mischief. She makes wild proclamations. It seems as though she only ever telephones in an attempt to rattle me with news of a new tattoo, a new piercing, a new scheme, a new scandal. "Do you only call when you want to shock me?" I regularly ask her. "Do you realize just how often you put me in the middle, making me swear to keep certain things from our family, asking me to deny what very few facts I know?"

This hasn't always been the way. The fact is, until I published my first book, I was the daughter who was generally regarded as the family problem. But somewhere over the course of the past four years, my sister and I have swapped coping mechanisms. In her effort to keep her feelings underground, she creates diversions with escalating displays of tumult. In my effort to do the same, I either busy myself with other people's feelings or I turn into a scholarly robot. Deadpan. That's the word my closest aunt and uncle often used to describe me.

At least before my breakup with the Lark, I was the daughter with a terrible habit of trying to finish other people's sentences, in an attempt to—what? Connect with them. Gain their support. Anticipate their needs. I felt like I moved around in a constant state of empathy or apology. When I wasn't listening, I was sympathizing. When I wasn't sympathizing, I was reducing everything to a detached, intellectual exercise (my anger book a prime example). I played the roles Satir called "the computer" (some Satir scholars call this the "super-reasonable") and "the placater." Satir said placaters hide their vulnerability by attempting to please others, saying yes not because we feel like it but because we're afraid that otherwise things will fall apart at the seams. For computers, every aspect of living becomes an intellectual experience; we hunker down in our brains and turn out the lights in the rest of ourselves, pretending, at least emotionally, that nobody's home.

Even our physical ailments align with Satir's model. Satir claims years of playing the distractor takes a toll on the central nervous system. I think, here, of my sister's chronic migraines. She also says computers have problems with the fluids in their bodies. Dehydration is my natural state. From the age of eight I was a chronic fainter, liable to cop a face plant anywhere from elevator to church pew. During my first-ever book tour, I'd wilted like a daisy halfway through a reading. I'd awakened, mortified, to find myself lying supine on the carpet while someone fanned my face with a copy of *Smashed*.

Why do we keep playing these roles if they are making us ill?

Satir says computers appeal to others through their intellect; placaters through their compassion; distractors through their headlong sense of fun. Deep down, I believe my chronic overthinking and motherly smothering are the qualities that endear me to people. (Or, at the very least, keep them from rejecting me.) In reality, they are the very affectations that exasperate people and make them avoid me like the bubonic plague.

———

There's a reason why my sister's announcement hits me as hard as it does; why it curdles my gut and pressurizes me right down to the bones.

My reaction has nothing to do with a baby.

It's more about the ordeals of the past two years—the catastrophes that have occurred as regular as clockwork. I still remember the abusive boyfriend, the dorm change after a college roommate allegedly threatened to stab her, the off-campus apartment from which she was "inexplicably" evicted, and, ultimately, the underhanded elopement.

All I can think is how it will fall on me to comfort my parents. I know that much from past experience. For the next few days I'm going to have to reassure them that my younger sister knows what she is getting into. I'll have to tell them to forget that she's newly married, presently unemployed and barely four months out of college. "You have to trust," I'll say. Or, "You have to let her do what she's going to do." I'll remind them that before all the acting out, she'd once been a gentle, thoughtful girl. She'd gone to piano lessons and Sunday school. She'd planted tiger lilies with her mother, fretted over her homework, and babysat the neighborhood kids before she was tall enough to reach the bathroom sink.

Tomorrow, I'll have to be composed and supportive—always supportive, doling out big-eyed nods and back-patting hugs. Even if my own head is about to open up and erupt like a whale's blowhole. For the moment, I don't have the energy. I climb the stairs and check my e-mail once more for word from the Lark (there is none).

12

Some part of me—the emotional part, which is just as stupid and stubborn as a barnacle—still wishes I could confide in the Lark this latest news. He was the one I'd turned to six months ago, during the hysterical weekend of my sister's wedding.

———

She had announced her engagement on the day before Christmas. Her betrothed had been her boyfriend for three and a half months (though they'd met one summer when they were fifteen and corresponded over the years with great depth of feeling). He was a twenty-one-year-old marine with an easy laugh, an innocent, blue-eyed gaze, and a square-shouldered air of chivalry.

I still remembered the way the pair had approached me to ask me when and how they ought to tell my parents. My sister wanted to wait until our mother noticed her diamond ring and pumped her for answers. (This was what had happened the summer prior, to a disastrous end, when my sister had started wearing a conspicuous third-finger ring given to her by her Cuban then boyfriend.) While they debated how to break the news, I held my breath, waiting for our mother to catch on to the way my college-age sister was walking around with a mischievous smile on her face and her left fist balled inside the sleeve of her sweatshirt.

Marriage was a very adult intention, I'd told them, and they needed to declare it in a very adult way. Why, I asked, didn't they fix breakfast for my parents? Why didn't they all four sit down over coffee and bagels and talk about their plans for a wedding? I hadn't been wrong, but I had been unnecessarily harsh for reasons I couldn't explain. I understand now how fearful I was of any scenario that triggered strong emotions in my family. Because few of us felt free to communicate our feelings, any life-altering event—whether positive or negative—was unsafe.

My sister nodded resolutely, and then what had happened? I'd awoken at the ungodly hour of 4:30 A.M. and heard them approach my mother—not at the breakfast table, but in the *foyer*—as she groggily prepared to leave for work at a local department store. My sister broke the news saying, "So we're thinking of getting married in February. Not with a big ceremony, just—like, you know—on *paper*. That way Tom will get a pay increase and I can get health insurance and we can both get on a list for base housing."

When my mother had flown off the handle, particularly over the bit about being married only on paper—"You did not," she shouted, "tell someone who's been married for thirty years that a union as significant as marriage was no more than a 'piece of paper'"—my sister had been quick to divert the blame. Her voice had assumed a tone of giggling fluster, and, even from my bed, I'd heard her pass off a wax paper bag, saying, "And uh, do you want a chocolate cruller? All this was Koren's idea. She said you wouldn't stay mad if I brought you donuts." Just like that I'd been implicated. *She'd sold me out*, I thought.

My boiling mother had called from the department store where she works and left me a shrill voice-mail message. And the placater in me felt compelled to drive over there immediately. I'd felt the need to apologize for both the shock of my sister's announcement and the part I'd played in it. I'd held both of her trembling hands while the PA spouted carols, and frowning Christmas shoppers stared, and the wounded woman whom I knew as "Mom" cried away the better part of her twenty-minute lunch break.

Stay out of it, I wish I could tell younger myself. *You're just mak-*

ing it worse. But at twenty-six, I was desperate to be closer to the mother who only recently seemed to like me. As Michele Baldwin, a student of Satir, wrote, "Human beings seem willing to pay whatever price is necessary to feel loved, to belong, to make sense, and to feel as if they matter, even if the price exacted doesn't really accomplish that."

In the end, my sister and her fiancé promised my parents that they'd wait until summer to tie the knot. It was only six months away, after all. And for their reasons, it meant a lot to my folks that my sister got her college degree before she donned the voluminous white dress. They were paying her tuition, after all, and was it really too much to ask to have her fully focused on her job hunt and her final exams? From what I heard, the couple had crossed their hearts, given their word, and veraciously shaken my parents' hands.

But by the time the New Year rolled around, my sister had begun calling home with far-fetched stories and strangely timed requests. Most memorably, she demanded her social security card, which my mother had been holding for safekeeping while she was away at college. As with most of my sister's stories, this one was long and muddy, rich in color but dim on details. She needed it immediately, she claimed, because her hip-hop dance troupe was "possibly" performing at the Super Bowl, an appearance for which she might "possibly" get paid. After my mother mailed the card, my sister's dance troupe promptly "canceled" their appearance. (This after my parents had bragged to family as far as Texas.) And then, some of my mother's military-savvy coworkers told her that the card was required to declare one's marriage to the marines.

Suspicions mounted that February when my sister flew up to North Carolina from her Miami university to spend her birthday at her fiancé's marine base.

As far as that weekend is concerned, I'll spare you the full story. Because it is a *tediously* drawn-out and oblique story, in which my sister repeatedly refused to answer our parents' calls, and I found myself volunteering again to play the role of the intermediary. Let it suffice to say that it had been the most chaotic of all recent family chaos. Who really needed to relive the way my mother had threatened to fly down there and stop the ceremony? Who wanted to think back on the conversation where my already married sister had lied to me point-blank, saying that as far as getting married that weekend, they "hadn't decided one way or another."

(*Cut her a break,* I think now. Like myself, she wants to be accepted by our folks. Unlike myself, she isn't willing to compromise what she wants in order to get it. It only stands to follow that she's found compromise by compromising the truth.)

In the weeks that followed, I'd tried to persuade myself that I didn't feel hurt that I hadn't been there. *Why should I,* I thought, *when obviously my sister hadn't been hurt by that fact? So what that she'd decided on a civil ceremony with no one but strangers there to bear its witness? Big deal if, in order to get married, she'd had to wait in the same line as people filing legal injunctions? That she'd found herself waiting behind a man who'd told her, "Y'all are getting married? That's nice. I used to be married. Now I'm gettin' a restraining order against my ex-wife."* I told myself that that was what my sister wanted. She'd *wanted* her first bit of marriage advice to come from the courthouse secretary rather than her mother: a woman who'd told her, "When you're married, your love for each other is like a sewing needle at the bottom of a trash dump. All this garbage will sure as shit get piled on top of it, but don't ever let yourself forget that—somewhere, way down deep— your love's still there."

As the weeks passed, the placater in me said my primary concern was for my parents, who were at that time too despondent to drive into town, shovel the snow off their walkway, or even answer the phone without crying. But beneath my caretaker's expression—a smooshed face of empathy—I nursed a sharp, aggrieved twinge. It was only in an early e-mail to the Lark (this was long before I'd moved to Brighton) that I'd been able to admit to feeling gypped:

I've gotta say, I feel a little cheated. I mean, my only sibling! I should have been the maid of honor, right? And worn a pretty dress, and snapped photos, and ensured good records were played after the cake was cut. Did they even have a cake? Who knows? The bride wore ripped jeans. Their witnesses were another marine couple. Last I heard from my mother, she was making these pained animal noises. You'd have thought there was a death in the family.

At the time, the Lark had sent me words that soothed my head and slowed my scrambling heart. He'd written:

Good grief. My jaw is still dropped. Marriage is such a permanent thing to do on a whim. Every time I think of what your family must be going through, my stomach churns a bit. You're upset. Who could fault you?

———

Hours after my sister announced her pregnancy, I gravitate to my laptop, then the Internet, then my e-mail account. When I see it there—the Lark's reply—in my in-box, I feel my whole body draw up and steel itself. The feeling is apprehensive and dire. In response to my 1,600-word e-mail, the Lark has written:

God, that final fateful night was awful. Do we have to go over it again? I spoke some of the most idiotic words to have come out of my mouth, which I will cringe about for a long time.

This is a bit unfair though: "being a waste of time, but nice to have on your arm, although on the whole not worth keeping around." By "wasting time" I meant that I couldn't see a future with you and that to pretend, to carry on hoping that it was a fleeting feeling would be worse for both of us—that to carry on would waste time, not that our relationship had been a waste of time. It was far from this. When we first started exchanging letters, you lit up a spark in me, and I was desperate to make it work and it did. We had some fantastic times. But when I realized that spark hadn't become a flame, I decided that I should be honest with you. The way it all came out, I regret sincerely.

"Nice on your arm"—by this I meant that all my friends loved you and I was proud to introduce you, although I seem to remember putting this differently. And "not worth keeping around"? I was gutted when you left. I still am. I've lost a future I thought was going to be brilliant.

As for my words about your book, I can only curl up. I seem to remember being wound up about a male/female crux, and then arguing myself into the darkest parts of my imagination. I can only hope you have enough faith in me to realize that this isn't the way I view the world at all. Or your work. But enough. Enough about that night. Thank you for caring about me and for being honest.

I read the message twice, puzzling over its contradictory tones, neglecting its subtle tenderness, wholly discarding its competence and honesty. I cringe at the patronizing "spark" and appreciate—in a writerly sense—the image about arguing with his imagination.

I try for a long time to figure out what he intends by reiterating "enough" in the final sentences. Is he mournful or exasperated? In the end, I decide on the latter. He must really mean "Enough!" I figure he's dropped the exclamation point out of a sense of chivalry.

13

I'm still convinced that Staphysagria has given me an allergic reaction.

So instead of taking it, I spend the weekend gulping Lycopodium—the homeopathic remedy for fear. Lycopodium comes from club mosses, and that seems to suit me. All those weeks at my folks' house are turning me into a kind of forest moss myself. What am I becoming if not a sodden blob? And my mood certainly seems to be spreading—reducing everyone around me to rot.

A little Internet research tells me that the Lycopodium patient is "saddened in the morning" and "annoyed by little things" all day. She is also "deficient of ideas" (something tells me my editor won't disagree on this point) and she "can't bear to read anything she's written." She is extremely sensitive to noise (like, say, the barking of her parents' idiotic, ill-disciplined dogs), and, even though she's averse to company, she has a debilitating fear of being alone.

As a little girl I'd had a real, violent, almost physical fear of being left alone. My father—who sometimes preferred to leave me waiting alone in the car while he ducked into a Stop & Shop to buy kitty litter—always returned to find me crying, hyperventilating, or eyeing the parking lot (not to mention the rearview mirrors and the dashboard clock) with a face of panicked vigilance. In the rare instances when I got off the school bus and swung open the door on an empty house, I would wait trembling with my backpack on the front stoop until my mother returned from her chat with a neighbor.

In adulthood, this phobia has more than loosened its grasp. For the past four years I've lived and worked alone, shirking crowds and dreading group engagements. In my relationships prior to the Lark, I'd been detached, guarded, noncommittal, and bound to a labyrinth of self-imposed rules that meant no one got close enough to wound or reject me. I told one boyfriend he wasn't allowed to stay over more than two nights a week. I also evaded the same brave soul whenever he proposed moving in together. And the few times he dared to push the conversation even further—to marriage?—I cut him off at the kneecaps with words as cold, sharp, and precise as a samurai sword.

In the days after the Lark writes back with the bit about the "spark that hadn't become a flame," some ghost of the old dread returns to me.

The fear hits me hardest at night, like a full-body blow, and I dread climbing into my bed. All night I lie awake and agitated. Those are the moments when the walls seem to constrict. When the floor fan makes an unbearable, pornographic slapping sound. I kick off the covers in fitful, twitching movements. But no matter how I turn,

I can't shake the feeling of being queasy, severed from the world, resentful, and panicked.

Why has this fear of being alone returned?

I convince myself that it must be because I'm Larkless. I'm too anxious to ponder what my present situation could possibly mean: I feel alone in the presence of my family.

14

Even worse than my sudden fear of solitude is the anxiety I feel about writing.

When I wrote my first memoir, my only problem had been trying to get my stubby fingers to type fast enough to keep up with the words that dashed like ticker tape through my head. The first draft of *Smashed* had skated out of me in four months.

My objective, journalistic little anger book, on the other hand, had already taken me four *years*. And I have little to show for it but a few ringed binders full of "research" and reading lists, a couple of usable scenes. Time is ticking on my deadline. And I can feel the people around me begin to lose faith in me. Pals, beginning to tease me, say things like: "It seems like you're never going to finish that book of yours!" Or, "Whenever we ask you how it's going, you always say, 'Almost done.' It's always 'almost done.'" (These comments make me hemorrhage with rage. Friends have no idea that these are the exact same phrases I punish myself with daily.) My computer's cursor sits still and pulses, as if tapping its foot in impatience with me.

Something has to change. I'm impatient for a revelation.

I can't relate to that doctor of Oriental sciences whose essay assures me the key will be revealed to me the moment I really feel "the pain and discomfort" that is "locked inside" myself, "energetically." I want to identify it. I want to exorcise it. If only it were as simple as a snakebite, I'd eagerly bite my own arm and suck out the dark venom.

One afternoon I finally get a hunch about what's holding me up.

In Virginia Satir, I read about and identify with a dysfunctional communication process called "nominalization." It's what happens when someone who is afraid of emotion replaces a process of being (a verb) with a static event (a noun). For instance, rather than saying, "I'm angry," a person talks about "experiencing anger."

The words seem to shine a spotlight on me at my desk, where I am sitting for the umpteenth day in a row in front of an empty Word document, holding one fist to my mouth and listening to the voice in my head that cackles *hack, failure, fraud* in a heartless loop.

For the first time I understand that I'm not trying to write about anger indefinite. I'm direly pissed and trying to understand my own. The time it takes me to arrive here makes a monkey of me, but the unconscious is riddled with blind spots that it doesn't want to acknowledge.

I sit down and try—just for my own private purposes—to write about leaving Brighton. Even if I'd ignored my anger there ("I didn't notice"), denied it ("I'm really not mad"), or distorted it ("I'm just disappointed"), I remember quite clearly the flashes of fury I felt just beneath the surface.

I start setting my teary exit into words, but I can't seem to stop going back, rereading, editing, and rewriting. Weeks pass and I manage to turn a perfectly fine (if truly embarrassing) story into something so tortured it's practically unreadable. *Pull yourself together,* I tell myself, as I hack the thing apart for the fourteenth time and Frankenstein it back together. *Move on. Get to the rest of the story. Handle your business.*

But I can't. The rewriting is compulsive. I drop the whole exercise and return to the safety of further reading.

———

I think I can elude my own emotions by crawling into my research and dying there. But in an anger-screening questionnaire I am cruelly confronted with the reason why I can't seem to write about my own individual anger:

"True or false," the question asks. "Being angry means being imperfect. Is it possible that I repress the emotion to maintain a mind-set of moral superiority?"

True, all around, I think. *A million times true.*

In psychological texts, I find the correlation between perfection-ism and anger. Freud frequently acknowledged how stingy the "anal character" was with anger. And in *Character Analysis,* Wilhelm Reich described the rather funny case of a man he dubbed the "aris-tocratic character," saying he had a "reserved countenance," "his speech was well-phrased and balanced, soft and eloquent," and "it was evident that he avoided—or concealed—any haste or excite-ment."

A perfectionist by any other name ("anal-retentive," "compulsive personality") smells just as bat-shit insane. I relate horrifyingly well to a perfectionist's MO. In recent years I too have taken on an ap-pearance that is "unrelaxed, tense, joyless, and grim." I've come to value "self-discipline, prudence, and loyalty." I prefer to do things myself instead of relying on other people. And I'm also stuck in a "repetitive life pattern" chock-full of wanton abandons like "me-thodical, meticulous work."

I get deeply depressed when I read about the way shrinks link repressed joy and closeted anger.

In the words of psychologist Theodore Millon, "the grim and cheerless demeanor of compulsives is often quite striking"; "they have an air of austerity and serious-mindedness"; and "their social behavior is polite and formal."

And according to Reich, the perfectionist is "usually even-tempered, lukewarm in his displays of both love and hate." How much of myself I see in those damning words. Not too long earlier, a friend had pointed out how dead I sounded whenever I called her from my parents' house; my voice was so absent of inflection it could have passed for the dial tone.

I'm so terrified to lend a voice to my anger, I begin to wonder if I've been holding back my affection too. Virginia Satir gave special attention to the ways families display both rage and affection. She saw them as two variations of the same theme. The same families that viewed anger as dangerous often had difficultly expressing affection too. Satir found children who grew up in families that expressed little affection also tended to behave angrily toward each other.

I start to wonder if I'd loved the Lark demonstratively. Had my eyes ever twinkled behind my poker face? Had I ever unknitted my troubled shoulders long enough to let my head melt against his shoulder? Even before what the Lark had called that "final, fateful night," anxieties had begun to express themselves in the corners of my mouth. My posture had taken on a quality that was guarded and withdrawn. I'd spent most of July treating the Lark with fussy politeness. From the moment I'd set foot in Brighton, I'd been afraid to contradict him, lest he see me as flawed. Our meals together had turned awkward and courtly in those final weeks together. I remember one meal in particular, where we'd done little more than clear our throats and smooth the linen napkins in our laps. Our stilted conversations might've easily been mistaken for small talk had it not been for the hot surge of expectation moving under them.

In the writing of psychiatrist Claudio Naranjo, specifically in an article called "Anger and Perfectionism," I come across the sentence: "It would be a mistake, however, to conceive of [the perfectionist] as a violent character—for it is on the contrary an overcontrolled and overcivilized interpersonal style." *In a nutshell*, I think. The same instinct that has my writing in a deep freeze is just as surely sabotaging my life. It's no coincidence that I am a writer. (This as opposed to a performer, a dancer, a singer.) Writing is an art form one can torture, "polish" to death, before it's ever exposed to the withering light of critique. In recent years, I'd brought that same stultifying attention to my character. Maybe it was no coincidence that the Lark and I had spent so much of our relationship connecting through letters.

I resolve to connect with my inner fool, to risk embarrassment, inadequacy, and imperfection. To that end, I send the Lark a text message even though I haven't heard from him in weeks. Something like: *I've been thinking . . . when it comes to you and me, the revolution failed because it was ill timed and poorly communicated. But I'm beginning to think I still believe in the cause.*

A few hours later, he writes back to say that he is, at that moment, playing the Reading Festival. But yes, as it happened, he would love to speak: "Why don't you give me a bell on Monday?"

I spend the rest of the weekend on a cumulus cloud. I credit Lycopodium, the fear remedy, for freeing me from my self-containment and making communication possible. *Homeopathy*, I think, *is sheer sorcery. It is out-and-out magic.*

"You seem better," my mother announces while we stretch out around a neighbor's pool. For the moment, she seems right. I find myself reclining in the same sunshine that I've been going to lengths to avoid, no tears on my cheeks, no impulse to evade my family, no wincing or teeth gritting or wringing headaches, no meanly shooing the dogs when no one is looking and letting frustration wrench me inside out. The bottom of the pool is as blue as an egg, and I lean over the side and plunge my arm in right up to my elbow. For the first time in a long time, I don't feel the urge to avoid phenomena that could move me. I take in the dragonflies brooding over the black-eyed Susans, beating their green-irised wings. I watch the light pitch on the water in jerky, golden flashes. I feel love, in a sharp pinch, when I look at my mother and see the easy beauty in her face.

In all my soul-searching, I think I've arrived at the answer to why the Lark and I had failed as a couple. I feel eager to share it with him, to make apologies, to make resolutions, to (above all) make up, move on, and resolve the whole fuck-awful mess. It's a bold move, bordering on insane given what he's said about not seeing a future with me. (Maybe the Lycopodium really has jacked up my courage.)

If only I'd read *Dark Night of the Soul*, I might have heeded the warning of St. John of the Cross and not acted quite so quickly: "There are others who are vexed with themselves when they observe their own imperfectness and display an impatience that is not humility; so impatient are they about this that they would fain be saints in a day. Many of these persons purpose to accomplish a great deal and make grand resolutions; yet, as they are not humble and have no misgivings about themselves, the more resolutions they make, the greater is their fall and the greater their annoyance, since they have not the patience to wait for that which God will give them when it pleases Him."

15

The very next morning, I sit in the front yard with a fully charged phone in my lap. I'm prepared. In my quavering hands, I juggle a prepaid phone card and a few bullet points I'd sketched out when 4:00 A.M. found me a-tingle and far too excited to sleep. I'm nervous and shaking very softly as I sit with my dusty, bare feet pulled up under me.

Moments earlier, I swallowed my day's shot of Lycopodium, imagining it might make me not as brave as a lion, but as brave as I'd need to be to tame the animal out of one.

Even I have to acknowledge just how wispy and New Aged I am becoming. My success with homeopathy has made me reconsider chakrology too. Mortifying to admit, but I am sitting outside because a chakrologist once told me fresh air could take away a person's "reserved, aloof, and distrusting energy" by opening a person's heart chakra, which was where the body stores unconditional love. (My research has moved on to the Zen-centric. Please be assured, though, this story doesn't end in an ashram. A woman with my degree of pent-up anger could never be as placid as a lotus flower.)

All rumbling stomach and heart, I carefully dial the umpteen digits in the Lark's international number. The world teeters on its axis as the line rings once, twice, three times before I recognize the befuddled and instantly lovable "Hello?"

The Lark tells me he's in London for the day. And though I assure him I can just as easily call him back tomorrow, he insists that I hold the line while he finds a quiet corner of the street. A smile lights my face as I imagine him moving through the crowd in his small, concentrated way—agile legs pumping, cigarette askew in his mouth, his blond lashes made bright by the sun, his mood always deepened or boosted by that city. I hear him approaching traffic, waiting to cross a street, humming absently.

"All right," he says. "That's much better. I'm in St. James's Park. And I've found a bench."

"First things first," I say. "Are you smoking a cigarette?"

"No, not yet."

"Good. Don't light one until I say it's okay. I've decided that cigarettes are one of those things that pull us out of the moment. And I'd really like us both to be fully here during this talk. So, no cigarettes. Swear?"

"Yes," he agrees with a laugh. "No smoking. I promise."

"Oh, one more thing. Will you close your eyes and put your hand on your heart?"

I'm prepared to explain. I have a little bit prepared about how I want us to focus on the beaten-down organ underneath our fingers. *The heart*, I imagine myself saying, *is the one valuable we are so careful with we let our shoulders tense up and roll over it in an ugly, self-protected posture.* But, as it turns out, I didn't have to go on.

"Okay," the Lark says trustingly.

"Okay? You mean, your hand's on your heart?"

"Yes, it's there."

Homeopathy seems like magic indeed. For the first time ever, I'm making demands of the Lark and he's responding in part. The moment feels confessional, and for a few minutes we sit together, secreted from the world, like two children hunched under a table-cloth fort.

I take a deep breath and begin. "The women you've known in the past . . ."

"Yes?" His voice is quiet.

"They bullied you."

"Yes."

"They belittled you."

"Yes."

"They betrayed you."

"Yes." This last yes comes out the softest, and I hear his breath catch against his teeth. I feel love for him like a small bubble rising to the surface.

Very gently, I say, "That's the past, honey. Do you hear me? It's over. It's finished. You've gotta tap into it, feel it, and then let it go. Because I'm not like those women. And that past has no bearing on our present. You know what I think? I think you were still fighting with them that night. Can you see that? You were arguing with the ghosts of girlfriends past, and I was arguing with my book."

I'm really circling It—the big Insight—with this final part. I am gleaning. The truth is, I hadn't been fighting with my book; I'd been fighting against my anger. I'd been desperate to avoid it, and then equally eager to chalk up my avoidance to my gender, my nationality, any generalization that sounded plausible enough and took the focus off of me.

When I ask him why he's never confided in me about his past relationships before, I hear him wipe his nose with the back of his hand. "I don't know," he says, in a voice that inches closer. "I thought that was a subject you were supposed to avoid. Doesn't it just lead to jealousy?"

"I guess sometimes," I say, and feel his surge of attention. "But it also leads to the bond you said your brothers have with their wives. It leads to the 'flame.' You never get to that unless you trust enough to share even the most misshapen, monstrous parts of yourself. The parts you long ago decided should never see the cold light of day."

What I am getting at is a level of trust that Virginia Satir describes best. Love, she said, best flourishes in an atmosphere "where individual differences are appreciated, mistakes are tolerated, communication is open, and rules are flexible." Before the Lark and I can be so accepting of each other, we have to acknowledge the parts of ourselves that we are still rejecting.

We talk for an hour, while the sun rises (on my end) and begins its decline (on his), and he tells me how the conversation just melts him. That's the word he uses, "melts." He says he's honed his defenses for years, living by what he calls a "Jack Daniels code," shaping himself to fit the mold of the pro musician who doesn't need anyone or anything besides work, the road, music. "We still have a geographical problem," he says. I'm American. He's British. We come from different sides of the Atlantic. If I move to Brighton permanently, then what happens? He's constantly away on tour. He's afraid a schedule like that will ruin my life.

We wonder aloud if we've ever been fully present with one another. We talk about how often we've been preoccupied with our pasts or distracted by anxieties about a future together. And it simply isn't true that we'd gotten along better in letters than we do in the flesh; perhaps we've just trusted ourselves more in writing. In Brighton, for whatever reason, we'd begun to tread lightly around one another—to say what we should, to do what we ought. But love isn't about peacekeeping. It doesn't mean agreeing on everything. And wouldn't that be as dull as a dust bunny? No, love has to be about supporting and, at the same time, challenging each other. And it really seems like we can figure this out. I mean, even morons can love each other from an unguarded place. We are intelligent people in many capacities. We're just emotional idiots.

But we are back to our original problem. I am on one side of the

Atlantic and he is on the other. But we decide that won't stop us. When his voice chokes with sniffles, I finally consent: Okay, yes, he can light a cigarette. We make plans to talk again tomorrow, and the next day, and however long it takes to work out our kinks, resolve the problem of geography, and talk through our fears and reservations.

I hang up the phone feeling honest and pure. I don't wholly know how to account for my pluck except to say that, for a brief window in time, my love overcame my fear. More agonizing than being rejected by the Lark again was envisioning a future without him. Maybe it was *tonglen* that first made me realize I missed all the virtues (and even faults) that were specific to him. Maybe it was all my reading that made me realize I'd been relating to the Lark the way I relate to my family. When we were in Brighton, our relationship had been what Virginia Satir calls a "closed system," a system dominated by neurotic dependency, obedience, conformity, and guilt. But we might be capable of something more. Maybe an "open system." A relationship where we can both honestly express a full range of hopes, fears, loves, angers, frustrations, and mistakes, and even appreciate each other for them.

In the wake of our conversation, the weight of all my past emotional failures—those times I played the stoic rather than exposed my fears, tolerated another of my mother's heart-on-sleeve lectures, or even listened in flushed-faced self-loathing while my ballet instructor took me aside and told me it was the mark of a weak character to let disappointment show on my face—lifts from my shoulders. *It is possible*, I think, *to emote without being rejected, to be honest and still be loved, to ask for what you want without seeking permission.* I walk back to the house with the phone in my swinging hand and my hair fluttering against the small of my back. My brain buzzes with endorphins. As I swing open my parents' screen door, every nook and knickknack looks new to me. The family photos that used to glare back from the walls re-create themselves moment by moment.

———

The buzz lasts through the night. I hold on to it through the dogs' barking and my dad's happy hour and my sister's latest phone-in crisis. But the next morning, when I call the Lark at our pre-agreed time, the person who answers is terse and unlike the confiding and tender man who just yesterday had been as wide open as a morning glory.

It shouldn't matter. It shouldn't prevent me from plunging into the conversation I've rung up to have. If anything, my deference to the unpredictable moods of others is the very habit I'm trying to break. I am confronted with my compulsive tendency to read people and size up what they expect of me. Here is my opportunity to keep my cool—not to censor myself based on the Lark's reactions nor let the quality of his voice determine what I ought to hold back. A cold bolt of fear pierces me down the center. I feel choked, liable to stammer, deeply embarrassed. Have I somehow gotten the entire thing wrong? What if the Lark has taken away something completely different from yesterday's conversation? What if, where I've been laying the groundwork for a new beginning, he thought we'd been saying a final and more reverent good-bye?

Again, I had taken the portable phone outside. The eleven o'clock sun is burning a hole in the sky and the afternoon is already too harsh and clammy. Fruit rots beneath the pear trees. Bees rape the rhododendrons. The world is already too sickly sweet with the smell of moist, fresh-cut grass.

There's silence on the Lark's end when I apologize for catching him at a bad time. "It's just . . ." I pace the brick walkway while I neurotically smooth the hair off of my sticky forehead. "It's just . . . I know we said yesterday that we were going to talk."

His voice flies up in a flare of white-hot irritation. "I'm not sure I understand what you want to talk about."

I couldn't be more stung if his hand had come through the receiver and smacked me across the mouth. Who *is* this callous ass, this childish, cow-hearted, posturing prick? And why is he rearing his head *now*, less than twenty-four hours after yesterday's communion? He's asking to be buried. He is begging for it. My heart begins pounding right along with my ears. The words that come to my mouth are nothing close to prudent or polite.

My hand shoots to my hip. My jaw is set. "You know," I say, "I've listened to you talk about how you're not sure I really 'see' you. But the truth is, I'm not sure that you, sir, *see* me. I'm not convinced you *listen* to a single word I say. So, fuck you. Really. Go on. Keep banging on about how I don't really get or appreciate you. Keep on writing about love in pop songs. The fact remains: You wouldn't recognize real love if it came up and bit your unmentionables. You don't take notice of *anything*! You don't consider *anyone*! I don't think you *see* anyone but *yourself*!"

With that, I hang up, trembling. A deep exhale rasps from my mouth. I've done it. I'm determined not to be swayed and not to feel sorry.

16

My subletters move out, and on Labor Day I go home to my apartment on Twenty-second Street, which looks solemn and clean-scrubbed but still smells strongly of someone else's perfume.

I'd complained of feeling displaced at my folks' house, but I am sorrier still to be home. I can't bring myself to slash open the mail, call friends, or hang my clothes in the closet. Even the crush and roar of the city—a sound I had pined for—does nothing to distract me from how little has changed in my absence. It is exactly as though Brighton has never happened. The sameness of it all only makes me feel crazy. Being home makes me feel as though I have no cause to feel miserable, as though I've never met the Lark to begin with and am hallucinating the slow, searing pain in my chest.

Still exploring homeopathy, I've switched to Natrum Muriaticum, which is a common remedy for grief and disappointed love. Internet research assures me that the remedy is nothing but common table salt. It's an obvious example of homeopathy's attempt to cure like with like. What do you take if you find yourself depressed? Sodium: the same substance found in your dribbling tears.

Homeopathy Web sites describe the Nat-Mur patient as someone deeply scarred, frozen in grief. She doesn't often accept help from others because she values her independence and "dislike[s] consolation or advice." She thinks grief is "an irremovable part of [her] life." Her past, she's decided, will "accompany [her] forever," and if someone has hurt her deeply, she opts to "completely erase [that] person from [her] life." I'm amazed by how specific the descriptions are and how much I can relate to them. Sparks dance in the Nat-Mur patient's line of vision. She has swollen eyelids, vertigo, sluggish speech, and a "deep crack in the middle of [her dry] lower lip." She submits to exhaustion whenever she tries to read or write. As it is easier to cry about other people's grief than it is to cry about her own, she is moved by sad, beautiful music or melancholy movies. The Brighton pier flashes through my mind as I read, "The Nat-Mur patient is drawn to the seashore, where [she] feel[s] much better or much worse."

I seem to hurt more under the effect of New York City, or Nat-Mur, or both. I avoid my friends. I forget how to talk to people. I cry when I should be working, sleeping, eating a real meal, or paying my bills in a timely fashion. Most nights, I pace the apartment, my eyes wild and a cigarette burning down to nothing between my stained fingers. Most days, I flounder in bed without the energy to even draw the blinds.

The few people that I can't shake (mostly family) grow increasingly concerned about me. Even my mother, who never goes near the Internet, begins surfing mental health message boards. Although she's never tolerated my anger, she entertains my despair. She calls to give me screening tests: "Has the joy and pleasure gone out of your life?" "Do you have thoughts that you would be better off dead?" One evening she announces that she thinks my depression is "situational" rather than "clinical." (In retrospect, it's hilarious the way she'd recited the symptoms like a college psych major: "Situational depression is sometimes called 'adjustment disorder.' That's when it comes on in reaction to a stressful event.") My well-meaning mama sends me articles about how B-complex vitamins can combat depression. She encourages me to write down the things the Lark has said that most hurt me: "Clearly, that man knew just where to hit you. He tapped into something you secretly believe about yourself. He triggered some anxiety that was already there."

Other people offer advice too, and miserable as I am, I try all of it. I trail my friend Max to the Church Street Boxing Gym. "Enough chanting," he declares. "I think you really need to punch something." At my sister's urging, I put everything that reminds me of the Lark into a box and stuff it under my bed. My pal and yoga teacher Rolf tells me to draft a list of "things I want the law of attraction to bring me," although I can't come up with any goals beyond "absolution" and "relief."

There are those who tell me to start dating again. One girlfriend in particular thinks it is (no joke) important to sleep with someone new as quickly as possible. "It's like a cleansing ritual," she says. "It'll clear away the Lark's energy." Where others advocate fresh air or vitamins, she prescribes the erotica of Alina Reyes, specifically "The Butcher." Finding a copy online, I discover it's a story of woman who consents to be slaughtered (in both senses) by her potbellied purveyor of meat for the explicit purpose of forgetting her ex-lover.

> *If I go to the butcher's house it will be like killing us, Daniel. By laying his fat body on my body the butcher will kill your thin firm body. . . . When the butcher is in my body Daniel we will be dead our story will be dead. . . . I will cry for you the butcher with his blade will cleave and cleave again . . . my stomach will laugh and I will not write to you one last time you have abandoned me.*

It's a ridiculous concept, a laughable prescription for good mental health. But when a friend of an acquaintance asks me out for a date,

I agree. It's unfair to accept, since I can't seriously consider him—can't consider anyone—as a real love interest or partner. But the placater in me doesn't do what she wants; she does what people tell her to do.

We meet at the Russian and Turkish bathhouse on Tenth Street. It's a testament to my unstable state that I arrange to meet a stranger there: half naked, in a clouded room, among the primitive smells of sweat, salt, mud, eucalyptus, and purgation.

The man I meet might as well be my fraternal twin: He has my small stature, pale skin, aversion to eye contact, and tendency toward silence. A fringe of dark hair falls protectively across his face, which, just like mine, looks so childlike for his age that I am torn between the competing instincts to comfort and reprimand him. My aversion is immediate.

Trying to envision sex with him makes me more depressed than ever. Far from anything "pure," I feel certain it would be a malicious act. I'd be doing it to obliterate the Lark, and to torture and eviscerate myself.

I see him only one more time before I collapse into full-on paralysis. We meet at Crif Dogs in the East Village, where I sip from a Dixie cup filled with water and watch him eat two tofu hot dogs with incensed energy. I notice his hands as he reaches across the table for a napkin. His nails are gnawed right down to the quick; even his fingertips are swollen and purple, masticated down to the knuckles.

"Oh my god," I say, taking his gnarled hand with a candor I so rarely bring to dating. "What is this? What have you done to yourself?"

He relaxes instantly, as though he's been uncorked, and I watch the shy strangeness leave him.

He tells me he's recently been through a breakup. And because he hasn't yet deleted the last text message his ex-girlfriend has sent to him, he leans across the table and shows me the screen, which says something eloquent and caring like *I hope you fucking die, you stupid motherfucker.* She constantly cheated on him, he says, as we drift outside and walk among the juvenile clatter of Friday night on St. Marks Place. He misses her, he says, even though she'd been controlling, selfish, jealous—your garden-variety nightmare. Does he resent her? Some. He pities her more. She drinks too much, he tells me, as we walk up Broadway and through Union Square. She's "got issues." When they were together he'd turned down work at her urging. He'd bought her gifts that put him into overdraft. During her blackest moods he had sat at her bedside, letting her humiliate and verbally abuse him.

As we near my front door, he asks me, "What do you think about someone who used to sleep with drag queens?" I search his eyes for the hint of a joke, but they stare back, earnest and expectant.

"Why?" I ask. "Is this something . . . I mean, are *you* trying to tell me that you used to sleep with drag queens?"

"Me? No. Not *me.* My *ex.*" (Forgive me, gentle boy, for revealing this here.) "Before I met her, she used to be involved with this guy named something like Sofonda Dix. He'd loan her stockings and do her makeup."

I didn't know what to say. It is one of those moments when life is a surrealist novel.

"So, I wasn't checking into you or anything. But, I heard from [So-and-so] that you broke up with someone too." He backs me into the doorway of a Korean nail salon and bites my lower lip with what seems like half-conscious aggression. I pull back from the mean approximation of a kiss, and instead I hold him close and lean my skull against his.

17

The next week is the worst in memory. Depression is too wimpy a word for it; this is nothing as manageable as a *mood.* I fester in bed, doubled over and steeling myself against grief so deep it seems to shallow my breath.

My family—which, as a general rule, doesn't believe in talk therapy but does believe in prescription drugs—begins to propose pharmaceuticals they've seen in prime-time commercials. They drop names like Zoloft, Wellbutrin, Cymbalta, Lexapro. They assure me that there's "no shame" in taking something that might, at the very least, elevate me to a condition where I am well enough to work on my book. And while I'm no Tom Cruise on the subject—I'd taken Prozac for six months in my early twenties—I am still on a vaguely homeopathic kick. I want to confront the malady head-on instead of simply treating its symptoms.

I have ideas about what is responsible for this large-scale collapse, and I want to understand what's causing these disturbances.

I try to write about my personal anger in the form of a memoir, but in doing so I suddenly resemble the students and lovers that the Philosophers of Coimbra used to talk about, people who "fetch up the spirits into the brain" as a side effect of their "vehement and continual meditation" on the ailments with which they were afflicted. All this self-dissection is making me "afflicted beyond measure."

I'm also distraught over the brief flash of anger I'd expressed to the Lark. I have a track record of feeling inconsolable after the rare occasions when I get upset. As a child, I was always drafting apologies for the most minor infractions and sliding them under my mother's closed bedroom door. "Dear Mom, I have been a bad daughter." My mother still has those letters of admission—they occupy the same bureau drawer as her collection of birthday cards and keepsakes. As a teenager, I gained a little more confidence during arguments with my family, but I've never fully shaken the misery that followed them. During my most angst-ridden year, I had recurring nightmares that my mother was dying of some unspeakable disease, and I would awaken racked with an earnest belief that I had caused her sickness. My outburst on the phone with the Lark is similar. I've lost my resolve and started berating myself for reacting at all.

My ongoing anger research reassures me that depression is "anger turned inward against the self." I'd read frequently that "denying one's own emotional reactions" landed a person in a trembling funk. Famed Swiss psychologist Alice Miller wrote, "It is easy to notice, if we pay attention, that [depressive moods] hit almost with regularity—whenever we suppress an impulse or unwanted emotion." And in the writing of psychoanalyst Walter Bonime, I learn that "A depression-prone person is distinguished by anger over the painful disturbances to his or her life." It seems possible that I have a great deal more anger to divulge to the Lark. For the moment, the feeling is still under-ground, fermenting somewhere beneath my depression in a place largely unknown to me.

I spin all these scenarios around in my mind until the day the man from my date at the bathhouse e-mails and calls me, among other things, a "cruel, selfish bitch."

The placater in me had been thwarting his proposed dates in a waffling way for two weeks. But in a rare stroke of directness, I've confided that I'm still a little too bent out of shape and don't want to exorcise any lingering feelings for the Lark on him.

Had I no consideration, this man demanded, *for the tough time he was going through?*

For some reason the question does a number on me. My rope has been swaying over the edge of the abyss for months, and this man brings me to its frayed end. *It's too much*, I think, *that a relative stranger—a man who is not my boyfriend, not even my intimate—would ask me to ignore my own emotional life for the purpose of comforting him.* The placater holds on tight to the idea that everyone puts their feelings before mine—a laugh, given *I'm* the one who never shares my own emotions.

I fall into a furor of despair and flailing rage, and then, fed up with homeopathy's tentative and uneven progress, I go hunting for a therapist.

FOUR *Anger Intellectualized*

When faced with life's needs and urges I used to begin by classifying, abstracting, and conceptualizing, until the classification became more important than life itself. . . . I need a stirring of the heart, a renewal of life, and not a new way of thinking. There are no new ways of thinking, but feelings can be ever fresh. . . . Words are good for shaping feelings, but words without feelings are like clothes with no body inside—cold and limp.

—AN UNNAMED MAN, *seeking the advice of Indian spiritual teacher and guru Sri Nisargadatta Maharaj*

18

My hunt for a shrink is not what you might call an informed search. I don't seek out recommendations. I don't ask for referrals. I select a woman on the sole basis that her practice is located three blocks from my apartment, which, in the death grip of depression, is the farthest commute I feel that I can undertake. (Let's call her Alice, since I followed her down my depression's rabbit hole.)

Under other circumstances, the fact that Alice is a dating coach in addition to being a board-certified therapist might have weakened her case in my eyes. But I'm still under the illusion that dating landed me in this mess to begin with, and so I entertain a fleeting hope that Alice is the perfect person to wrench me out of it.

It's raining as I wait for Alice in a nondescript suite of a non-descript building on a hectic avenue. She rents and runs her practice out of a small room in what I can only guess is an employment agency. Phones trill. The air smells of ink toner. I watch a woman in an open room down the hall nod in profile while a lumpish, sweating man slumped behind his desk gives her a lecture about her résumé, which should be "like a thirty-second commercial." "With your résumé," he says, "you are trying to convince the employer to *buy* you and your future potential."

I sit fidgeting on a wobbly metal chair. Although the office is noisy with people returning from their lunch break, no one passing gives me a glance. I'm grateful to feel hidden. I've shampooed and dressed for the first time all week, but I know there's still something damaged and off-putting about me. My lips are cracked. My red eyes are runny. Although I'm immune to the smell of my own chain-smoking, I suspect I stink like an ashtray.

The woman who comes out to greet me looks impossibly young under her fine dusting of freckles. "Are you Koren?" she asks.

I nod and stumble to my rain-soaked feet.

"I'm Alice," she says, extending her hand. "I'm so glad to meet you. Why don't you follow me?"

I trail this terribly well-adjusted-looking woman—she is as nimble and blond as sawdust, with high, wholesome cheeks—back into the intimate quarters of her office. Following her lead, I lower myself onto the overstuffed pleather sofa opposite her chair, where I spend a few seconds folding and unfolding my hands. I quickly survey the room's sparse furnishings. There's an Oriental rug on the floor with a complex, threadbare pattern. On the wall: a diploma. At my left elbow: a table. On top of it: an unlit sandalwood-scented candle and a ready box of "ultra-soft" tissues.

Tissues. These were always my mother's main criticism of therapy. As a teenager she'd brought my sister to a counselor for the explicit purpose of getting her untimed testing on school exams (this required a letter from a psychologist, confirming conditions like anxiety or learning disorders)—not, she would have you know, because my sister needed someone to talk to. But my sister hadn't been in therapy a month before my mother began railing against the doctor's tissues. "They're just sitting right there on the table in front of her, almost as if he's encouraging her to cry! As if she'd been so abused and boo-hoo!" Shortly after, my sister quit going, because she would later say, "He kept wanting me to talk about our family, and that wasn't why I'd gone to see him."

As we talk, Alice seems awfully interested in what I consider to be the tangential details of my depression. She knows I've sought her out as the result of a recent breakup. Yet she keeps enticing me to tell her more about my parents, my childhood, my life since my first book and what compelled me to choose the anger topic for my second. I respond out of a sense of obligation, but my answers are brief.

As for my parents, I tell Alice that they are very supportive, particularly of my writing.

She nods meaningfully, taking a sip from a small carton of juice and again fixing me with her sparkling eyes.

I tell Alice my childhood was so average and uneventful that I have few distinct memories of it. I tell her I played with the other girls in the neighborhood (leaving out what an unwelcome tagalong I was, how I was frequently excluded and bullied). I say I've always had a roof over my head (but leave out how desperate I had been to sneak my way out of it). I tell her my parents had never divorced or anything (but not about the endless arguments with my mother, fights I had frequently tried to cope with by boozing to blackout).

I'm not trying to be rude, but I firmly tell Alice I didn't have any childhood woes. "Maybe we can just skip ahead in the interest of time?"

Regarding my first book, I tell Alice I'd written it at twenty-three in a fit of urgency. What the rush was, I still can't say. It had seemed imperative that I write it, that I'd felt the story might leave me if I didn't get it down right away. The words had run through my head and I'd panted along after them, typing nothing short of eighty words per minute and composing sentences even in my dreams.

And finally we get to my book-in-the-works. I admit to Alice that I set out to write a book about anger because I sensed I was conflicted about it.

"Why do you think that is?" Alice asks me, bringing the stub of her pen to her mouth. (In eight months together, this will be the only time she sits back and takes notes.)

"I don't know," I say, shrugging. "Maybe because I'm a woman? It's not very feminine to get angry."

"So, let me just make sure I have this right. You think your femininity is responsible for your writer's block?"

"No, that's not right. The fact that I'm a woman has nothing to do with my ability to be a productive writer." I feel uneasy, confused about how we arrived at this topic of conversation. I rub my face with my palms.

"Is there a chance that the repressed anger that led you to write this book is the same force that's preventing you from seeing it through?"

It seemed more than likely. Later, at home, one of my researching jags leads me to look up the word "fury" in my *Oxford English Dictionary*. There beneath the first dictionary definition—"fierce passion, madness, wild anger, or frenzied rage"—is an obsolete definition. There was a time when "fury" also referred to "inspired frenzy; (artistic) inspiration." Maybe, in all my attempts to stave off a fit of emotional frenzy, I've also cut myself off from a creative one. I learn that some psychotherapists, including Beverly Engel, believe "Repressed and suppressed anger can thwart creativity and motivation."

It makes me a little nervous to sit in a one-on-one session with Alice. My only previous brush with therapy was an anger-management seminar I'd attended two years earlier, and I won't yet admit that that was anything more than research.

That seminar (in the interest of protecting the people I met there, let's call it SAP and say it stands for Self Actualization Program) was what its Web site described as a "group experience." "Angry people feel alienated," the sponsoring institution claimed during one of my first sessions there. And its program aimed to replace that isolation with feelings of inclusion and camaraderie.

I felt sick as I wheeled my pull-along suitcase into a budget motel off of the Interstate. All weekend our therapy was interrupted by the sounds of couples in the throes of extramarital affairs, midday ass smackings, and appeals to "fuck me harder." I still remember the fishbowl on top of the check-in desk, where a fish floated three days dead in a bowl of rainbowed gravel, and the way the night manager suppressed a smirk when I told him I was there to attend the SAP weekend.

My SAP coattendees slouched on their patio chairs in all variety of maladroit poses. They were round-shouldered, cross-armed, cross-legged, and crooked, with their hats pulled down over their noses and their hands turtled into their sleeves. To avoid eye contact, we studied the wall's "Feelings Chart" as though trying to select an appropriate emotion. Listed in one column were "Unpleasant Feelings": Bitter, Weary, Wary, Fuming, Vulnerable, Humiliated, and Lost. In another were "Pleasant Feelings," the ones we'd never enjoyed: Calm, Certain, Sure, Assured, Satisfied, Fortunate, and Free.

Danielle, a woman with the habit of writing into her leatherbound notebook whatever the therapists at SAP said, was in her midthirties, Chinese, and beautiful in a way that seemed packaged too tightly, what with the high-chinned, sharp-shouldered, and tooerect way she delivered herself. "It's human frailty that endears people," one of the therapists told us during our first night at SAP. "You guys have to learn to let people in. To show the world your imperfections." I felt an affinity with Danielle. She traveled just as far as I did to attend SAP.

Danielle confessed to the group that she'd enrolled because she and her husband were fixing to get pregnant. And when the time eventually came—when their gametes fused, her breasts ballooned, and the smell of the morning coffeepot began to flex her gag muscle—Danielle didn't want to project all her unappeased furies onto the tiny person doing somersaults in her uterus. It struck me as a nice thought, and perverse in the way of all things brilliant. I mean, whose mother was that considerate?

Beside Danielle, there was Carly and Daryl, sitting in milk-white sneakers and matching tracksuits with the American flag embroidered over their hearts. They were attending SAP to doctor their long-ailing marriage. Their union, they said, resembled a flaming sack of crap. Should they stamp it out? Let it burn? They hoped the SAP team could help them decide.

Next was Nico, splaying his legs into the center of the circle and fanning his brown toes over the edges of his flip-flops. He was my age at the time, twenty-five, and Hawaiian, with a breadth and might to his frame. Even at Nico's most inconsolable—even when he talked about the horrors of his childhood, about the time his mother made him chew on the contents of his own soiled diaper—his sloe eyes stayed backlit, as though they'd retained the violet-red flare of the Big Island sunset.

Bev and Tate both stood at the brink of retirement and wanted to exorcise their anger once and for all. To puke it out of their systems, so to speak, so they could enjoy their post–nine-to-five lives in fraternal good humor. To hear them tell it, they'd spent decades seething, socking pillows and spending as much on therapy as they might've spent on lush summer bungalows. And yet they still found themselves flaring up over the smallest annoyances—wrong change, telemarketers, long lines at the post office—because they couldn't seem to pardon the massive ways they'd been mistreated by the people closest to them.

Finally, there was Raquel, who fast became my cohort, my angel and friend there. A San Francisco native, she was a hairstylist of the rangy, perfumed, gravel-voiced variety. When it was her turn at introduction, Raquel revealed that she was there at the insistence of her fiancé, who had attended an SAP seminar one month before.

These were SAP's primary players, those who monopolized most of the conversation because they enthusiastically chose to be there. But there were also a few barrel-bodied men enrolled because a court had required it. Some were road ragers. Others nose breakers. Many confessed to having pending sentences and prior arrest records. A spattering of soft-spoken and small-wristed women sat as far away from the convicts as our cramped room would allow. They hailed from households rife with domestic anger, and over the course of the weekend a few resolved to leave their abusive husbands, whatever it might take.

I suspect that if I'd been more forthcoming at SAP, I might have come to a few revelations that could've kept me out of Alice's office. But it had been easy to take a backseat to so many big characters.

———

Alone with Alice, without anyone else around to divert the conversation, I feel uneasy, exposed.

I can't fight the feeling that she is trying to trick me into incriminating my family. Anytime I make some blanket statement about the Lark, Alice seems to minimize the importance of my relationship with him. Instead, she asks me for what feels like the hundredth time, "Who does that remind you of?"

When I tell her I wanted to be close to the Lark but was afraid he'd think I was demanding, she challenges me by asking, "Is there someone else in your life who tells you that you're oppressive?"

When I tell her that I felt responsible for the Lark's moods when I was living in Brighton, she drills me. "Who else passes their emotions off on you?"

Although I sense the answer she's fishing around for, I flat out refuse to take the bait. I grow cautious and inarticulate whenever she begins this line of questioning. I begin to respond with gems like, "I've never given it much thought." I'm aware that I am throwing out a lot of shrugged shoulders and muddled looks. Revealing anything about my family feels like a betrayal. I'd always lived by the idea that the first rule of the Zailckas family is like the first rule of *Fight Club* (don't talk about it).

Alice seems to sense my reluctance, so she switches tactics. She wants to know which of the Lark's words had hurt me the most. These things are sometimes retraumatizations, a.k.a. "the domino effect," also known as "collapse." She suggests (very gently) that my experience in Brighton might have reminded me of experiences when I'd been insulted or invalidated as a child. Perhaps memories I've ignored or minimized are making the current situation more agonizing than it needs to be. Later, in psychologist Alice Miller's work, I will find a further description of the kind of collapse that my own Alice is hinting at.

> *These people have all developed the art of not experiencing feelings, for a child can experience her feelings only when there is somebody there who accepts her fully, understands her, and supports her. If that person is missing, if the child must risk losing the mother's love or the love of her substitute in order to feel, then she will repress her emotions. She cannot even experience them secretly, "just for herself"; she will fail to experience them at all. But they will nevertheless stay in her body, in her cells, stored up as information that can be triggered by a later event.*

I look into Alice's blue-gray eyes, which are gentle with effusive kindness. She certainly doesn't fit my image of a therapist. I could try, I suppose, to talk to her like a girlfriend, even though she couldn't be less like my actual girlfriends, most of whom would laugh wildly at a phrase like "retraumatization."

I tell Alice that I keep coming back to what the Lark said about us "getting along better in *print.*" He'd said my *letters* "sparked something in him." What really hits me in the jugular, I tell Alice, is the implication that he prefers the professional me to the real me sitting here in flesh and blood.

Alice burbles sympathetically. She makes some distinction between being admired, like a possession, for our talents, and being understood, taken seriously and loved as human creatures—humans who are, in turn, sometimes lonely, jealous, helpless, anxious, and, yes, even angry.

I'm intrigued, but I internalize too readily that feeling of inadequacy. Just the mention of it and it blossoms in me so furiously that I can't concentrate on Alice's bowed mouth.

Hot tears force themselves into my line of vision, and if I don't regain control soon, immediately and magically, I'll be forced to lean over and withdraw a tissue from the "ultra-soft" box that taunts me. I was just as skeptical about therapy as I was about homeopathy, but for the first time I wonder if there's something of my mother in me after all. Even here, where I am paying for an emotional outlet, I hear her voice saying, "You think you've had it so hard. Do you have any idea what I went through when I was a kid?"

———

I had collapsed into tears just as quickly at SAP. The group barely finished with introductions when I turned lachrymose and cried me a Nile.

"What are these tears about?" one of the therapists asked me with all the compassion of a drill sergeant. Her name was Sheila and she was the founder of SAP, the casher of checks marked "Pay to the Order of." Not more than five years ago, she'd been a registered nurse (more Ratched than Nightingale, if I had to wager a guess). But at SAP, she stood before us as a board-licensed shrinker of craniums. She was Freud in Stuart Weitzman heels.

I felt silenced by the power of everything I might say. SAP was a place that subsisted on words. Every feeling had to be defined, qualified, and dismantled by the group at large. A person couldn't simply shrug there or let a brief spasm of emotion pass without comment. My embarrassment expanded with the widening pause.

I was crying as a result of a get-to-know-you game that Sheila and her partner, a woman named Trish, had devised, whereby we took turns sharing our first impressions of one another, both good and evil. "It seems harsh," Trish said. "But out there in the world, everyone's making snap judgments about everyone else. Only in here, we're more open about it. In here, we're privy to what our peers think of us."

According to my eleven coparticipants, I struck them as "meek," "frail," "wimpy," "hypersensitive," and "overwhelmed," as though "everything was too much to take." In addition, Daryl, SAP's resident metaphorist, described me as "a baby bird that needed taking care of." This analogy hit me particularly hard. (Was it because I'd always felt like my mother resented how much I needed her as a kid?) I kept picturing myself wet, widemouthed, big beaked, and cadging at high pitch for a mouthful.

My counterparts had said things that were complimentary too. The rules of the exercise required it. But, by some stroke of selective amnesia, I simply can't remember the praise. And I don't just mean now, as I write this. I mean I couldn't remember the niceties a split second after they were said. It was what Trish, who had a habit of treating us like lobotomized turkeys, called the "Velcro/Teflon" phenomenon. Too many of us let the criticisms stick and the kudos dribble off.

———

Whereas my interactions with Trish and Sheila left me feeling humiliated, therapy with Alice is a far more tender thing.

That is not to say that Alice doesn't have me pegged from the first tear that rolls down my cheek. I sense she knows what ails me, but she must also sense how reluctant I am to accept her conclusions, ones that I don't ferret out myself. She lets me journal, research, and present conclusions I arrive at "on my own." She avoids diagnoses. She eschews pathologies. She tries her best to encourage me when I am hot on the trail to some uncomfortable truth (she has a certain smile that says "you're getting warmer") and rein me in when I go too far astray. She even appeals to the overachiever in me by assigning me homework and drafting up goals.

"So, just to get it straight, here's a list of things that we hope to accomplish," Alice says as our first meeting tapers off to an end. "We would like to get you to a place where you can work again and sleep through the night. We would like to try to understand why you are what you describe as 'sensitive to rejection' and generally 'reluctant to reveal too much of yourself.' What else do we want to make sense of? The need to do things 'perfectly.' Your difficulty lending words to your emotions. The rift between your 'public' and 'private' self. We want to help you find some empathy for yourself. To remember more of your childhood. Oh, and we want to find a way for you to really experience your anger. [*Looking up brightly.*] Did I forget anything?"

19

I'm sure I didn't tell Alice that I wanted to do anything as mortifying as "tap into" my anger during that first meeting. In fact, I'm pretty sure I didn't mentioned the big A at all, except to say that—until depression had emptied me of every idea and purpose—I had been researching and writing a book about it.

I begin to fear Alice is a "ventilationist"—a term I'd first come across in the work of Freud's nemesis Wilhelm Reich. His disciples had grown out of a small group of renegade psychoanalysts who worked in New York in the 1950s, and in a time when other thera-pists were preaching the value of self-restraint, ventilationists en-couraged their patients to kick, scream, bash mattresses with tennis rackets, and generally go to town with their feelings. Whereas Freud thought it was society's job to manage people's primitive instincts, such as anger, Reich believed the human unconscious was a virtuous thing. Only society's repression turned ordinary people into ogres.

The ventilationist movement gained momentum in the late 1960s, riding the coattails of self-improvement and sexual freedom. Its proponents argued that it was unhealthy to bottle up any emotion, particularly rage, that could, in turn, cause high blood pressure, disease, depression, neuroticism, addiction, and (ye olde floppy) im-potence. Ventilationism gave way to the kinds of retreats you often see in grainy documentary footage: people strewn around grassy fields in various degrees of undress screaming primally or complaining about the bourgeoisie values of cookie-cut parents who'd imprisoned them in patterns of "self-control" and denied them the outlets to vocalize their rage. Michael Murphy and Dick Price formed the Esalen Institute in a poolside motel in northern California, and within seven or eight years, there were nearly two hundred such centers in America urging autonomy and the liberation of anger, encouraging attendees to just let it bleed.

Critics of the ventilationists cite Sigmund Freud, who believed giving full rein to our angers, egos, and desires would have devastating social consequences. Some naysayers suggest that the selfishness ventilationists herald has created a culture of isolated and greedy individuals who are unusually vulnerable to politics that exploit their fears and advertising that preys upon their desires.

Today, ventilationists claim we repress our anger with the help of a number of addictions. They contend we stuff it down along with a bag of cheese puffs or light a cigarette, convinced our rage too will go up in smoke. They say compulsive spending can be an attempt to squelch feelings. Likewise, gym rats, workaholics, sex fiends, and gamblers abuse their long-suffering treadmills, BlackBerrys, privates, and savings to escape from the long arm of rage.

The ventilationists insist entertainment is the biggest of all American addictions. For that reason, SAP made each of us sign a contract vowing we would abstain from newspapers, television, radio, and Internet for the full course of our stay. "Emotions will be surfacing for you," Sheila insisted. "And you aren't allowed to detract from them, not with YouTube, CNN, stock indexes, or the Sunday *Times*." We weren't allowed to make phone calls either. Trish told us, "If you need to talk about something, talk about it in here, in this room. If you think something is bullshit, say so. If something's not making sense to you, please let us know. What we want to build is a loving and receptive environment, where your hearts can open up in a tremendous way."

I broke as many of SAP's rules as I possibly could without straining something in the process. Just one day into the program and I became the archprincess of multitasking, surfing Internet news headlines with my cell phone cupped against my cheek and speaking in clipped, furtive whispers.

I had gone to bed the first night with every intention of following SAP's rules. But a curious thing happened that morning. I awoke to the orders of a bull-horned voice, saying, "Put your hands in the air! I repeat, put your hands in the air!" It was 6:10 A.M., according to the splintered integers that stared back at me from the motel's clock radio. And when I parted the room's putrid, plastic curtains, I saw a police chase straight out of *The Driver*. At the intersection less than a stone's throw away there were twenty police cars and as many drawn guns. Sleep weighed heavily on me at the time. I had not yet reinhabited the world of conscious logic, and it took me a second to realize they didn't have their 9 millimeters aimed straight at me, but rather at the man who tumbled out of his bruised Chevy pickup and sank onto his knees.

In the clutches of a death sweat, I went about packing my bag. At that point, SAP hardly seemed worth staying for; I mean, what kind of self-respecting psychologists practiced in this kind of no-tell motel? Why had they selected a location that, a local woman would later inform me, was a drug drop house and an infamous site on the city's guided tour of streetwalker stabbings?

Then, abruptly, a wave of indignation surged over me, narrowing my eyes and steadying my hands. I thought about the price of enrollment. I thought about the aims of my research. I spewed the contents of my suitcase back out again. I felt threatened at SAP. But perhaps I had felt threatened from the very start of the seminar and too frightened to reveal my feelings. I wouldn't glom onto one pesky shoot-out and use it as an excuse for escape.

I had, however, found a suitable excuse for some harmless transgression. Sheila and Trish's rules seemed patronizing, dictatorial, and outright cultish.

I might have looked like a child to Sheila. The day before, I had overheard her telling Trish, plain as day, "So, about Koren. Was she ever molested? It's just—look at her. Her development's so arrested. She looks so much younger than she really is. Poor thing, I don't even think she's aware of it." But she could go suck a copy of *The Ego and the Id*. I was the quintessence of the autonomous adult. And as such, I was fully entitled, if not civically bound, to read the morning paper over a sticky stack at the neighborhood IHOP.

———

"So, did anyone break the rules last night?" Trish posed the question a couple of hours later. She stood in her sensible heels and eyed the room with tilted-head amity. "It's okay if you did. Sheila and I are forgiving. But SAP is an exercise in communal confession. You owe it to your peers to be honest."

Owl eyes all around the sharing circle. The air swelled with a taut, guilty pause. The men folded their arms in shows of tough-guy defiance. A few of the women chewed the ends of their hair.

"Wow, no one slipped. That might well be an SAP first," Sheila said in a combative tone. "Okay, yesterday was what I call the locker-room experience. It was all about stripping down, sizing one another up, making a game plan for yourselves, and bonding. But today . . . today is the most important game of your life. Fern, can you please bring out the bats?"

———

My reading about the ventilationists had assured me this was coming. But even as I watched SAP's assistant, Fern, lug an armful of aluminum baseball bats into the center of our sharing circle, I kept praying that the sporting equipment was some inside joke between shrinks. I half expected Trish, the sole humorist in our sullen group, to announce something like, "Only kidding! Do you take us for some kind of amateurs? You didn't really think we would be so cliché?"

But no, Fern went on to drag an eighty-pound boxing bag across the grimed carpet and arrange it, supine, like a sleeping human body. And for the next two hours I watched my cooperative co-attendees stage mock beatings of their fathers, mothers, spouses, siblings, and anyone else who had wronged them. I listened to their booming monologues and free associations. I heard "fuck" and all its derivatives—employed as noun, verb, adjective, adverb, interjection, and gerund.

"Dad, I'd pitched a perfect game! A perfect fucking game!" Daryl howled as he beat the bag like a rented mule. "Would it have killed you to say, 'Son, I'm proud of you'? Would it have killed you, you tight-assed wad of shit?"

There was a chilling moment when one woman, Bev, addressed the punching bag as though it were her childhood sex offender—the man we'd been talking about all weekend with the blackest repulsion. Bev turned to Trish with the expression of a woman possessed, like someone who was having auditory hallucinations. She was tall and queasily thin. Through the stretched-out neck of her tank top we could see her sternum like a glockenspiel. "He's here again," Bev told our instructors. "Can I please hit him?"

"You want to hit the man who hurt that four-year-old girl?" Trish was wearing her soft mouth, her do-good eyes. You could say what you wanted about Trish's high-camp mottos, but as the weekend went on, I began to think she was genuinely concerned about us.

Bev's throat betrayed a shriek that could have damn near peeled the paint off the walls. After hoisting the bat high over her silvered head, she let it fall with a murderous thud. She convulsed and screamed, "I want to get it *out!*"

Everyone, Trish, Sheila, and my eleven co-angries talked about anger the way you would a crowning baby. Their expressions lit up whenever someone like Bev appeared to have her feet in the stirrups. People coached her with Lamaze-like enthusiasm, shouting, "Breathe, Bev! Stay with your feelings!"

As ventilationists, SAPers believed strongly in catharsis. Not only did Trish and Sheila think it was essential to shout, howl, stamp, and beat out any pent-up aggression, but they also believed it was pos- sible to purge all our resentments in a single, uninhibited go. Sheila urged one of my peers, a man who still couldn't forgive his abusive mother, to rent a cabin, alone, in a jerkwater town and not come out until he'd shed every last tear about the ordeals of his youth.

"Eventually, you will come to the end of those feelings," Sheila told him in her single flash of humanity. "I'm gonna tell you a story. Some years back, I met my dream guy, my perfect man, and he broke my heart. Cheated on me. I was going to marry him. And I told myself, 'Sheila, you can let this anger ruin your life or you can unburden all of this anger once and for all.' So that's what I did. I checked into a hotel, and I didn't go home until I didn't have a single tear left to shed. I didn't leave until I'd thrown everything that wasn't bolted down." After I broke up with the Lark I thought often of this speech. A few times I almost walked down the street and checked into the Hotel Chelsea for this purpose.

At the time, I didn't dare mention the psychological studies that I had come across in my research. The ones that said venting aggres- sive feelings could actually become a cathartic habit. I didn't men- tion the clinical trials that found that this kind of battering and bawling not only failed to make participants less angry in the future, but it in fact made them more inclined to repeat their tantrums. I didn't tell Trish and Sheila that these studies validated my hesitations about rage. If I allowed myself to lose control once, I really might never regain it. I kept a well-guarded lid on my misgivings, sarcasm, and contentiousness. Who wouldn't? Those people had bats and, sweet Jesus, did they know how to use them.

"Do I have to?" I'd whined to Sheila when she told me it was my turn at the plate.

"So let me be clear here." Sheila smoothed her blouse with an obvi- ous air of contempt. "Why are you passing up your turn at the bag?"

She suggested I pretend the bag was my father, and I told her I didn't think I was angry with him.

Sheila continued to eye me disapprovingly and I felt a rouge fury wash over my cheeks. There was a curious shift in my thinking. Yes, I was jam-packed with aggression, not for my dad, but for Sheila, who seemed to remind me of someone.

"You expect us to believe your father was the perfect man, huh? A saint? Never did a thing wrong a day in his life? Well, pardon me if I'm the first one to say 'bullshit.' Fathers are violent; fathers are negligent; they drink too much; they say too little; they express love only through their bank accounts."

I must have given Sheila a blank look. "Fine. If not your father, let's pretend the bag is this mother of yours," she said. She made a move for her files, in search of my preweekend questionnaire. She began to flip pages noisily, licking her thumb and saying "hmm" whenever she arrived at passages she deemed incriminating. Eventually, she found what she was looking for, where I'd written that I felt more rage for women than men. "What does it say here? That you 'carry grudges for women' because you 'expect better from them.' Because 'women should not pass on to girls the same disrespect that they themselves suffered.' Sounds to me like you're addressing Mother. So hop to. Let's pretend the bag is Mommy Dearest."

I contended that the sounds of the day's violence, all the thwacking, clawing, cursing, and kvetching, made me uncomfortable, made me feel less instead of more expressive.

With evangelical conviction, Sheila turned and announced to the group, "Koren's very good at playing the victim."

20

Talk of parents was an important part of SAP. Trish and Sheila had this idea about rewriting our childhoods. They wanted us to acknowledge the "unconditional acceptance" and "loving support" our parents had denied us, so they could teach us how to mother and father ourselves. Their method was madness, but their logic was far wiser than I gave them credit for at the time. We were furious, they said, because we were too dependent on our friends and lovers to listen and enact all the tenderness our families never had. While I was there I treated this idea with relentless mockery. But when I begin seeing Alice, my mind returns to one of those grotesque mid-August e-mails to the Lark, in which I'd told him: "I'm beginning to think if you subtract the dumb-fun of sex, romantic love isn't all that different from the love that we feel for our families or our children—the people for whom we'd rather die than see injured." How clear it seems then that I wanted to wring from the poor man all the validation I'd felt my family had never given me.

But at SAP, the phrase "inner child" came up in conversations just as often as slogans like "stay with your feelings" or "just let it out." The inner child referred to the childlike aspect of our psyches—our emotional memories and earliest childhood experiences. The twelve-step community considers healing the inner child one of the essential stages in recovering from addiction, abuse, and trauma. Charles L. Whitfield, who calls the inner child "the Child Within," writes: "The Child Within has been part of our world for at least two thousand years. Carl Jung called it the 'Divine Child' and Emma Fox called it the 'Wonder Child.' Psychotherapists Alice Miller and Donald Winnicott refer to it as the 'true self.'" Like Rokelle Lerner, Sheila and Trish use "inner child" to signify our authentic selves, the person buried inside us who is unburdened by the "intolerable cruelties" they're convinced we've experienced.

In order to get in touch with our inner children, Sheila had instructed us to bring along a childhood photo from home. Every so often Trish forced us to pull it out of our folders and give it the old once-over. This taking-out-the-photo routine was difficult, especially for people like Bev, who had brought hers in a sixteen-inch gilded frame.

Mine was the only childhood snapshot I could find in my New York apartment. In it I am four years old, standing at an easel and pondering an abstract paint smear. When I look at it, I see a serious girl. A girl aggrieved. I'm not sure she looks particularly oppressed by her parents. She is certainly healthy, and her mother obviously put a lot of effort into her appearance, although a taffeta party dress and patent leather Mary Janes aren't exactly the right ensemble for painting. She seems far more distressed by her own incompetence, and by the asshole preschool that had entrusted her with a paintbrush in the first place. Her brows are stressed. Her mouth circumspect. She certainly looks like a perfectionist. She might well be a tiny curator for MoMA.

For the SAP gang, this talk of inner children was almost unanimously embarrassing. When Fern passed around handouts of four hundred possible activities we might employ to "play with our inner children"—never in the history of homework assignments has one sounded more pedophilic—most of us smirked or exhaled mournfully, full of discomfited resignation. The suggestions included everything from the reasonable ("take a hot bath," "go for a hike," "flip through an old photo album") to the clinically bonkers ("count your beauty marks," "play percussion on your kitchen pots and pans," "masturbate in an unlikely place"). Additionally, the activities were divided into categories that required under five dollars ("treat yourself to a banana split"), under ten ("get a manicure"), and over thirty ("buy a convertible," "rent a houseboat," and, most alarmingly, "have a baby").

Daryl was the only one of us who could raise his inner lad in a cinch. Following frequent praise from Trish and Sheila, he'd made a habit of showing off his talent. By the end of the weekend, the ghost boy called "Little Daryl" had been referenced so often, I wondered if Fern shouldn't fetch him a chair.

"Little Daryl wants to say something to his dad," bearded Daryl announced with a raised adult hand.

"Good!" Trish enthused. "Lend that little boy a voice! Let him say everything he needs to say! No harm can come to him now."

And in the trembling falsetto the full-grown man had assigned to his younger self, Daryl stuttered something like, "Dad, all I wanted was your approval. I did everything just to make you love me. To make you tell me that I am a good son and a good boy. I've lived my whole life thinking I was a fuckup inside. That I can't do anything right. That I can't be loved by anybody."

"Was your dad right, Little Daryl?"

"No!"

"Tell him."

"You were wrong!"

"Tell your dad who you really are, Little Daryl."

"I'm just a kid! I just wanna be happy! I just wanna be a baby! I don't wanna always be worrying about you!"

Following that, Trish made Big Daryl address Little Daryl and the conversation took a turn that felt vaguely schizophrenic.

"All right," Trish said. "Little Daryl is really scared right now. What does Big Daryl need to say to reassure that kid he's safe?"

"Little Daryl? It's me. Big Daryl talking right now. I ain't gonna let anything hurt you. You don't need anybody's fucking approval, and I don't give a shit what anyone else thinks of you. You're awesome, Little Daryl. You're the most loving, innocent little kid. You're fair. You play. You play hard. You're smart and talented. And you really love people. You're a people kinda guy."

I hated them both and spent most of the weekend imagining various scenarios in which Big Daryl ate Little Daryl like an after-dinner mint so the rest of us could get a moment's peace. But my malice came from a place of jealousy. If by some miracle of imagination I'd actually been able to envision my inner girl, I would've wanted to drop her on the doorstep of the closest fire station with a note safety-pinned to her best winter coat, saying, *Sorry, but I just didn't know how to be a parent to her.* I couldn't imagine being able to talk to myself with Daryl's patience and compassion.

———

I had just about had it with this talk about inner children.

Unfortunately, just as we were preparing for our evening group meal—we were joking, wiping our last snotty tears, and cursing a hard day's psychological "work"—Trish pulled out (I shit you not) a child's fairy wand. It was a spangled dime-store monstrosity trimmed with sequins and pink marabou. She walked around the circle, bopping each of us on the hairline with it. Its magic, she said, transformed us into our six-year-old selves.

We stared into the middle distance, aghast. What did Trish expect from our six-year-old selves?

She instructed our inner children to go to the forlorn plush toys that Fern had piled in the corner and remove the stuffed animal that was "most appealing." Raquel plucked a lamb. I selected, for lack of better options, a bunny. Nico grimaced and grabbed what he thought might pass for the smallest and least effeminate bear.

"Are you feeling good, kids?" Trish asked us. "I hope you're feeling pleased with your toys. Because these are going to be your dinner dates tonight. Fern will escort you across the street to the Down Home Buffet. And while you're there, I want your inner child to order whatever he or she likes. French toast for supper? You got it! Want a banana split? You, my sweet babies, are entitled to anything you like! I want you to color on the place mats or throw a tantrum if you feel like it. You're six now, remember? And the only thing you need to be concerned with is what game you want to play."

All eyes were on us as we slinked into the Down Home Buffet: twelve terminally mortified adults with an array of playthings clutched to our chests. Upon seeing us, busboys dropped silverware. Small children giggled while their slow parents gaped.

I suppose the point of the exercise was to teach us to take ourselves less seriously. But the only thing we took less seriously was the lesson. Most of us, myself included, acted mutinously adult. Only Carly and Daryl spat spitballs, told knock-knock jokes, and ordered root-beer floats off the kids' menu. We told them things like, "You kids play nice," and otherwise positioned ourselves very far away.

Fern cornered me that night. "I have told you that I study chakrology, right?"

"Yeah, You mentioned it. That's has to do with the feet right? Like, qi and stuff? Like squeezing the pressure points?"

"No, that's reflexology." Fern seemed vaguely offended that I'd confused her pseudoscience with another. Little did I know just how soon I would take my own active interest in these things. "Chakrology divides the body into seven parts, seven chakras, seven forces of energy. Only sometimes an emotional wound that we've left unattended blocks these chakras. I've been thinking a lot about you these past few days."

"You have?"

"Yes. I think your *anahata*, or heart chakra, is too open. I think it's strangling your *vishuddha*, or throat."

I had only the smallest clue what she meant by this. And beyond that, I had no idea how to respond. Fern wasn't exactly the first person to call me aloof. Trish had taken to saying that I wore a "lid." Sheila insisted that by repressing one emotion (my anger), I was repressing any inkling of personality and animation, any sparkle or fire. Like, Walter Cannon—the physiologist who coined the term "fight or flight"—Sheila thought anger was the door to all the other emotions, and mine was padlocked shut.

Fern examined me behind the smudged lenses of her bifocals, and I took a contemplative sip from my drink's bendy straw.

At the other end of the table Carly was childishly shrieking, "But I don't wanna put my shoes on!"

———

Even though the motel was only across the street from the restaurant, I got a ride back from dinner in Raquel's tobacco-brown Lincoln.

"Can I show you something?" Raquel turned slowly to ask me as she silenced the engine.

"Sure," I said and followed her around to the rear of the sedan. It was a steamy night, rain falling like a noxious vapor, glooming windows and misting the roofs of the cars in the lot. Although it was only around eight, the motel was swinging with the sounds of a party or a drug cartel. House music thundered from the third-floor balcony, a monotonous beat.

I don't know what I expected as Raquel twisted the key in the lock of her trunk. Probably something contraband at SAP. I expected to see crates of records or piles of DVDs. I hoped she might reveal a whole bundle of newspapers, novels, and periodicals with which we might stun our senses stupid and wipe away the tragic events of the day.

After all, Raquel and I were SAP's heretics. Like me, she refused to defame her parents. She refused the bat when Sheila tried to make her beat the boxing bag. We were the contrarians, the ones unacquainted with therapy-speak and slow to learn, much to everyone's frustration.

In fact, what my new friend removed made me realize that I was the only one at SAP unwilling to examine my own relationship with my family and my childhood. Raquel handed me a child's scooter, painted bubble-gum pink and with silver tassels spewing out of either handle and Hello Kitty decals affixed to its sides.

"It was my fiancé's Christmas present to me after he attended SAP last month. I didn't understand it at the time. Before I left for this weekend, he said, 'Don't worry, you'll get it by the time SAP is over.'"

"So your fiancé wants you to embrace your 'inner child'?"

"I think so," she said. "I've been too embarrassed to take it out of the trunk until now. But, I think, after all this is over, I might be ready to take it for a ride."

As I walked back into the motel lobby it was with an adult's sense of isolation, a grown woman's miscreance in a place of pure faith. The desk manager choked on a giggle when he saw the bunny that I held by one pink velour ear. I passed a herd of small kids—children of the night staff by the looks of it. They'd been engaged in a game with the vending machine, trying to stretch their reedy arms up through bottom and dislodge whatever goodies they could reach.

"I like your bunny rabbit, ma'am." The most cherubic-faced boy turned and told me in earnest.

Why did I feel neither bond nor love for the girl at the easel? Why did I want to tell her cruelly to handle her business, paint her crappy picture, and do a better job pretending nothing was wrong?

———

Our final day at SAP fizzled out into a graduation ceremony. The culmination in panorama: SAP threw the whole lot of us a birthday party meant to symbolize our rebirth as compassionate, calm, and healed individuals, and to mark that twenty-ninth of January as the first day of our fury-free lives. We wore worn conical hats with strangulating strings. Fern toted in a wide, buttercream cake gleaming with trick candles. Trish made us gather around the confection and sing "Happy Birthday to Me."

After the flames fluttered out in our shared exhale, Danielle revealed her morning pregnancy test had shown her a positive sign and then dropped her slice of cake in excitement. The slimy mess was stepped in by Nico, who told us he realized that he wasn't a bully, and was mopped up by Bev, who concluded she wasn't a victim after all. In profile, Daryl abused an earsplitting noisemaker. One of the men finally removed his much-loved Yankees cap, which Sheila claimed he wore "like a shield," like part of his "tough-guy macho act." The instant this man revealed his bare cranium, the room spit whistled, wahooed, and jumped to ovation. Shrugging, he said noncommittally, "It's not a big deal. I don't know why everyone's acting like I'm dressed in black tie."

More than half of my co-attendees seemed genuinely transformed. I wanted to believe they were just putting on a show, but I think SAP's catharsis really had made a difference. I'd spent all weekend condemning the meal, but by the time I said my good-byes and hailed an airport-bound cab, I didn't doubt anything but my palate.

21

In the writings of Alice Miller, I will later find this warning: "Experience has taught us that we have only one enduring weapon in our struggle against mental illness: the emotional discovery of the truth about the unique history of our childhood."

But back in New York, where I am having my second real experience with therapy after SAP, I still feel extremely put off any time Alice tries to broach the subject of my family.

Sure, I'm coming off a difficult month at my parents' house and—in the month since I've been back in New York—I've failed to tell my parents about a few things that have been nettling me. But I want to take responsibility for my emotions, to focus on myself, and I feel like Alice is goading me to pass the buck and dump my anger about my breakup on my parents. I concede that they might have unintentionally laid the foundation for my anger, but I came to therapy because my heart had been broken.

I agree to talk to Alice about my frustrations with my sister by way of compromise. For the moment, it's the best I can do.

My sister comes to stay over one night that September. The visit begins when she calls me repeatedly from somewhere under the Manhattan Bridge, saying, "Okay, I'm at Oliver Street. Which way should I walk?"

I tell her to just get herself in a cab and I'll pay for it when she reaches my place.

She calls back ten minutes later to report, "No fucking lazy, asshole cabbie will fucking stop for me, and what the fuck am I supposed to do?" I lead her through a brief lesson about how only the cabs with "the lit-up numbers" are available to take fares. With all the patience I can muster, and that's not much, I tell her to wait on the corner and hold out her arm whenever she sees a cab that fits that description.

Ten minutes after that, she calls to say, "Look. I don't know where the fuck I am and no cab will fucking stop for me even if I *am* pregnant, and I don't know your fucking address anyway."

Maybe I could have forgiven her if it was the first time she'd ever come for a visit, but a couple of years earlier she had *lived with me for a whole month* while she worked in an internship at a downtown film production company. "Look yourself," I fire back. "I'm not going to come down there and hail a cab for you. You're an adult. You're a college graduate. It's not nuclear physics. Just face traffic and stick your fucking hand out. Don't call again until you're in the backseat."

These are the kinds of huffy outbursts that often arise when dealing with my sister. It has always been easier to get angry with her than with my parents. Maybe because, being my little sister, she reminds me of my inner child whose emotions I am always eager to keep in check. Or maybe it's because we grew up in a house where approval seemed rationed; starved for my mom's affection, we are used to squabbling for it, even if it occasionally means turning our backs on each other.

She arrives at my apartment looking forgetful. No jacket, despite the approaching autumn chill. No shoelaces in her white Converse sneakers. She pushes her sunglasses back on the moussed crown of her head. She rummages through the metallic handbag that weighs down her elbow. From the moment she walks in, my apartment grows dense with the scent of her perfume, the smell of citrus rolled in sugar. I look at her and feel touched by her youth, enraged by her helplessness, and amused by what she thinks is her don't-effing-F-with-me swagger. You might mistake her for some impetuous Disney Channel star if it weren't for the three pounds of baby jutting out of her abdomen.

She collapses on my bed with an exaggerated sigh and thrusts a pillow between the holed knees of her jeans. She curls her hand over the round of her belly. "Ow," she yelps, addressing her navel. "*You*— quit it!" For some reason I can't name, I feel tense already. And I wonder about that, about how I could at once feel so protective of this person and yet so thoroughly rejecting of her.

I imagine the feeling is mutual. The month we'd lived together had been a specific hell, wherein she hadn't been able to resist behaving like a thankless, disparaging child any more than I had been able to refrain from acting like her overbearing mother. When she stopped consuming anything but Red Bull, menthols, and pink Necco candies, I started packing her a daily paper-bag lunch. When she complained of being bored, I dragged her to concerts, book readings, and yoga classes. Instead of walking beside me when we went for a "stroll," she insisted on traipsing half a block behind me, all the while smoking a cigarette and whispering conspiratorially into her cell phone.

What hadn't she found fault with? She'd whined about my "yuppie, organic, all-natural food." She'd called my boyfriend at the time as "exciting as milquetoast."

In response, I'd slammed her on her rather astonishing ability to rot on my pullout sofa for days at a time, watching *Friends* episodes she'd brought on DVD. I bought her a small closet's worth of office-appropriate clothing and watched her eschew it all in favor of tank tops that revealed her bra's upper ambits. At the time, nothing I could do or say or buy for her could wipe the condemning look off her face. Listen to me: *Wipe that look off her face.* I'd started thinking in mean-mom-isms. And she, in turn, had barked back in the language of the spoiled punk ("You don't own me"; "I am so out of here"). No one knew as well as me how convenient it was to use me as our mother's effigy. I often employed the very same method.

We'd shared the same five-hundred-square-foot space that summer, but any real communication between my sister and me had been triangulated, passing entirely through the specter of our mother. Whether she mediated or pitted us further against each other I'm still not sure. She'd call to tell me, "Your sister likes it when you pack her a lunch." Or, "I hear you made your sister clean the kitchen." After a particularly vicious fight on my twenty-sixth birthday, Mom had called up and lambasted me for—abuse of all abuses in our family— "trying to make my sister talk about why she was upset."

During this visit, I take my sister baby clothes shopping. We ride the subway to Park Slope and I give the snake eye to every man and able-bodied woman who doesn't offer my sister a seat. I am careful— perhaps overly careful, perhaps obnoxiously careful—to make sure she has enough water and cereal bars to sate her between meals, to make sure she sits occasionally and puts her feet up, to make sure she doesn't carry any bag that is too heavy. I'm aware that I'm acting like her mother again, but the placater in me just can't accept that she's an adult fit to take care of herself.

In a store on Seventh Avenue, I watch her finger a tiny white bunting suit and feel my pulse flux with envy. I'm not envious that she's having a baby, but rather that she feels equipped to do it. *How does she feel secure enough? How does she know she won't delegate her suffering to her children? How can she be sure that she won't revenge herself on what her latest ultrasound showed was her baby girl? Or make her daughter feel as though it is her sole responsibility to make my sister feel validated?* I am fully aware that I'm already controlling and overly critical of my sister, averse to the helpless devotion of pets, and indignant to the neediness of my dates, and frankly I doubt my potential as a mother.

When I think of myself as a mother the image that comes to mind is that of someone lipsticked and powdered, someone formal, forceful, faux friendly, and frigid, with a homemaker's apron tied over her cocktail dress and an autocratic look on her face. This image, rightfully, fills me with terror. I've long ago let it convince me that I don't want kids. I've let it persuade me that I can and will be perfectly happy delivering not babies but books.

That night my sister and I order take-out Chinese and play Battleship while the TV plays white noise in the background. She shares my aversion to stillness and quiet, and, together, we make an effort to fill every minute with distraction.

After credits roll on a late-night talk show, I loan her a pair of flannel pajamas. We curl up on opposite sides of my bed, back to back, an invisible force field between us.

Were we really so opposite? My parents conditioned us to believe that we were stark, polar opposites: one dark and gaunt, the other golden and dimpled; one woeful and sensible, the other uninhibited and flaky. This is just another fiction, very much like the one that insists we aren't close because we're five years apart.

I awake the next morning, still beside my sister, swathed in the afterimage of a dream. In it I was lying in a coffin at my own open-casket wake watching a procession of people approach, kneel beside me, mouth a few silent words, cross themselves, and go. I had been at once factually gone and clinically present. My heart had beat loudly in my ears. I'd felt deficient, self-conscious, and judged. I'd felt like I couldn't trust myself enough to even *know* whether I was really dead. Even embalmed, I'd been convinced that I wasn't exerting enough, wasn't *doing it right*, that I could do better at this business of being a corpse.

———

Discussing my sister with Alice is a bit like working on an impressionist painting. It's progress for me to describe things in resentment's blunt language, to dip into the shocking and unadulterated color of memories I've tried hard to avoid.

I say: "I can't trust her, I hate that."

Or: "It's unfair that I'm the one who has to attend every holiday because she misses them."

"Maybe she misses holidays because you're always there," Alice counters.

It's my what a painter friend would call my first attempt to let my eye "view the subject" of my emotions instead of "re-creating" it.

And yet even my riff of complaints isn't without a conscientious structure. I still think out what I want to tell Alice in advance and walk in with a mental order of business.

This approach doesn't allow me to think any differently about the Lark, my depression, or the truth of my family. If anything, therapy begins to feel like those phone calls from my parents, the ones in which they ring to discuss my sister's latest dramas and traumas, skipping what's going on in their own lives and asking nothing about mine other than the ever grating question, "How's work?"

———

I tell Alice about our trip to Hollywood.

Shortly before my sister eloped I booked two round-trip tickets to LAX to coincide with her spring break. In my mind it was a kind of early graduation present, and I planned it because I'd thought it was outrageous that a film student and aspiring screenwriter had never seen the vapid beauty of LA.

There might have also been some logic hard at work beneath my conscious mind—something that said the trip could win her acceptance, her friendship, and make us close in a way that we'd never been. And maybe that's why we were both so angry while we were there. I was desperate to prove that I could be sisterly and spontaneous. And sensing the strings attached to the trip, she decided she'd have none of it.

I had picked her up at her gate in a rented candy-apple-red Mustang. I had chosen a gaudy hotel in Beverly Hills. I arranged a meeting for her with a well-regarded film agent—someone who might agree to look at her scripts. I knew only that I wanted to show her a glittering, glossy, and magical time. Excuse me while I reach for infamous last words: I wanted everything to be perfect.

"Young hockey players with unhealthy perfectionist tendencies are particularly prone to fits of anger." I would read this later in a paper by researchers at the University of Alberta who had studied fighting that occurs among child hockey players. "We found that players run into trouble when their standards are too high. When these athletes make a mistake, they get angry at themselves, but they also get angry and frustrated because they feel that their parents or coaches put an unfair amount of pressure on them."

In retrospect, I think my sister and I sought in each other a depth and quality of love that no sibling can ever provide. This intensity of affection should come from a parent, and, even then, it has to come in childhood. We needed it, well, needily, and yet we couldn't accept it from each other under any terms. At the core of the matter was not love but anger, a grudge against someone and something else entirely.

I thought she'd been ungrateful, even judgmental. She hated the convertible ("too hot") and the hotel ("ridiculous"). The local radio station, 103, was "boring." Pinkberry frozen yogurt was "weird." At the Troubadour, where I'd brought her to see a band, she'd shot me a withering look between songs and said, "It's like you think you're still a kid."

Unwilling to tell her off directly—this would have meant surrendering my idea of a perfect, sisterly trip—my road rage expanded exponentially. I revved, swerved, and shrieked by way of the horn while she sat beside me, texting her new husband about what a psychotic I was, her face a sullen mask. At one point on Mulholland Drive, I had to resist the urge to give us a Hollywood end to our misery and plunge us both over the vista.

In the parking garage after the meeting I'd arranged with the film agent, during which my typically swaggering sister had been as friendly as a closed clam, I imploded.

Suddenly all veins, teeth, and bulging eye sockets, I clipped along in a pair of agonizing heels. I had reached the stage of fury where I was gesticulating madly and narrating out loud.: "Did I not set up that meeting explicitly so you could ask for career advice? And what did you do when that agent leaned in and very nicely asked you what you want to do after graduation? You puckered your face, looking totally disinterested, I might add, and said, 'I'm not sure.' *I'm not sure!* As though you were palm-up at a Venice Beach fortune-teller instead of in a networking meeting!"

I was being controlling, rejecting, almost bullying, but I felt beaten, and bitter, and more matronly than any twenty-six-year-old I'd ever had the misfortune to meet.

In the meeting, I'd indulged an impulse I despised and spoken for her like the pushy stage mom I remembered from my youth: "She's being modest," I'd told the agent. "She's studied screenwriting at school. She has some incredible scripts. Maybe she could send them to you sometime?"

It would've felt so nice to abandon my role as sister-as-mother. And I'd have loved just as much to see my sister ditch her own as a punk-ass kid.

———

For some reason, when I recount these events for Alice, I find it much easier to guess what my sister had been feeling than to talk about how the mess had affected me. "She's suspicious of strangers," I say. "I think we acquired that from our parents." And, "Perhaps she just collapsed in on herself in that meeting. We were not raised to sing our own praises."

Confiding in Alice about my sister helps me come around to the idea that I can't focus on myself without addressing my ongoing issues with my family.

But even as I begin to open up, my language on the subject remains detached. In addition to referencing Satir—"She's our family's distracter," "I'm its placater/computer"—I quote from the stacks of family psychology books I've begun withdrawing from the New York Public Library. When I speak about the Lark, and boy do I, I say I've decided our relationship fits Robert Sternberg's definition of "fatuous love," "strong on passion and commitment but low on intimate involvement." When I talk about my relationship with my mother, I reference Nancy Chodorow, who said that girls never separate from their mothers as completely as boys do.

Alice, in her bubbly way, expresses a growing concern that our conversations are becoming "too academic," and my anger "too intellectualized."

I'm willing to admit our sessions are beginning to feel like an adult education class. Yet, instead of using our time together to tell her what I'm feeling, I find myself responding by reading up on "emotionology" (the way a group of people thinks about and describes their emotions). The next week, I tell that Alice that she's right. I am responding to my anger like a quintessential American. I'm depressed because I live in a time when Americans are freer than ever to express tenderness, passion, or fear but not serious anger. (I've read this in Carol and Peter Stearns, who coined the word "emotionology" to begin with.)

I watch Alice's mouth make a hyphen of itself. This is the closest she ever comes to actually frowning.

I imagine she privately combs her own experience and studies, looking for a fix: What to do with someone who avoids rubbing up against her emotions by turning them into endless theories and philosophical debates?

I tell Alice I've been reading a lot of linguistics books. I appreciate the detached, mathematical tone of semantics—the way linguists can reduce a feeling to a word and a word to a formula. Did she know there are a number of tongues (Russian, for one; Polish, for another) that have no exact equivalent for our English "anger"? From Anna Wierzbicka's *Emotion across Languages and Cultures*, I've learned "the view of *anger* as something that can be manipulated—'controlled,' 'vented,' 'released,' left 'unresolved,' 'directed' at this or that target, 'stirred up,' 'repressed,' 'expressed,' 'suppressed,' and so on" are untranslatable elsewhere in the world.

When the long-suffering woman wants to talk specifically about my anger at the Lark, I take issue with the word itself. I tell her the anatomy of "anger," at least linguistically speaking, goes like this:

X is angry (at/with) Z:
Something is happening inside of X

The kind of bad thing that happens to people
When they think:
"Someone (Z) did something bad to me"
And because of that,
they want to do something bad (to Z).

(I've taken to spending afternoons cowering in my apartment with the blinds shut, tearing through this emotional arithmetic. I devour these sentences that sound like caveman-speak, like the forlorn gruntings of Earliest Man.)

According to this, I tell Alice, my feelings about the Lark don't have all the hardware to qualify as anger. Most notably, the last step (payback) is missing. Sure, I want, in my own way, to rouse him, to convert him, and to persuade him to give our relationship another try, but I feel too limp, vacant, and unimaginative to attempt any kind of vengeful thinking.

I even pin my reluctance to get angry on a larger culture. "Anger," Wierzbicka writes, cannot be taken for granted as "culture-free" or having a "universal standard." I tell Alice our English anger is specific to us. According to linguists, the English "anger" reflects our perception that the emotion is internal, involuntary, and unbecoming. In a case study by linguist Cliff Goddard I see my own fears reflected in the words: "English 'anger' includes an implicit negative evaluation—it is bad (or possibly merely not good) to be angry."

In all my reading, I miss the part where linguists say that the fact that an emotion word is missing from our language doesn't mean we can't and don't experience the feeling. The fact that words like "rage" don't cross my lips doesn't mean the feelings aren't in me, lying dormant, waiting for a moment when I'm too distracted or weakened to guard the cage I've locked them up in.

I sense my dedication to my research list is maddening, but it isn't any more disingenuous than when I told Sheila at SAP that I "didn't know" why I was crying. The computer in me still thinks she can eke out a little bit of security by intellectualizing everything. I talk around subjects, restricting my language to generalizations and abstractions. I'm used to avoiding words as direct as "I" and "you" whenever I talk about my emotions. I'd been a child when I'd dug a hole for my emotions and now, over twenty years later, I don't have the slightest clue under what bush, stone, or flower bed I might have buried them.

It's a problem in my writing, just as it is a problem in my life. According to my editor, my first drafts are always stoic accounts of the facts. It is only in editing that I remember to include what I am feeling at the time of the story.

FIVE   *Anger Displaced*

A good scapegoat is nearly as welcome as a solution to the problem.

—UNKNOWN

22

There comes a point in October when it seems as though everyone has a guru they want me to meet. I simply *must* visit "Iviana, the Park Slope acupuncturist." I *have* to make an appointment with the city's best psychopharmacologist. If I don't go see "Brother Blackstone, the West Village energy healer, I'll never restore my 'core frequency.'" My yoga teacher, Rolf, thinks a retreat at a Costa Rican coffee plantation will get me centered. Alyssa keeps urging me to fly out to the Peoplemaking center in Colorado and submit to therapy with its director, a man who is trained in Virginia Satir's "Human Validation" method.

They're only trying to help. But homeopathy taught me that the Staphysagria patient, an independent and introverted idiot, avoids social interaction. "This is a very introverted type, a fugitive, who runs away from people in order to avoid a repetition of his past, a childhood in which [she felt] helpless or worthless."

Hunter is the only person I ever consent to call. Frankly, I am curious. My friend Devon describes him as a twenty-seven-year-old Catholic seminary student from the rural South who is trained in Reiki healing and quotes liberally from the *Yoga-Sutra*.

I've also been thinking more about what Fern said to me at SAP, about my heart chakra muffling my throat. I've become a lot more accepting of alternative medicine since that long-ago weekend. I'm even a little more open to the idea that emotion can be stored in the body as "energy." And Devon has described a profound experience in which Hunter has "cleared away the blocked energy in her root chakra."

In the years Devon and I have been friends, she's often described herself with words like "logical," "analytical," "unromantic," and "pragmatic." Given all that, I'm surprised she'd spend time lying on her back while Hunter applied his "touchless healing" to her.

"It was the strangest thing," she confesses. "While Hunter was working on me, I became really conscious of my feet. I'd never realized just how alienated I had been from them. Sure, I walk around on them all day. I stuff them into boots. But I don't think I'd ever really *felt* them before. They've been floating down there in deep space."

I might have thought Devon was certifiable if I hadn't felt the same way about my throat. Some part of me still wanted to shrug off Fern's diagnosis, but another part had begun to realize that I rarely *felt* my throat in my day-to-day life, not even when I spoke, choked down dinner, or cleared it with a tidy *a-hem*. Alone in my apartment, I found myself tracing my voice box down from my cocked chin with a fingertip. Reiki practitioners call the throat the "midway point between the heart and the tongue"; they say it is the energy point that determines how we communicate, express ourselves creatively, and voice our emotions. I'm aware of my neck, and in a cerebral way I know my throat exists somewhere in there. But most of the time it feels as though my head hovers three inches above my clavicle, unmoored and indifferent to the rest of me.

Perhaps there's some connection between my numb throat, my lack of self-expression, and my unspoken anger. In a 1915 meeting of the American Psychopathological Association, G. Stanley Hall claimed "anger is the acme of self-assertion." And Virginia Satir often referenced the throat when she encouraged people to speak their truths: "Just let the words come out of this beautiful throat of yours and see what happens."

I think too about my vocal cords. My voice fluctuates between the qualities Virginia Satir ascribes to computers and placaters. It's either "dull and monotonous," or it's "squeaky," as if lacking the air to maintain a "full, rich voice."

One Tuesday afternoon I decide to call Hunter. I turn the phone over and over in my hands in a state of livid anxiety. I have no social graces. In the weeks since I've begun seeing Alice, I've felt terribly exposed, and it's kept me dodging situations in which I have to confront new people. I feel my embarrassment mount as I began to dial. I realize I'm hoping to get an answer from Hunter, yet I don't know what question I am hoping to ask.

As it happens, I have little cause to worry. Hunter picks up the phone as if he'd been anticipating my call at precisely that moment. He pauses humanely while I sputter through my prerehearsed introduction. When it's his turn to speak, I relax at the sound of his gentle voice and receptive demeanor. I have no idea what he looks like. I imagine him as a lithe young man with a halo of kinked hair and a shock of beard on his weak, boyish chin. I imagine him shirtless and shoeless, fingering a corncob pipe in a cottage by a creek. I suspect he strings wind chimes and whittles wood for fun.

We talk for a bit about Reiki, a spiritual practice developed in 1922. Hunter talks about its creator, Mikao Usui, who spent three weeks fasting and meditating on Mount Kurama in Japan, where he claimed to receive the ability to move people's healing energy around with his palms, redistributing it between the seven chakras, the energy points found in the coccyx, ovaries or prostate, navel area, heart area, throat area, pineal gland (or third eye), and the top of the head (in the part where you find a newborn's fontanel).

While I used to think Reiki stank of charlatanism, I've realized that a similar concept exists in psychology. In treating families, Virginia Satir used to say that her goal was to redirect "blocked-up energy," allowing people to deal with their self-esteem and to establish communication and rules for being human that relate to the eight levels of the self. Even her eight levels closely resemble Reiki's seven energy points. She sees everyone as made up of a physical level (the coccyx), intellectual level (the fontanel), emotional level (the heart), sensual (the ovaries or prostate), interactional (the throat), nutritional (the navel), and the contextual and the spiritual (the pineal gland).

I tell Hunter what Fern had said to me at SAP about my heart standing in the way of my throat.

"That would make sense," Hunter says with a voice as Southern and moist as fresh tobacco. "Especially if you're the kind of person who is so sensitive to other people's emotions that you deny your own."

There is a poignant little pause. "Let's just say, for the sake of argument, that I am that kind of person. Out of curiosity, how would I open my throat?"

There is another long pause. Hunter doesn't have most people's aversion to dead air. Just when I begin to worry that my cell phone has dropped the call, his previously soft-spoken voice bursts open and blooms bright.

"Some people say to gargle with saltwater," he tells me. "If you're into yoga, you could spend some time in fish pose. Or plough pose. Or shoulder stand. Whenever you meditate, you could envision a turquoise sunburst. You could sing. You might chant 'ham.' Whatever you do, you should make noise. Hum. Scream. Create a vibration. From sound comes communication, and communication is the main point of the *vishuddha*, the throat chakra. The throat is connected to our idea of who we are. It's the place where the affairs of the mind meet the feelings of the body. The throat allows us to describe our experiences. It's the source of all art and creativity."

"That sounds about right. These days, I can barely write a check, let alone my next book."

"Balancing your chakras is a life's work," Hunter says. "So is facing your fears and asserting yourself. Emotions aren't things you experience once and then check off your list."

He says he makes an effort to pay attention to his own energy points every day. He attends to them when he meditates, goes to therapy, studies religion, and meets with his spiritual adviser.

Because Devon told Hunter about the book I was writing, we also talk about anger. When I tell him that I think the Buddhist approach to emotion seems repressed, Hunter tells me I've missed some very important passages in my reading.

Yes, Buddhists generally value patience, warn against the faults of anger, and discourage retaliation, but they also warn against being a human doormat. A person has to establish boundaries and practice a little self-defense, he says. The word "no" has to be in her vocabulary. She can't placate, abide violence, or absorb everybody's blame, because in the end that would make her a broken warrior and "a broken warrior is of no good to anyone."

"Have you heard the story of Sadhu and the Snake?" I tell Hunter I haven't. "In India, *sadhu*s are wandering monks who travel from village to village teaching, chanting, praying, and helping people burn off bad karma. According to legend, one of these *sadhu*s visited a village where a huge snake was terrorizing people. So the *sadhu* sat the snake down and taught him about *ahimsa*, or nonviolence, and the snake seemed to take the message onboard. A year passed. The *sadhu* visited the village again and, sure enough, he ran into the snake. Only this time, the snake was bruised and skinny. He had stopped terrorizing the village, but in an effort to be nonviolent and openhearted, he had allowed the village children to taunt and throw rocks at him. He was so injured that he could hardly hunt and so scared that he couldn't leave his hiding place. The *sadhu* shook his head in disappointment, and the snake said, 'What? You told me not to bite.' And the *sadhu* said, 'Yeah, but I never told you not to hiss.'"

I listen as Hunter goes to his bookshelf and opens to a passage in Gandhi. "'[Nonviolence] does not mean meek submission to the will of the evildoer,'" he quotes, "'but it means the putting of one's whole soul against the will of the tyrant. Working under this law of our being, it is possible for a single individual to defy the whole might of an unjust empire, to save his honor, his religion, his soul and lay the foundation for that empire's fall or its regeneration.'"

Unlike Sheila, Hunter doesn't think a person can process all her rage in one weekend. "Thich Nhat Hanh compares anger to a crying baby," he tells me. "Whenever we feel it we need to pick it up, embrace it, speak quietly to it, and try to figure out what's making it anxious."

"That's from his book *Anger*, right? I've read that. The only trouble is, I think my 'anger baby' died of SIDS. Forget crying. I can't even hear its *breath*."

I give a hot, dry laugh, but Hunter stays quiet. There's another long silence, this one loaded and portentous. "Empathy's my gift too," he finally says. "I've always been very sensitive to other people's emotions. I absorb them. They affect me. I can't seem to help it. The whole time we've been talking, I've been getting this really sad vibration from you. Like, it's making me feel really depressed."

The old me realizes this statement is ripe for mockery, but Hunter has seen me somehow in the course of one phone call, and I feel my eyes mist over. "I didn't think I felt sad when I called you." I crush the cigarette I've been smoking into a leaf-shaped soy sauce dish. "But, now that you've said that, I feel like I could cry."

"I know. I feel like *I* want to cry."

"Shit," I say, feeling my breath catch like a bone in my throat. "Maybe I am. Sad, I mean." Amazement briefly illuminates my misery. A *stranger* is more in tune with my emotions than I am.

"Stop trying to get angry," Hunter says. "All of that will come later. For now, I think you need to go cry for however long it lasts. If you can, clear the afternoon for it."

Alice has suggested the same concept. She calls my humiliated, depressive mood my "gremlin," after the mythical creatures responsible for sabotaging aircraft and causing inexplicable accidents during flights.

Alice is always encouraging me to devote fifteen minutes a day to "sitting with" said creature—this so the emotions won't subvert the rest of my day.

But for as much as she wants me to "feel" my gremlin's disappointments and "write down" all the panty-waisted scrawl the varmint has to say, I prefer to tell the gremlin to shut its yap. Or even better yet, I tell it what I had always been told as a child: chin up, shoulders back, put on a smile, don't let on that you're upset, think about how your behavior reflects on *me*.

My method doesn't work. By neglecting the beast, I pretty much ensure that he'll distract me. Where concentration is concerned, he adds static to my radio. Saner people, like family therapist Karyl McBride, have put it this way: "The grief process begins with a decision: to let your feelings be there." I can't yet relate to my "gremlin" or understand where he comes from. But I know I can acknowledge his pinched, reptilian face. It's small progress, but unlike my occasional stabs at *tonglen*, I don't turn away from the loneliness that arises, to the shame that I can touch and smell and hear and taste. A tendril of indignation pushes itself up beneath grief's surface, carrying with it *those* emotions, my feelings, hale and tingling.

After I hang up with Hunter, I cry until my cheeks are fevered, my eyes are slits and my nose is raw. Then I go to my medicine cabinet, looking for Natrum Muriaticum, for grief, only to find its little brown bottle dry.

23

I can't understand anything I am feeling, and, at the same time, I can't talk myself out of this state. I feel exhausted and lost, almost as though I am walking a long blank highway. I have no idea what revelation I'm walking toward. I am too far gone to turn back. What's worse, I'm losing the incentive to keep trekking. I can't bear to think or talk about emotions anymore. Talking doesn't change the landscape. I ache to call it quits and absorb whatever ruin comes my way. Only my book keeps me going.

With Alyssa's help I call her mentor, a woman named Stowe, to beg her for more Nat-Mur. She wants to know how much of the other remedies I have left.

I am also out of Lycopodium (for fear). I have at least four more doses of Lachesis (for envy). And, although I have two spoonfuls of Staphysagria (the anger remedy) left, I'm avoiding it due to the bad reaction it gave me.

This last statement piques Stowe's interest. "Tell me more about these negative reactions."

I mention the vomiting, the headache that felt more like a brain injury. I ask her if she thinks the reaction was healing aggravation.

"For sure," Stowe says in a slow, blissed-out voice that wears on my nerves, even though, in recent months, I've been warming to alternative medicine like hers. "Don't be discouraged. That's an auspicious sign! Your body is clearing out and airing old toxins! The headaches are probably temporary. I'm gonna send you more Staph and encourage you to keep taking it."

Stowe also urges me to take more Lachesis, the remedy for jealousy. She says I'll know when I need it because I might develop a tickle in my throat or feel an urge to get what she very clinically calls "all gossipy."

From what I've read in my homeopathy books, Lachesis is the poisonous venom of the bushmaster snake (albeit in a highly diluted form).

"Most women take all the other remedies before they take Lach," Stowe tells me. "We don't like to admit when we feel jealous, vengeful, kind of bitchy. My husband always reminds me to take Lach, usually right around my period. We'll be bickering, and he'll say, 'I think you need to take your Lach.' And I'll tell him, 'Fuck you.' Then, a few days later, I'll cave in and take it."

I picture Stowe as a tall, handsome woman, bohemian and rich thin, with streaked red hair tumbling down the back of her caftan.

She asks if I have any other concerns that she can help me with. Eventually, I confide that I'd like to stop smoking again.

"A few cigarettes are fine," Stowe says in her wistful, Hollywood voice. "But they'll make you sick if you don't know who you really are."

I'm not entirely sure I do know. Stowe agrees to include some detoxifying droplets in the box of remedies she will soon mail me.

———

For the next two weeks, I follow Stowe's advice religiously.

On Monday morning, I swallow a spoonful of Staph. I stay inside most of the day, nursing a cigarette between my yellowing fingers. I try to write and find myself just as numb and confused as I was when I tried to "meditate" on my throat.

On Tuesday, I take Lach. On homeopathy Web sites, I read that a person who needs Lach is like "a highly strung bow, taut with sexual energy." "A sexually frustrated Lachesis woman" is liable to be "touchy and highly emotional," one site said. Evidently, she'll need an outlet for all that stamina (art, career, spirituality, or sex) so that it won't backfire against her.

Something in this passage reminds me of a word I came across in the huge stacks of semantics books back at my parents' house.

The word I am thinking of is *liget*, a concept that has terrific importance to people of the Ilongot tribe of the Philippines. According to linguists, *liget* refers to anger, but also to energy and passion. The word is ascribed to forces of nature like chili pepper, liquor, wind, rain, fire, even a man's seed. Although *liget* is often born of envy, it is not always destructive. On the contrary, it frequently implies vitality and fierceness. Psychological anthropologist Michelle Rosaldo wrote that *liget* represents a will to compete and a desire to triumph; it is "realized in activity and purpose, in a willingness to stay awake all night and travel far when hunting, in a readiness to climb tall trees or harvest in hot sunlight, in an aura of competence and vitality."

Depending on how *liget* is channeled, it can "generate both chaos and concentration, distress and industry, a loss of sense and reason, and an experience of clarification and release." There was no exact

English translation for *liget*. Yet the Ilongots say there would be no human life without it.

———

I stick to my homeopathy routine out of curiosity. I do it out of desperation, and because I have a masochistic desire to play the part of the guinea pig. But, computer that I am, I still put much more stock in therapy. It's far easier for me to believe that horrible experiences become entrenched in our psyches than imbedded in the tissue of our body as dark "energy."

Once a week, I find myself back in Alice's office with its canned, deodorized air, and on the black leather sofa that droops in the center as though it too were about to collapse into tears.

I can tell the saintly woman is frustrated with me. In an effort to arouse the anger beneath my avoidance strategies, Alice has taken to treating me roughly. But no matter how she prods me, I won't lash out, challenge her perspective, or raise my voice above a polite murmur.

Alice begins to engage me in role-playing exercises. When she plays my mother—hoping I will tell her how much it bothers me when she gossips about my sister to me and about me to her—I spend a quarter of our session describing how doing so would make my mother feel as abandoned as she did when my grandmother made her move out at nineteen. When she tries to play my father, I insist my dad is too fragile to hear my criticisms until he finds steady work. When she suggests I coddle my family and repress what I really want to say, I cry with self-loathing. When she calls my "sweetness" inauthentic, I absorb the criticism and resolve to be meaner.

One day she claps her hands together and cuts off my string of excuses. "Koren!" she yelps. "There is no 'right' or 'wrong' time to open up and reveal the real you to people! Get real. Be authentic. If you wait until a 'better time' to tell them what's bothering you, you'll be waiting forever!"

"Give it time," Alice used to tell me at the start of our sessions. "You grew up in a family where you learned very early that anger was dangerous. You learned it would compromise your parents' love for you. That it would upset the balance of your family and interfere with everyone's ability to cope. I'm trying to prove to you that you can have a safe and positive experience with anger. It just takes time. Hopefully, through the process of transference, you'll be able to start by getting ticked off at me."

Weeks pass with Alice trying to provoke me. Instead of letting anger fly, I apologize. Therapy becomes just like those notes of apology I used to write my mom as a child. Only instead of groveling for being a selfish daughter, I apologize for being a submissive woman.

———

Because I still think of the Lark, I try to follow the advice friends gave me. I try to make a list of my good points. I try to make a list of his bad points. I pack everything that reminds me of him into a cardboard box and shove the whole caboodle under my bed.

A few times, I meet up with girlfriends of girlfriends—theatrical women, pale, emaciated—and listen to them talk about their sex lives in crude, exhibitionistic detail. But I much prefer to spend Friday or Saturday nights helping Devon take long exposure shots of religious displays in her Brooklyn neighborhood.

We work between 10:00 P.M. and 1:00 A.M. in at least partial silence. I idle in the street, chain-smoking and making a show of guarding Devon's equipment while she trains her camera on a flood-lit statue of the Virgin Mary.

The saint is positioned in a familiar pose: chin aimed down in a way that says "I'm here to serve," upturned palms always saying "whatever you need."

———

One Thursday, I write the Lark the first e-mail in months.

My book keeps roping my thoughts back to last summer's mess. What I'd been trying and failing to tell you, even on the night whose name we dare not speak, is that the essays I've been writing are really just about how uncomfortable anger (my own and others) has always made me. What dumb lengths I've gone to in order to deny it, or avoid it entirely, or convert it into something gentle, helpful, like empathy. Any anger that arises, naturally in my life? I've tried to rub it with patchouli oil and give it some mala beads.

I tell the Lark that I'd left Brighton—in a flash, like my ponytail was on fire—to dodge his anger and avert my own. Maybe worse, I never confronted him about the things that weighed on me while I was there. The prospect of arm wrestling my only ally in a place full of strangers was just too daunting.

I tell him how sorry I am for the few times when, from one end of a telephone line, I tried to choke my anger down and hung up too abruptly. I write:

The more writing this book informs the rest of my life, the more I realize that the idea for it is just some doomed attempt to keep any frustrations inside and still them on my own. This is like the rhythm method of anger management techniques: um, not effective.

I ask the Lark if he found being assertive challenging too. He'd never told me why he was piqued the first night I arrived in Brighton, and he'd never let on about what I had done to miff him while we were visiting his hometown.

Whatever concerns you had about me, I had to hear them once removed, from your brother or whoever else was stepping in as your emotional interpreter. Are your feelings in a little-known dialect too? Sometimes I feel like mine are.

I end the letter with an apology:

I got everything the Buddhists taught me backwards. I thought those robed tyrants were telling me to say nothing in dissent, accost myself exclusively and whenever possible. I really did have their mantras ass-backwards. They were trying to tell me to address the things that were bothering me, at precisely the moment they arise, and not wait until I couldn't shoulder them anymore.

24

Almost immediately after I send my mea culpa to the Lark, I feel the first flutters of regret.

Apology, therapy has taught me, is my nervous tic. It's an old habit, what I do instead of expressing what I want. All day, every day, as I wander the public library or the stretch of thrift stores on Twenty-third Street, I'm atoning for one assumed sin or another. I don't know how many times, on average, the word "sorry" escapes my lips in an hour. "Sorry to trouble you." "Sorry for interrupting." "Sorry for getting in your way." In *Homeopathic Psychology*, I read about and relate to the "Sweet Staphysagria:" "If a stranger steps on her foot in a queue, she will apologize."

"*Sorry*'s a game by Parker Brothers," a grizzly of a man with a Fu Manchu and a bar code tattooed on his neck once responded. "Don't ever say you're sorry. I can tell just by looking at you, you've never done anything bad enough to be that sorry for."

Not more than a day after I write to the Lark, my in-box registers his reply. "You didn't smash up our friendship," he writes.

How could you? I've thought of you every day since our last conversation, but never knew how to say, "I'm sorry. I'm still here." I think it scared me. I'd been so closed off for so long, I wasn't sure I knew any other way.

He also tries to explain why he'd seemed short-fused during my first weekend in Brighton (to hear him tell it, the pressure of my arrival coincided with the stress of a family visit and his performance at Britain's largest music festival).

I had my folks down, and had to take care of them for the whole Battle-of-the-Somme-like weekend, I didn't think you'd enjoy a weekend of two-foot-deep mud and rain having just arrived jet-lagged and weary, and there wasn't room in the van to take you there which would've meant you catching a train and a bus.

In closing, the Lark asks for advice about a professional problem, giving a detailed explanation of the circumstances surrounding it.

I immediately begin to type back my prescription to the problem at hand. I do it ebulliently, lit by the unavoidable instinct to help, appease, head-stroke, and nurture.

Then I remember Hunter's story about the snake that refused to hiss.

I think of Fern's advice about lending equal time to one's throat and one's heart, about balancing self-expression with empathy.

I think of Alice urging me to set boundaries.

I go back to the beginning of the e-mail and insert a provisional clause before the paragraph where I give the Lark my advice.

Okay English muffin, here is the best career advice of its kind, but I'm giving it to you on the following condition. You ask frequently about and show insatiable interest in my writing from here on out, okay? Because, from the very beginning, this here alliance was founded on unconditional moral support in the arts. I don't know when exactly it started to feel a little one-sided. And it's probably equally my fault. I don't know when it first claimed me—this perverted desire to take care of all the people in my life and look out for their interests—but it sometimes comes at the risk of protecting my own. I know I don't share my work often. My writing process is just so damn different from yours. So much slower, quieter, and, at least the way I do it, a little more private. But I need my own pep rallies sometimes. Especially since some of the things that have happened have cowed my (already crippled) confidence in the second book department.

Then, wishing the Lark good luck with his big decision, I tap the button marked "send" and go back to my day with a feeling of wistful fulfillment.

I take my Staph, which, thankfully, is no longer giving me symptoms that resemble the avian flu.

I head uptown to Kara Walker's exhibit at the Whitney and feel strangely stirred by its title: "My Complement, My Enemy, My Oppressor, My Love."

I go home, open my mail, and find a Hallmark card from my mother. Inside some preprinted message of encouragement I find a handwritten footnote telling me she will be proud of me when I finish my book because she knows how difficult it has been to write.

———

In my next session, Alice asks when in my childhood I made the snap decision to stop getting angry.

"You're looking for a single memory?" I ask.

"If you have one. If you describe it to me, we can decode it together and lessen its power. Can you think of a moment in your past when you made a command decision to stop revealing your emotions to people? Or a time when you stopped asking for help?"

I inhale and look to the ceiling. I close my eyes, trying to will my memory back to the house where I spent most of my earliest childhood. No immediate story lines come to me. I puff my cheeks, bewildered.

"Well, just think about it," Alice says. "It may come to you."

No memories emerge until a few days later, when a mouse scuttles out from behind my bureau. Over the summer, while I was away, a new restaurant opened on my building's ground floor, and now my apartment is an occupied state. At night I've begun to hear the vermin squeaking and scampering in the wall behind the radiator, a sound I don't want to investigate but can't seem to ignore. I've even wondered if their incursion could be healing aggravation. I've always been irrationally afraid of mice, but like my cholerophobia I've never traced the fear to its source memory.

Oddly, seeing the little pest scuttle across the hardwood brings me back to an afternoon when I was two or three years old: I was alone in my bedroom when I saw a small wooden sign lying upside down on my bedroom floor. Printed with some aphorism, this same artifact was usually tied to my doorknob by a pink satin ribbon. Thinking I would bring the plaque to my mom and have her retie it for me, I picked it up. Repulsion rippled through me. Instantly, I realized that what I'd mistaken for the sign was actually the underside of a snap trap. And I wasn't holding what I'd thought was its "long pink ribbon"; I was clutching the tail of a dead mouse our mean tomcat had dragged into my room. I felt panic in a white-hot spasm. It wasn't the mouse that terrified me so much as its deadness. Its neck was broken. Its cloudy gaze gaped at me like the X-ed out eyes I recognized from dead animals in cartoons. I dropped the thing in an existential panic.

"There's a mouse in my room," I told my mother when I ran to her. Maybe she thought I was playing an imagination game, or maybe I said it blankly—the computer in me already taking shape—because she hardly looked up from her basket of laundry. "Uh-huh," she said with disinterest. Lacking the vocabulary I needed to describe the trap or the way I had touched it by mistake, I could only clutch her thigh and repeat myself. "Right," my mom said sarcastically. "There's a mouse in your room. Very funny."

My frustration surged. I raised my voice and stamped my bare feet, but this only made my mother harden. Maybe she was overwhelmed. It seems likely that my father was traveling at the time. Whatever the reason, she yelled at me for yelling at her. She told me it was wrong to "fib" and make a mouse up. She threatened to punish me for my outburst. Did she follow that warning through? I seem to remember being exiled to a tiny, wooden step stool positioned in an alcove (from that angle, I frequently pored over the helixed pattern of the wallpaper). Even after she'd scolded me, the mousetrap remained. Did my mom apologize when she found it? Did she explain death to me? What I remember most was her laughing when she realized I'd been earnest all along (a joke I hadn't found particularly funny).

Even if my phobias—fear of emoting, fear of mice, fear of self-expression—weren't born out of that exact memory, it seemed likely they were born around that time in my youth. Before I'd even fully learned to talk, I'd learned to doubt my perception of the world. I suspected people would sneer at my emotions if I let on about them. If I asked for help, I worried they might hold it against me. I struggle to remember another time when I held my ground with that kind of conviction.

———

In the week that follows, I feel myself grow suspicious of the world. I'm unreasonably shaken. I flit around my apartment like a trapped black fly, distressed and disorganized even in my routine movements.

I begin to break things. Not purposely. The destruction is careless and accidental. In the kitchen, a water glass loses its footing. In the bathroom, a bottle of makeup slips from the medicine cabinet and streaks the tiles with an oily, flesh-colored sludge.

I screen phone calls and avoid the mail. I feel myself growing paranoid. I grow certain there's someone in my life who doles out injuries under the guise of gifts, who does not and cannot love me in the way I need to be loved, who seems to have no use for me if I'm not obliging them, absorbing their criticism without comment, stroking their ego, writing, striving, achieving. I suspect this person taught me that I couldn't be loved if I was sad, dependent, emotional, furious. They taught me to reveal only what is expected of me. They need my attention and admiration, the kind they never received from their own lunatic mother, and their strength, stability, and self-esteem seem to hinge on me behaving in a particular way.

Naturally, I assume that person is the Lark.

I had answered his call for advice—answered it with all the care and compassion in my oozing, unshuttered heart—and yet he hadn't so much as acknowledged the gesture with a response.

I decide the Lark never noticed or understood me, has never taken me seriously. Perhaps I was just the mirror in which he admired his image. This isn't true, not remotely. But in the absence of information the mind concocts its own stories. Once the idea is formed I feel rage open in the pit of my stomach and roar through me like a howl.

I sit down at my desk and return to my book. Specifically, the stilted, overworked account of the way I'd left Brighton. Now that I can admit I am angry with him, the story seems relevant. The pages that come out of me crackle like a fire I could warm myself by. Words come easily, swaggering, strutting, slitting their eyes, and snapping their forked tongues. How good it feels to call the Lark "tantrumic" even if it isn't fair.

Of God, I write: *If* "He" exists then He is surely a sociopath.

Then, just to be certain "sociopath" is the exact word that I mean, I go looking for a nuanced definition. Sociopaths are charming and spontaneous (these seem to fit) but also reckless and impulsive. They're manipulative; covetous; controlling; they appeal to our sympathy but themselves lack empathy; they have an "intense, predatory stare."

In Martha Stout's *The Sociopath Next Door,* I am struck by a passage about the kinds of women who make great prey for sociopaths:

✗ *A part of a healthy conscience is being able to confront con-sciencelessness. When you teach your daughter, explicitly or by passive rejection, that she must ignore her outrage, that she must be kind and accepting to the point of not defending herself or other people, that she must not rock the boat for any reason, you are not strengthening her prosocial sense; you are damag-*

ing it—and the first person she will stop protecting is herself....
Do not set her up to be gaslighted. When she observes that
someone who is being really mean is being really mean, tell her
she is right and that it is okay to say so out loud.

I read Stout's book all night, from cover to cover. I know I have
felt both discounted and used, and in grasping for a convenient answer I carelessly finger the most obvious candidate. By sunup I've
quit thinking about whether God is a sociopath. I've convinced myself that the Lark is.

I do this, in part, because I'm a latecomer to anger. *Once the*
Staphysagria's old, subconscious anger has been brought to the fore,
it "attaches itself" to the present circumstances, generating seemingly
endless resentment toward the one who rejected him. I blame the
Lark because, at least in my mangled mind, he is less threatening
than the other available antagonists.

Like repression and depression, displacement is just another
arrow in my quiver of defense mechanisms. At the heart of the reaction is a reality I'd been avoiding as long as I've lived. Deep down is a
truth that I can't confront for fear it will level me, rob me of the ability to function even in what has become my sleepy, stupefied way.

I concoct this story about the Lark because it's less painful than
admitting the things that have been unspeakable for most of my life:
I often feel stifled and manipulated by my mother.

My rage is still curled, fistlike, around the Lark on the Thursday
evening when his response finally arrives:

Yes—to uphold my conditions—let me know where you are with
your book. Let me know what you're worried about—you always
seem so unjustifiably worried about it. Thank you deeply for your
advice, I couldn't have asked for more. I owe you. Send me pages and
I'll try to help you through. Send me your worries, and I'll try to set
you straight.

I march into my bedroom, wrest the cardboard box from under my bed, and upend the jumble of preposterous mementos, and letters, and small, thoughtful gifts the Lark had once tentatively given me.

There is, in the pile, one particular photo of my man reclining in his parents' garden a week before our fight: In it, he is handsome and distracted, pinching a cigarette, beetlelike, between his fingers, and he reads the *Sunday Telegraph* with cold intensity. Separating it from the others, I bring the photo to eye level and try to decide if the Lark has what could be described as sociopathic "shark eyes." Are they "sadistic"? "Intense"? "Emotionless"? "Predatory"? "Unblinking"? "Feral"?

Moreover, is he really on my side? I didn't realize it, but this is a question I ask of almost everybody.

I reread the message through the lens of defensiveness and built-up fear that I mistrust as my intuition. When I had confided in him in the past, had he used it against me? Part of the truth that I can't yet face is that other intimates often have. I'm sure my gut is saying to ignore his message and respond when pigs fly passenger jets. But my second response sounds more like Alice's cheeping, inspirational voice urging me to "be genuine," "tell the truth," and speak my dim mind.

I do. Two days later, with my teeth still gritted and my pulse firing like a Ford piston, I find myself seated at my laptop again. Convinced it is sane, I type:

Thanks for making the courtesy call. This may seem like an abrupt change of heart, but I guess you could say I started thinking about things in a new light since my last note. How glad I am that I could pony up whatever professional I've got in me, but when it comes to soliciting any morale from you, I guess you could say I opened my biggish browns. Not only don't I need your support, but I'm not convinced it's even possible. For you.

I guess the more I got to thinking about it, the less certain I was that you ever had my best interests at heart. I'm not convinced you ever had any of those: interests (in me, unless you were considering how I might add to or diminish from your experience, unless you were considering me, first, as a possession and, later, as a hindrance) or heart (for my rendering of "heart" is not the blipping organ, but rather a person's capacity to understand what the people around him are feeling).

I know this must seem like a 180-degree pirouette after recent appeals and apologies. But I got to asking myself, why I was so willing to believe that a man was capable of any real loyalty in the present or in the future, when the past proved so contrary? Why would I continue to entrust him with my livelihood—my book, my stories, my personal history—the things that mean most to me?

I don't know why, even after all that's happened, I've felt compelled to cling, like a raft at high seas, to the version of yourself that you sold me in the beginning in letters and, yes, spoken words too. Why have I wanted to preserve this story about the empathetic Lark, the sensitive artist, the man who tells me that he grieves sometimes, that he doubts, that he loves, that he takes triumph in other people's successes and feels concern when they're on the skids? I realize now how like lyrics those were. As often as I've heard legends of these things, this girl has never once seen them, not in action and not with her eyes. With her eyes, he's shown her only callousness, aggression, avoidance, deceptiveness and a kind of staunch self-serving.

I'm not sure which is worse, the month of July, which I spent fearing you, and backing down to you even in moments when facts were on my side, and giving you far more leeway than anybody deserves. Or the weeks and months that came afterward, when I've been so quick to hurt for you, or rescue you, or understand you, or try so desperately to lend you my support and see things from your skewed perspective.

How much nicer it would be if I had the opportunity to tell you all of this in my speaking voice. But I realize it's not me that's bound to written words. It's you. It has always been you, hiding behind language and substituting it in the moments where action and emotion ought to be. I'm not sure you're capable of acting any other way, but I think I am. I think I don't have to go to such super-human lengths to rationalize and tacitly accept it.

A sudden change, I know. But such is the nature of revelations.

———

I am aware that this message, following the bleeding-heart tone of my last, will probably make me look like a paranoid schizophrenic. I don't care. I imagine the electric-blue sunburst Hunter told me to envision in an effort to open my throat. Although I talked to Hunter only once, I still think often of his prescriptions. Closing my eyes, I picture a blue burst exploding before me with sickening power.

25

In the days after I write to the Lark, I feel wild and weightless. During the day, I work on my book, or mystify my neighbors by banging and clanging away at my kid-size drum kit.

The latter is my newest experiment in anger management, my attempt to channel my growing anger in a positive way. In G. Stanley Hall's 1915 speech, I'd found a passage about angry women excelling at musical instruments: "Girls often play the piano loudly, and some think best of all. One plays a particular piece to divert anger, viz., the 'Devil's Sonata.'" I mostly play the Ramones and baby beats a drum teacher once taught me. Even then I am so out of practice that my "playing" sounds more like a dozen pots and pans falling down a flight of stairs.

At dusk, I bound down the sidewalks at full swing, letting the wind lick my hair and tug the tails of my coat. My expression is confident if not exactly happy. My thoughts are blissfully distorted. I feel free, a planet unto myself, no longer orbiting anyone, a feeling I'm certain will last forever. I still can't see that my anger is displaced— directed not at the person who actually provokes me but at someone I thought resembled her.

During my next session with Alice I describe the e-mail exchange. Idiotically, I expect her to be impressed by my progress.

"Wow," she says, widening her eyes and blinking a few times in surprise. "You don't do that often. How did it feel?"

"Great," I say. "It feels like tapping into my power."

"So you're certain the Lark is your anger's home?"

"Yeah, sure." I pause for a second to reconsider. "What exactly do you mean by its *home*?"

"I mean, do you really think all the anger that's been floating free in your head all this time belongs there, with him? Do you think there's even just the smallest possibility that something he did reminded you of the original object of your anger? Did anything in particular happen before you sent the Lark that message?"

"Well, I'd sent him an earlier one, giving him a whole heap of advice, for which he'd never thanked me or responded. I guess that made me feel kind of shitty. I also took some Staph. I got a card, out of the blue, in the mail from my mother."

"What did the card say?"

"Just that she was glad I was back to working on my book and she'd be proud when I finished."

"Did that make you feel angry for any reason?"

"I suppose. Just a little. I'm sure she just meant to be supportive, but sometimes it feels like my family only relates to and . . . " I pause here to take a deep breath. " . . . *likes* the part of me that's the writer."

"Any idea where that feeling comes from?"

"No one seems to have much patience for talk about anything else in my life. And, of course, there are only so many emotions I feel like I'm allowed to share with them. You and I've already figured that part out."

Alice nods.

"I was also the black sheep of my family until the time I was twenty-three and first started publishing what I wrote. Before that, I always felt like I was a problem. Like I was the one thing disrupting their lives. The fact that they only accept me now makes me feel like I have to constantly perform in order to earn their love. I suppose I resent that. But then, maybe it's not their fault. You say I withhold my emotions, and what do you call it—my essence?—with them. Maybe I've never given them an opportunity to get to know me through anything but my work."

"Did the Lark somehow make you feel as though you had to perform in order to be accepted by him?"

"Not really. I think I was the one who tried to woo him through writing. But there was that thing he said about us getting along better through letters." The weight of realization begins to settle on me. "You think it's possible that I've been using him as a stand-in for my family?"

"What do you think?" Alice asks. "You can tell displaced anger because its magnitude doesn't seem to fit the situation at hand. Do you think it was *fitting* that you reacted the way you did to his e-mail? Do you think there's any possibility that you baited him on an unconscious level? Do you think you might have created a situation where he felt compelled to express his support for your career— one of the few ways you feel your parents are supportive—and then unleashed all the angry rebuttals you're so convinced your parents won't let you say?"

My hands fly to my mouth in horror. "Yes," I say. "That's more than a possibility."

"Let's just say you're going to address your parents right now," Alice says. "You're going to thank them for thinking of you and giving you their support, but you'd like to share with them some of the things about your relationship that don't work for you. What would you say?"

"I suppose I'd tell them that it hurts my feelings that they're so dismissive anytime I reference my personal life. Sometimes it feels like they only entertain talk about my career. And that makes me feel less like a person and more like a commodity."

"Is there any chance that it goes both ways? Any possibility that *you* only confide in *them* about work?"

"Only because *they* have always made it clear that they find emotion so unacceptable! My mother, in particular. Any talk of feelings and she turns her back on me."

"So tell her right now," Alice urges. "Pretend she's sitting right here."

I sigh audibly. I still haven't warmed to role-playing. I always feel like I am faking it. Like a kid covertly nudging the planchette on an Ouija board, I spell out the words I suspect Alice hopes to hear in order to preserve her faith in the exercise. But privately I can't seem to conjure up the spirit. I can't envision my mother in Alice's office any more than I can imagine such frankness ever hurling from my lips.

"Follow me," Alice says. "Mom, I really appreciate your concern . . ."

"Mom, much obliged for your concern. I know that you think I'm overly emotional."

"But I need you to know . . ."

"I need you to know that I'm totally healthy and . . ." I pause. ". . . halfway happy. I'm not sick. I'm not off my rocker. I'm not a saint and I'm not a demon, either. I'm a human being and things move me. Things disappoint me. Occasionally, they devastate me. I have emotions. I'm not a machine, all evidence to the contrary. Out there in the world outside your very limited orbit, everyone else thinks I'm aloof and impossible to read. The only person who thinks I'm a hysteric is you."

———

After my session with Alice I need to purge my head of the horrifying realization that I am using the Lark to act out my relationship with my mom, so I drag my maladjusted ass to one of Rolf's "hot" yoga classes, the kind where he heats the room to a temperature more appropriate for roasting a rack of lamb.

I come back to my apartment wet as an eel; sweat is crawling down my breastbone. Before showering I collapse into my desk chair, more out of habit than with any explicit purpose, and log on to my e-mail.

I'm half-expecting a retort from the Lark, but that's not what I find. Instead, I discover a notification from the same social networking site we'd met on. It says I've received a message from myself or, at least, from a person who shares the name Koren Zailckas.

For a few moments I sit, paralyzed with foreboding.

Strange as it sounds to the rational ear, this is the moment I'd been expecting. A few days earlier I'd given myself freely to fury. And every moment since I've been waiting to be struck down, as if by a lightning bolt, and punished for the things I unleashed.

Where I'm from, anger never came without consequence. I think of all the people my parents have disowned over disagreements: my uncle, my maternal grandfather (who is my last living grandkin).

At sixteen, after a particularly vicious verbal fight with my mother, I was lured downstairs by panicked footsteps, clangorous wails, and the sobering words "emergency room!" I remember the reddening rag that she held between her hands, and that she'd made a point of telling me that she had sliced her hand (and a few tendons, a doctor would later determine) because she'd slammed a crystal bowl against the sink in her frustration with me.

I log on to the Web site. Sure enough, in my in-box I find a message from myself. I take a deep gasp and open the note, feeling damned. It reads:

People are sending me messages of support. That's not what this was meant to be about.

Do I gag? Time freezes. For a moment I can't hear the roar of traffic outside my window. As I bring my hands to my mouth in shock for the second time in one day, I notice, in a dislocated way, that they've gone cold and jittery (*the Staphysagria patient often trembles when she is enraged*).

At the top of the message, an oscillating orange symbol indicates that my alter ego is online at the moment. When I bring my cursor to her name and click, I am treated to my own face in her profile picture.

It's a regrettable shot, but one that has been posted online elsewhere: In it, I stand wild-eyed against a bloodred wall, my hair rising from my head in a thorny crown of static and one corner of my mouth curled into an impish smirk.

I scan the rest of the page with a hot flush of horror. According to the profile, my "interests" include: "rimming," "fisting," "deep-throating," "shit-eating," "being punched in the prissy, fucking face," "boozing," "shagging," "swallowing," and "making disgusting, nasal, moaning sounds" while I fornicate like a "stray dog."

In the part designated for "friends," this person has already contacted, among other people, Alyssa, my sister, and my brother-in-law.

I am struck by the British slang "pleb." In the space set aside for "favorite books," it reads "nothing that a pleb like you would know," betraying the origin of the page's creator.

I've heard that acknowledging a hostile stranger is the worst thing a person can do in these situations. But then, I am not convinced I'm dealing with a stranger. My spine chatters against the back of my chair. I stab the keys madly as I type the following response:

This is clearly the Lark. Or his brother. Or both. (Here's a hint: next time you might want to disguise your British spelling.) This is a personal matter. So let's please deal with it personally. And in a manner that's a bit more adult.

My alter ego reads it immediately and dispatches "her" reply:

I DIDN'T REALISE (OOPS, REALIZE) AMERICANS SPELLED THINGS DIFFERENTLY. WHO IS THE LARK? I AM JUST SOMEONE WHO READ A BOOK AND HATED ITS AUTHOR SO MUCH I WANTED TO MAKE HER PAY.

In a state of deep panic, I take the L train to Devon's place. The subway car shimmies and shrieks in the tunnel, carting a cast of people who totter foal-like in their high-heeled boots and laugh as the subway poles slip away from their mittened hands. Beside me an off-duty firefighter hits on a young girl in a minidress as tight as a compression bandage. "I know a place off the next stop," he tells her. "Just a scummy, roughneck neighborhood place where you and I can get a beer."

Everyone seems selfish and secretly cruel, a recurring side effect of any rejection. For the moment it's as though Alice has never helped me to see the childhood memories where these feelings first took shape. Instead of being present, where the fake profile might exist to me only as a childish prank, I am stuck like a barnacle to the past. And in the past, the mean messages constitute further proof that when I reveal myself I will be hurt for it.

I take my cell phone from my pocket and send the Lark a text message. It reads: "I know we're not on good terms right now, but did you contact me by Internet today? I really need to know." How much I want to believe he's the cause of all emotional turmoil. It's less painful than admitting my life feels chaotic because Alice is slowly making me acknowledge the childhood lessons I've never wanted to admit. Because she is slowly and systematically stripping me of my defenses.

Devon squeezes me hello at the door to her apartment and helps me out of my scarf and coat. She has a pot of something warm bubbling on the stove. Her boyfriend, Jeff, one of my friends from college, moves between the stereo and the sofa, changing a record and loading something on his laptop. The light is warm and the radiator hisses under its breath.

"So you think it was the Lark?" Devon asks once we're settled on the floor around the coffee table, drinking hot apple cider from footed teacups.

I tell her I'm not naïve enough to think that there's only one person in the world who hates me. But it just seems a little too coincidental, didn't she agree? Two days ago, I said the harshest things I've ever said to the Lark, and today I get an unmistakably *British* message from someone who seems to know my nasally speaking voice.

"Your voice isn't nasally," Devon sweetly insists.

Jeff takes a sip from his delicate teacup. "The Lark seemed like a decent enough guy when I met him," he says diplomatically. "But I can't lie. You make a strong case."

———

The next morning, a text message comes through from the Lark. All it says is: "It wasn't me. Sorry."

Within the same half an hour, the vilifying Web page is taken down. Or rather, the profane details are wiped from it and my picture is replaced by one of a green-faced grim reaper, cackling as he brandishes his scythe.

Another hour after that, another message appears in my in-box. This one reads:

I APOLOGISE. I REALISE THIS STUNT WAS A BIT IMMATURE. I AM MENTALLY ILL. I TAKE MEDICATION FOR IT AND IT MAKES ME BEHAVE STRANGELY SOMETIMES. LOL. I HAVE TAKEN THE PROFILE I MADE FOR YOU DOWN. MY NAME IS HENRY. BELOW IS A LINK TO MY REAL PROFILE.

I write a few short lines to the boy at the Web address he's provided, just to verify, in my own way, that he really existed and isn't the Lark in disguise. His profile picture is that of a wiry eighteen-year-old boy with what looks like a hearing aid. He has twelve friends. He says he enjoys smoking pot.

"So this is really Henry?" I type. "The Henry who wrote to me yesterday under an account with my own name?"

He writes back:

YES, THIS IS HENRY. I'M SORRY AGAIN FOR FRIGHTEN-ING YOU. IF YOU HAVE A MOMENT I'D LIKE TO ASK YOU FOR SOME PUBLISHING ADVICE.

I go slack with relief, stunned by the coincidence in the absurd timing of Henry's message. Because I'm so relieved, or because I have a soft spot for young writers made stupid by hormones and illicit substances (time was, I had been one), I spend the next twenty minutes messaging with my new, manic-depressive friend. I explain book proposals. I tell him to read Frank Conroy's *Stop-Time*. I teach him about literary agents, and I secretly fear for ones that he might solicit, using his fine-tuned skills as a stalker.

There is barely time to get my bearings after that resolved conflict before I have to address another. Moments after I've wished Henry good luck and good-bye, I discover the Lark has responded to my e-mail.

I open the message, I sit back in my chair, and I try to breathe slow as I feel my pulse drumming in my ears. The beginning of the message reads like a script, a dialogue between characters A and B:

A: Can you help me.
B: Yes, I'll help.
A: I don't need your help. Oh, and fuck you too.
B: ??
What should B's reply be?
I don't know what your game is. Do you think that by hurting me you'll make yourself feel stronger? Part of me didn't want to reply to you, but I feel so aggrieved at your revisionist take on our relationship that I have to reply.

I'm "incapable of any real loyalty"? What the fuck? I was faithful to you before we even met face to face, and remained faithful until the end. Long after the end if you want the truth. I was and remain proud of you and take pride in the knowledge that you can only better yourself with your writing. Do these count as loyalty? I think so. It seems as though the phrase "no man is capable of loyalty" popped into your mind and you've tried, by the simple fact that I was born into a male body, to squeeze me into your repellent idea. I don't believe that revising the past to justify present emotions does any good at all, especially not for your own peace of mind.

As for the rest of the message, there is a "How dare you?" An aptly placed "Fuck you." A bit about how I'm positioning myself as a victim.

There is a list of memories the Lark claims to cherish: "meeting you in Boston after weeks of pining and ache," "introducing you to Brighton and my friends and family," "reading papers in the Chelsea whilst the sunlight poured in."

You haven't managed to tarnish these memories for me. Because what you are accusing me of has no part in them. If you want to look back on our year together as a time of hatred, insecurity and awfulness, that's up to you. It won't make you happy, and will probably ruin any chance you have of finding true love in the future. But if this is how you feel, then that's your choice. It isn't how I look back on our time together.

I'd like answers to all my questions, but I fear that any more contact will just ruin any respect I still hold for you. I want you and expect you to do amazingly well. But in your current state of mind, I don't want to hear from you again. I hope you will understand why.

I grab my keys and take off down the stairs in my slippered feet. It's late afternoon, but the lobby of my dingy high-rise is congested with familiar (if not quite friendly) faces. I tear past the scowling mailman. I pass the bestselling author who lives in the penthouse and treats me suspiciously whenever I say hello. I dodge and dart around the superintendent—a flannelled sadist who'd once told me that he drowns rats for sport.

Outside, it's a consummate autumn day. Shrill light splinters off mirrored storefronts. A barbed wind rakes the avenue. In my head, I roll around the Lark's words: "I don't believe that revising the past to justify present emotions does any good at all." He's right to feel used. Alice has showed me that.

The Lark has touched me deeply, even in his harsh assessment, and I enter the drugstore on the corner of Twenty-third and Park with a sharp jolt of urgency. I need an international calling card. I'm sick of the one-way conversation of e-mails. I want to communicate with the pink instruments of my lungs and my throat.

I ferret through the aisles until I find what I need. I shift my weight with a nervous bounce while the cashier counts the bills I slap down in a slovenly bunch.

I find a pay phone on the corner of my block.

As I pick up the receiver, a street-sweeping truck monsters past and drowns out the dial tone. I dial the Lark's number after a gritty cloud of dust settles and I absently bite the corner of the calling card. I hold my breath as the line rings once. Twice.

"Hello?"

"It's Koren. Don't hang up. I just want you to hear me out, okay?"

"Okay."

"You were right. I accused you of some things that were unfair and I blamed you for some feelings that weren't entirely about you. I know you were loyal to me."

"Yes."

"I can recognize that now. But I'm not a man hater. I need you to know that. God knows, I'm miserably flawed. I've got a million other even less becoming defects. But if you think I hate men, you might want to consider how you feel about women. No one would blame you for being distrustful of them. It sounds like you've known some horrible ones."

"I've known some brilliant ones too." He laughs, not unkindly, as I tell him about my eighteen-year-old hacker and confess that I'd thought it was the Lark in disguise.

"When you asked me if I'd contacted you, I thought maybe you were just looking for attention," he says. "I've dated girls who did things like that."

It has been two months since I've heard his voice. For three-quarters of an hour, I idle on the corner in my slippers, pressing the greasy receiver to the side of my face. As we talk he stops being the saboteur of my imagination. We talk about the position I'm applying for at a nearby university and the toy piano he's recently bought in an effort to help with his songwriting. I feel the blood bloom in my cheeks when he asks if I am dating anyone.

Whereas the last time we spoke, he'd sounded testy and preoccupied, now his voice seems soulful. He seems so much more present and receptive—perhaps we both are—and I tell him as much.

It's hard to say whether the fact of my honesty has unlocked his or vice versa, but instead of letting my fear speak to the Lark, I'm letting my humanity talk. Where does my sudden confidence and flexibility come from? I feel some twinge in my chest and think of Reiki. Odd as it sounds, it feels as though plates are gently sliding around there. Something new is being revealed. Though the hurt hasn't gone away, it's shifted a few small millimeters, making room for the possibility of love.

The Lark asks if I'd ever consider another visit to Brighton.

I pause. An elderly woman in a leopard print coat passes the phone booth and frowns at me under her thick mask of putty-colored makeup.

At the mention of Brighton, I feel my knees stiffen. I've only just begun to feel appreciative about being back home. Work is going better. I've finally put my apartment back together after packing things up to make room for my subletters. I realize I'd miss Devon. I'd miss yoga with Rolf, and even boxing with Max. I wasn't sure I felt strong enough to be a stranger in a strange land again. For once, the placater doesn't pop up to say, "I will if you want me to."

Instead I say, "I'm not sure. I'd have to think about that. I'm not sure your town brings out the best in me."

"Well, I hope you'll call anytime," the Lark says. "I've missed the sound of your voice."

A truck slams into a pothole. A hard, stinging wind blows my hair across my face. I hang up the phone, feeling a mix of relief and regret. I worry that I may never see or speak to him again. Dusk falls around me as I walk home with muted, dragging steps.

26

The part of me that emerges in the briefest flashes since I've started seeing Alice—a pure part, untouched by fear or past criticisms—feels like the Lark is still meant for me. But at the same time, I've never truly loved him and can't do so yet. I can't love the Lark until I see him for the person he really is. And I won't be lucid enough to recognize and appreciate the man in full until I acknowledge the whole of my biography.

The weekend after I speak to the Lark, I return to a passage by Alice Miller. "Without free access to these facts [of our life history], the sources of our ability to love remain cut off. . . . We cannot really love if we are forbidden to know our truth, the truth about our parents and caregivers as well as about ourselves."

As far as therapy is concerned, I know I have to stop approaching it like such a good student. I've done enough anger research. I've done too much of it. Instead of bringing me closer to understanding myself, my inquests have only widened the distance between my emotions and me. The computer in me remains convinced that research can fend off the painful truths Alice wants to reveal.

In past sessions I've said, "There's this anthropologist, Robert Levy, who talks about 'passive optimism.' He says in Tahiti people have less anger because they expect to have less power over other people. Nature teaches them this. If you try to control nature, she levels you, but if you relax and accept nature's bounty, you will be taken care of." To this, Alice asked, "Who is 'nature' in this case? Your family? Your mother?"

I asked, "What if my presumed 'anger' doesn't come from anything that's happened in my personal history? What if it's just a biological predisposition? There's this Harvard pediatrician, Daniel G. Freedman, who studied Cantonese American newborns versus Caucasian newborns of North European stock. Their mothers were all the same age and had the same number of children, the same prenatal care and type of drugs during birth. And Freedman found the Chinese babies always fussed less than the white babies. They were always easier to console. Why should I go around ranting at people if there's a chance anger's just in my genetic code?"

"Do you have memories of being a baby?" Alice asked.

She said, "You can't see it, but you're already ranting at people. They're just not the *right* people. They're not the people the hurt kid in you really wants to blame."

I'm just starting to put together the pieces a more adult woman would have realized from the first word: I elected to write a book about anger because I was brimming with it. I've been trying to give myself the license to unleash what I secretly agreed was "the most hideous and frenzied of all the emotions" (this from Seneca). But my fear only let me get close to my anger under the pretext of a scholarly exercise. It was like I couldn't access my emotions without a press badge. The more furious I got, the more detached I became from the source of my fury. I was quick to turn clinical; to categorize, or rationalize, a fit of temper; to transform my personal journey into a course of study.

I'm going to have to drop the shtick that I wear like a chignon and a pair of tortoiseshell glasses. I'll have to stop treating sessions like a night-school psychology course and my psyche as a case study in emotional maladaptation. Before I can be any sort of companion to the Lark, and I'd like to be, if he'd have me, I'll have to engage in a real relationship with Alice and tell her every petty, puffed-up, odious thought that flashes through my head. I will have to look into the woman's nearly cherubic face and let rip without exception.

Alice has been trying to charm my rage out of its coil. But the stubborn serpent never fully raised her head. Instead of striking, I've always bowed to Alice's provocations like an obedient child. Whenever she calls my bluff, I smooth my high-necked blouse and brightly vow to be more beastly.

After my conversation with the Lark not only do I realize that I've never trusted him enough to reveal the part of me with the potential to be just as rash and petty and inarticulate and snarly as any flawed human thing, but I haven't trusted Alice that way either.

———

"I don't think I trust you enough to show you my anger," I admit to Alice during our next session. "I mean, no offense. It has nothing to do with you. You've never been anything but compassionate, even when you're trying to be tough on me."

"Well, something's changed," she says. "At least now you trust me enough to tell me you don't fully trust me. So if this distrust doesn't have anything to do with me, where do you think it comes from?"

I puff my cheeks, blowfish style, and then let a sigh out. "My parents," I said. "After I got off the phone with the Lark the other day, I realized I've always seen the world in binary."

Alice gives a smile of sweet relief. "Go on. What do you mean by that?"

"Like, ever since I was a kid I've thought the world was divided between scapegoats and bullies. Between people who dish out blame indiscriminately and those who scarf it down and apologize for not eating faster. I've never really trusted that a relationship—any relationship, not just a romantic one—can survive if both people are equally honest. I never knew I thought that way. I mean, I wasn't aware of it. But I do."

"So where did you get that idea that people had to be one thing or the other? Either always angry or always ingratiating?"

"From my parents. I know you've known that from the second I walked in here. My family doesn't express much emotion to begin with. But with anger especially, my mother seems to be the one who lets it fly while my father truckles to her."

"That's your blueprint," Alice says. "You model your relationships after how you've perceived your parents. Every time you enter into a new romantic relationship, or even a new friendship, you choose whether you want to play your father or your mother."

"Whether I want to be all heart or all throat."

Alice nods. "That's why you find yourself swinging between enormous outpourings of emotion and periods where you are blank and robotic, as though there weren't a single emotion in you."

Because I've been attempting to love without an awareness of my past I've only been able to behave as if I were loving. Alice wants me to see how hypocritical and deceptive that is. How confusing is to the people I might have used for that purpose.

I think of the part of the Lark's letter where he asked, "What should B's reply be?" No wonder he's been bewildered. No wonder my angry accusations seemed to come from out of nowhere. I know in my heart that the Lark was not the first person I had used in this way. He was simply the most recent in a string of boyfriends, acquaintances, and friends. All my life, in almost all of my interactions, I had either selected people who were controlling and critical to begin with or withheld my emotions, catered to these people, and tried to trick myself into thinking they were self-absorbed and stifling. Then I staged the rebellion I'd never been able to work up as a kid.

"When you were growing up, did your family piggyback their

anger? Like, because you weren't allowed to say what you were really angry about, you took all that anger and heaped it onto a smaller, safer target?"

"Totally," I say, shocked by how intuitive she is. "We still do. If my mom wants to yell at my dad for something of real consequence, but she can't because we have company, she'll turn and scream wildly at him for letting one of the dogs out without a leash. Because I feel like I can't acknowledge the ways my family's rejected me in the past, I dump it all onto the Lark, where it feels safer to scream about it."

Alice hallelujahs like it's church Sunday. "Can I ask what brought about this revelation?"

I tell her about my phone conversation with the Lark. "It was the first time in a long time that I opened up in an honest way. I didn't say what I thought I ought to or do what I should. I tapped into my feelings," I say. "It occurred to me that there might be a middle option between blind fury and total blankness."

Alice says, "That middle place is where we find love."

SIX   *Conniption*

Let us picture anger—its eyes aflame with fire, blustering with hiss and roar and moan and shriek and every other noise more hateful still if such there be, brandishing weapons in both hands (for it cares naught for self-protection!), fierce and bloody, scarred, and black and blue from its own blows, wild in gait, enveloped in deep darkness, madly charging, ravaging and routing, in travail with hatred of all men, especially of itself, and ready to overturn earth and sea and sky if it can find no other way to harm, equally hating and hated.

—SENECA, "On Anger"

27

After I begin to open up to Alice about my family, my dreams become varied and graphic. From a flickering parade of nightmares, one emerges as the dreadful centerpiece. In it I am staring face-to-face with my mother, who is as she looked at age thirty-five: trim, energetic, and powdered, her face framed by a wreath of mahogany-colored curls.

In the dream, it's dusk, and we are standing in an empty parking lot beside an idling sedan. Suspiciously, the car is the same shade of dusty blue as the Datsun that she drove in my earliest youth.

On the side of the car that faces me, both doors yawn open. Keys dangle in the chugging ignition. In the backseat, my sister sits on one ankle and watches us. She is about eight or nine years old—the age at which she started entering beauty pageants and modeling for mail-order catalogs. Her blond hair hangs in a persnickety braid down her back, and her cerulean eyes hold me in a look of accusation.

Based on the ages of my mother and sister, I should be about fourteen in this dream, the age when my relationship with my mother became particularly wrenched, and also the time in my life when Mom's relationship with my sister began to seem clubby, if not downright exclusive. I alone am my present age: twenty-seven, self-sufficing and pissed.

There's an argument in process. My mother and I are fighting about something unknown and unknowable, though each of us is sure as hellfire she's right. The spat is still civil enough for the moment, but some terrible threat seems to loom beneath the surface. I'm aware that there is something more that I want to say, something so unacceptable, self-indulgent, insensitive, and *wrong* that it will immediately drive my mom into the arms of my dimpled and obedient sister, who seems to be waiting in the car for exactly that purpose.

I simply can't choke the blasphemous statement back. With a sharp hiss of hatred, I tell my mother than my feelings are valid, a statement that sprays out of me like a sheaf of sparks. She rolls her eyes. I tell her that I'm entitled to them. She tosses her head wildly and shouts at me to stop. Across the parking lot the streetlights flicker and abruptly blow out. With a full-throated scream, I ask her why she won't just let me say what I need to say. In response, she shooshes me quiet.

I punch her square in the mouth in what feels like sedated slo-mo. The world grinds on its axis. The moment has the finality of shattering glass.

The instant my knuckles make contact with my mother, she begins to shriek. She shrivels until she's two whole heads shorter than me, nearly the size of a school-age child. The dream ends just as I'd suspected it would. With guilt and jealousy, I watch my mother embrace and fuss over my sister. And soon after, the pair swings the car doors closed and drives into the approaching dark, leaving me alone in the gray landscape.

———

"On a scale of one to ten, how likely do you think you are to express rage in a physical way?"

I am sitting on Alice's flabby leather couch, watching her features pinch together in worry.

"You mean, what are the chances that one day I'll get angry enough to let loose and clock somebody?"

"Since you put it that way, sure. On a scale of one to ten, how realistic would that be?"

I think for a moment. "Zero. No, make that negative two. I'd say that's totally unrealistic. I've gone my whole life and never smacked anybody."

Alice looks at me askance. As part of my ongoing resolution to confide in her without censor, I've opened up an inch and told her all about my dream.

"Negative two," she repeats. "That sounds pretty unlikely. So, if you're not afraid you'll get violent, then what's holding you back? What's preventing you from bringing your frustrations to your family?"

"I'm afraid I won't ever come to the end of the feeling. Like, if I turn my anger on, I won't ever find the off switch. I'm afraid getting mad will literally drive me mad. I'm terrified I'll end up like Charles VI—the bat-shit lunatic king of France. His schizophrenia all began with a feud with the Duke of Britain. I'm afraid that's how it works. One day you're pissed off at just one person, and the next you're spending the rest of your life drawing your sword at every bystander that you pass in the street."

"Drawing your sword," Alice repeats, with an abstracted look on her face. "I thought you said you could never get violent."

"It's just a metaphor."

Alice brings her hands together and sighs. "You and I both know it's holding anger back that's driving you crazy. It's refusing to acknowledge the source of the feeling that's turning what you call your 'bystanders' into enemies."

"Fair enough." My eyes wander to the window. Outside, it's a shaggy, wet dog of a day. I pause before turning back to look at Alice's patient face. "I'm afraid my family will leave, go away, divorce themselves from me. It's obvious to me why the car in my dream had its engine running."

"Why?"

"Because my parents have cut ties with a lot of people they've had arguments with. I've lost track of the relatives my mother has disowned—everyone from her father to her oldest brother."

"So it's a very real possibility your family could go away."

"I don't know." My throat constricts a little. "Maybe."

"All right, we know you're angry at your mother. Let's take a minute to focus in on your sister. What's her role in this dream?"

"I'm pretty sure she's there to back my mother. That's why she's in the car's *back*seat."

"Would you say this is something that happens a lot?"

"It used to. There was a time, a long time, when it seemed like any tiffs I had with my mother only brought the two of them closer together. It was like the more I asserted myself, the more my mom needed validation from my sister. Sometimes it seems like we can never both be in Mom's good graces at the same time. One of us is always on the ins while the other's on the outs."

"If you had to choose, which side would you say you are on right now?"

"I'm on the ins, but, relatively speaking, I've only been there for three years or so. In fact, it wasn't until I had this dream that I remembered how it felt to argue with my mother and how challenging her used to cast me in the role of the supposed 'problem daughter,' how it used to secure my position as my family's black sheep. I never used to try so hard to be careful, be sweet, be diplomatic, to be dutiful and high achieving. Adjectives like those belonged to my sister. The role's so exhausting, it feels like I've been playing it forever. But the part is comparatively new for me. For twenty years, before I published a book and became a success in my parents' eyes, I was what my mother called her 'strong-willed' child . . . or her 'short-fused' daughter." I scratch quotation marks in the air with my fingers.

It's still difficult to talk to Alice this way. *Grow up and shut up*, says the same internal voice that used to abuse SAP's Little Daryl.

But with Alice's help, another voice is taking shape in me too. One that knows I'll never be able to face the world as an adult until I acknowledge the feelings I wasn't allowed to express a kid.

"So when did you and your sister reverse roles?" Alice asks.

"Four years ago. When I wrote *Smashed*."

"A book about your experiences as the 'bad' daughter."

"Ironic?"

Alice steals a warm, amused smile. "In your dream," she asks. "Why do you think you and your mother are having your argument outside of the car?"

"That's easy. It's a fantasy. It never really happened that way. In real life my mother seemed to store up all her own anger until we were in the car. As a kid, I took ballet classes every day after school. The studio was a forty-five-minute drive from our house. The car was a private place, and my mother seemed to relish the fact that I was a captive audience in the passenger seat. I accused her of using that commute as an opportunity to jaw me about everything from my bad skin to my bad grades. When she was driving, I couldn't argue back or upset her too much. As long as she held the steering wheel, she literally held my life in her hands. One day I couldn't take it anymore. I was thirteen. I demanded she pull over so we could have a conversation instead of a monologue, so we could argue on equal footing. When she refused, I reached for the wheel and tried to wrench us onto the shoulder of a back-country road."

"What happened then?"

"What always happened. She told me I was dangerous. She suggested I was crazy. She hinted that 'behavior like that' could get me institutionalized. She'd say things like, 'If you get angry like that out there in the world outside of this house, people will lock you away.'"

"Was she right? Were you a danger to yourself or your family?"

"I probably shouldn't have made a grab for the wheel, but I really wasn't trying to cause a crash. It wasn't the first time my mom told me that I was mentally ill. It seemed like something she trotted out anytime I disagreed, stood up for myself, or fought back."

I take a breath and say, "There was an underlying warning there: Anger could get me 'sent away' the same way a neighbor girl's parents had recently turned her over to the state. If I slammed a door or raised my voice—you know, just typical teenager transgressions—I feared the men in white coats would come to strap me to the bed and cart me away to the Waltham sanitarium, where I'd spend the rest of my life humming 'Surrey with the Fringe on Top' and eating butter sandwiches."

Alice laughs. "It doesn't quite work that way. It's not the nineteen twenties. Did anything like that ever happen again?"

"No, it wasn't long after that incident that I quit ballet. I went to high school. I said I needed more time to focus on other activities. But a part of me wonders if I gave it up because I dreaded that drive." I can still remember the way dread pooled in my stomach as I waited after school for my mom to pick me up. I remember the way, after she dropped me off at the Acton School of Ballet, I looked into the studio's wall-length mirror with a renewed loathing for my hands, my expression, my hairline, the shape and very fabric of my face.

I tell Alice there's still one part of the dream I can't make sense of. "Why did my mother shrivel like a sea anemone when I hit her?"

"Maybe she's not as formidable as you seem to think."

"Maybe," I say, though I'm not entirely convinced. I still can't imagine a scenario in which I could ever tell my family the real source and depths of my rage. *Why would I do that?* I often ask Alice. *Why, when it wouldn't change anything? Why, when it would be like beating my thick head against a brick wall?* Alice's response was always: *You wouldn't do it to achieve an effect. You'd do it because it's honest.*

Alice had told me that the brick wall I mentioned was very common. Virtually everyone who has some repressed childhood beef uses the image of a "high wall" to describe the experience.

In Alice Miller I'd recently found descriptions of a patient whose "[r]epressed memories of the shy, distant mother produced in her the feeling of a wall, one that later separated her from other people in such a painful way." Another patient had no advocates growing up; he had been in "the unfair situation" of being opposed "by two big, strong adults, as by a wall." A third patient's feelings were so enormous his repression of them had to be even larger: "The stronger a prisoner is, the thicker the prison walls have to be." Miller suggests we internalize these constraints even after our families aren't around to reinforce them. They become defense mechanisms, walls that "impede or completely prevent later emotional growth."

I'm beginning to wonder if the wall is just another version of the lid that Trish and Sheila accused me of wearing at SAP. Maybe I worry I'm the one who can't change. Maybe I'm afraid of confronting not my family but a lifetime of fears, habits, and self-imposed rules— the very system that keeps me self-contained.

Alice's jam-colored BlackBerry trills loudly from the table by her elbow. "Just enough time left to give you a homework assignment," she says, looking at its LCD screen. "For next week, why don't you make two lists? In one you'll describe your parents' marriage and in the other you'll write down what you want your own relationship to look like. The lists might look the same in some places and very different in others. Remember, you don't want to automatically do the opposite of what your parents did either. That's still letting your future be defined by your past, and we really want to get you to a place where you're solidly in the present. Part of being an adult is consciously choosing your own vision of what you want to create."

28

While Alice plumbs the uncharted depths of my rage—most days it's still buried so deep I think the poor woman might need a pickax and a headlamp—she also agrees to help me ditch what she calls the "internal blocks" that prevent me from "realizing my heart's desire." To this end, she employs some of her expertise as a dating coach.

The computer in me wants to dismiss Alice's romantic advice as cheap and patronizing. But a more honest inner voice knows the lesson's seeming childishness speaks more to my own. It's a sad testament to my romantic complacency that a question as remedial as "describe your ideal relationship" brings me to the very end of my faculties. The computer in me can come up with reams describing what I don't want. The placater in me is accustomed to asking only what the men I date want. When Alice asks what's important to me, I tell her it's like asking a color-blind person to write her an eighteen-hundred-word essay describing a Monet.

I hardly know where to begin drafting what Alice calls my "relationship vision." Aside from my parents, I know few couples intimately enough to emulate them. Even films offer few examples of responsive, affectionate, cooperative, witty, and passionate pairs. Movies give me either Juliet of Verona or *Juliet of the Spirits*. They pay tribute to either love's tender beginnings or its embittered dissolution. But how do two people who love each other live their daily lives? How do they fight, compromise, remain faithful, and endure straight through to their diamond anniversary?

"So tell me," Alice says at our next session. "What do you want in a partner?"

I must give her the blank-faced blink I perfected in childhood because she says, "Go on. If you could toss a personal ad out into the universe right now, how would it read?"

"Stunted rage-a-phobe seeks mother substitute for validation eternal? Must enjoy impassivity, mixed messages, and occasional blasts of displaced aggression?"

Alice laughs. "You're finished with that. How do you really want your next relationship to look?"

"Okay, don't laugh, but I had to go back to basics. I was at a loss for how to describe a word as simple as relationship. I had to go look it up to get some ideas." I pick up the notebook in my lap and begin to read. "A psychotherapist in California, this doctor named Alan Rappoport, writes, 'I define a relationship as an interpersonal interaction in which each person is able to consider and act on his or her own needs, experience, and point of view as well as being able to consider and respond to the experience of the other person.' So I wrote that down. I thought I'd like to have that."

It's a basic definition and as dry as a Saltine, but Alice says, "Good. You want to be able to share your emotions with a partner and have him share his. What else?"

"Well, in Virginia Satir, I read that love flourishes in 'an atmosphere where individual differences are appreciated and mistakes are tolerated.' I'd like that too."

"See, you're making your own blueprint now. What else do you want?'

"Passion," I say. "I got my final inspiration in an essay by Laurie Lee. I want my relationship to be what he called 'a meeting place, an interlocking of nerves and senses, of constant surprises and renewals of each other's moods.'" I say I'd like it to grow over time, to rise and branch out like a great, weeping beech under which kids might eventually grow, play, climb, carve their names, and scab their knees.

"This is going to sound crazy," I tell Alice, "but I miss the Lark. Or rather, I feel like I *missed* the Lark. Like I missed the opportunity to see who he actually is. We were together a year, and yet I feel a little like I was acting out this script the whole time. Like I dressed him up in my own neurosis and fed him his lines. I pushed him away and then convinced myself that I was surprised when he left."

"So you think you were a little passive-aggressive?"

I nod.

"Like maybe you forced him into a situation where he had to express the emotions for the both of you?"

———

And so it happens that I find myself sitting cross-legged on my splintered windowsill, simultaneously biting a cuticle, ashing a cigarette into a blue, footed teacup (I refuse to buy a real ashtray, as if the very act means admitting I've become a daily smoker), and sandwiching a cell phone between my shoulder and ear.

As I listen to it ring I try to fill my head with the meringue-sweet voice of Alice. I hear her telling me to be spontaneous for a change. I haven't told her what I'm up to, but if she were here, I'm sure she would say: *Be authentic. Be honest. Express what you're feeling regardless of whether the voice on the other end of the line negates or affirms your gushing outpour.*

Adrenaline bubbles up in my veins. I'm not exactly sure what I'll do if the call goes through, but to hear the "Hi, I'm not in" of voice mail would be disastrous. For the first time in years I find myself writhing with urgency, and I don't want to waste another minute waiting to say what I have to say. The line rings twice, three times, and then an agonizing fourth. And just as I am about to give up, hang up and talk myself into thinking it's all for the best, the voice I've been waiting for comes over on the line and says "hello" in a tone like a slow, shy smile.

I don't take a breath. The words hemorrhage out of me as though in a rolling billow. I tell the Lark there's something I need to tell him. "Pay close attention," I say, "because you might never hear it again."

I tell him, "You were right." And repeat the admission. I say I wasn't entitled to love him back in Brighton because I hadn't seen enough of him to confirm that feeling. But I still want to. I want him to show me all the things I've been too childish to notice. I want to ask him all the questions I'd been afraid to have him answer. I want him to tell me the story of his childhood, the reality of his present, and, finally, what he visualizes for his aforementioned and oft-referenced "future." In spite of everything that has happened between us, he still has that certain *je ne sais quoi*. And I'd like to get to the bottom of it. I want to know the fucking *quoi* of the matter. Because ever since I met him, I've felt like the rest of the world's men are in monochrome while he alone is in kaleidoscopic color.

I pause for his response and realize I'm practically panting. I can't remember the last time I was this honest with anyone. Speaking this openly makes me realize just how often I tell people what I think they want to hear. Relating to people that way negates both of us; their demanding personas don't really exist anymore than my sham-obedient one.

"This is really embarrassing," I say. "But I realized I don't even know your middle name."

He laughs and says, "It's Peter."

That's how it happens. That's how the Lark stops being the empty theater in which I reenact the dramas of my youth. That's how I stop using him as a scapegoat in order to disguise the unspeakable anger I have left over from my childhood. I quit demanding that he fill a mother-of-a-void, and I allow for the possibility that we might forge a different relationship than I have with my family. Which is to say that, in time, the Lark might love me without my pandering to him or sacrificing any essential piece of myself. That's how I learn to see him for who he is and has always been: Eamon. An Irish name, which to my once Catholic ears always sounds a bit like the closing of a prayer.

—————

Once a week I speak explicitly about my family to Alice, and once a day, usually over my morning coffee, I spend a tender hour on the phone with Eamon. With the former, I try to express all the feelings I'd held back as a kid, and with the latter, I aim to strike the right balance between my throat and my heart, between being supportive but also assertive.

Even though Alice still worries that I haven't addressed my parents directly or experienced my anger in what we've come to call a "visceral way," I feel a little more at peace. There is more color in my face and the smallest trace of a skip in my step.

It's November, and I bear little resemblance to the deferential stoic who fled Brighton in a passive-aggressive huff. And still less to the feeling-stuffing depressive who'd literally been sick with rage in the month that followed, or to the austere academic who footnoted her way through her first weeks of therapy, or to the hurting, hurtful lunatic who once used her e-mail to vomit up all her displaced aggression. Where there used to be no one it was safe to express myself fully around, there are now two people in my life who really know me. And one tells me he'd known I was the one for him ever since that phone call in August when he'd spoken to me from St. James's Park.

Something in Alice's schoolgirl smile tells me she takes my progress with Eamon as something of a personal triumph. From doomed beginnings, she's helped us create a coupling based on truth, passion, and conscious thought.

———

My first hint that my anger is not fully diffused comes when Eamon visits in December.

For two weeks we fill my apartment with the sounds of music and confession and laughter. During the week we work side by side and come away with three songs and two chapters to show for it. On the weekend we go to a friend's holiday party in ill-fitting second-hand garb and nuzzle beneath a sprig of plastic mistletoe. We read the papers and eat sushi in bed with our fingers. We have one rather ridiculous but terribly heated fight over whether or not the term "housewife" is offensive. I insist the word places too much emphasis on the house instead of the family. To my ears, it sounds too much like "housekeeper." But we weather the spat just fine and spend the rest of the visit holding mittened hands, curling in each other's arms atop a steep rock in Central Park, and mocking the ice-skaters who totter around Wollman Rink.

"We're really doing this, right?" I ask one night while we sit on my living room floor, exchanging early Christmas presents. "I mean, I'd like to really find a way to be a couple, in spite of past history and current geography."

"We're doing this," he says, pushing away the wrapping paper between us and pulling me in for a hug.

I'm feeling awfully accomplished, amazed by how much I've grown in the last four months, and how my transformation has transformed the people around me.

But a few days later the bubble that holds me, love-struck and cocksure, bursts a little when a rosy rash buds and breaks open on my rib cage. Eamon has it too, but to a far lesser degree, and while his clears up quickly, mine begins to twist up my back and sprawl down my arms, until I'm rasping and clawing myself like a dog with a case of red mange. I take an oatmeal bath. I guzzle Benadryl. I douse myself in hydrocortisone and Gold Bond medicated powders, but nothing that I find on a drugstore shelf seems to slow the bizarre outbreak's course.

I reach the height of agony on a Saturday afternoon, when my doctor's office is empty but for an on-call nurse.

The good woman runs through a series of screening questions by phone. Scratching myself like an animal, I respond in part. I tell her: *No, I haven't switched laundry detergents; I haven't recently traveled outside the U.S. nor have I been frolicking in the type of wild, wooded environment where I might've made contact with poison oak, ivy, sumac; yes, I've had the chicken pox before; no, my building isn't infested with bedbugs and, uh-uh, I don't use tanning beds.* I don't mention Eamon's brother, a doctor, who suggested we might be allergic to each other.

At the end of the interview she tells me the hives might be the result of a virus. She urges me to call back later and schedule an appointment if Monday morning still finds me inflamed.

Something about the word "inflamed" gets me thinking about something Alyssa once said. Back in her first attempts to explain homeopathy, she'd claimed: "The first place anger reveals itself is in the skin. A fear that anger will destroy the love in your life causes agitation and panic. The result is skin allergies. An angry rash is like the 'check engine' light coming on in the dashboard of a car—it's your body's way of drawing your attention to what you're feeling."

I then remember that one of the girlfriends I made in Brighton suffers from psoriasis. Once, when we were discussing the subject of my book over tea, she'd rubbed a silvery plaque on her arm and told me, "I've always thought it might come from some unresolved emotion, most likely anger."

Perhaps I'm not as cured as I'd thought. Alice is always claiming fear of fury is my default mode. "In your family, anger wasn't safe," she says. "You've gone your whole life operating under that assumption. You can't expect to change the pattern overnight; the most you can do is be aware of it."

Although I haven't touched a remedy in months, I go to my medicine cabinet and remove a half-empty bottle of Staphysagria. It's little more than a last-ditch effort to quell the itching just enough to survive through the weekend, but two doses and two days later I don't need a doctor. Unbelievable as it seems, by Monday the rash has vanished to a chafed memory.

Maybe the remedy worked or maybe what I experience is just a placebo effect (even sugar pills occasionally "cure" ulcers). Either way, the flare-up draws my attention back to my feelings. It reminds me that although I'm finding ways to access my anger, I'm still a loaded gun, my chamber filled with years of pent-up rage. I fear for the next few weeks. Eamon is returning to England for a string of gigs, and without him around to remind me that anger can be a positive force for change, I worry repression might return and undo my work.

Before Eamon boards his train to the airport, he holds me tight amid the crush of Penn Station's rush-hour mob. There he says the words I would have walked five hundred sun-scorched miles to hear last August. "I love you," he says, touching his forehead to mine. "I really do, Koren. I love you so deeply."

I don't walk back to my apartment so much as fly. All of the ways in which I've tried to become better acquainted with my childhood and my emotions—especially sessions with Alice—have helped me accept love as important as Eamon's. Being gentle and loving with myself has brought me to a place where I can embrace him with that same integrity and compassion, where I can confide in him what I actually think and feel as opposed to shaping my mouth into the words I've decided I ought to say.

Our differences, when they arise, no longer seem like a looming threat so much as an opportunity to grow, explore, and know one another better. Though our ideals align, we will inevitably approach some things differently, seeing them through the lenses of our own individual memories and perspectives. But even conflict can bring depth and insight to our lives as individuals, as writers and as a pair. From the newspaper, I clip a nature article that says lovebirds sing both in harmony and discord; even their conflict drives a coordinated duet. For the first time in a long time I'm trusting, even hopeful.

———

For all my progress with Eamon, I remember that Virginia Satir thought that there will always be aspects of ourselves that we do not know—puzzles we'll spend our lives attempting to solve. Every so often, I chance upon a hint (an image, a sound bite) that clues me in to my childhood anger. But most days, those long-ago emotions are still difficult to access and unnerving to look at squarely.

I know the extent of that fury is hidden from me, but is it obvious to others? Was Seneca right? Does rage always show itself openly, whereas other emotions can be "concealed and cherished in secret"? Is it true that the greater fury is, "the more visibly it boils forth"?

In "On Anger," the Stoic said every creature makes its anger known in some way: "[B]ulls toss their horns in the air and scatter the sand by pawing, lions roar, snakes puff up their necks when they are angry, and mad dogs have a sullen look."

Yet every time I wonder whether I'm walking the streets with quivering lips, knit eyebrows, and a furious red flush, the world assures me otherwise. To the outside acquaintance I'm about as hard-edged as saltwater taffy. Hardly anyone guesses what brews beneath my sprightly, chirping surface. Whenever I divulge the topic of my book-in-the-works, my listener says something like: "It's hard to imagine a sweet girl like you has a drop of anger in you." To which I always laugh and reply, "That's just because it's closeted and repressed."

———

Eamon moves in on the twentieth of February—a date etched in memory also because it is the same day my niece, Riley, is born.

We decide to share my place on Twenty-second Street, at least until its lease expires in April and we can hound around for a new home together. It feels right. It feels like it was intended to be. Brighton's fight has been downgraded from "hemorrhage" to "hiccup," and although we're not yet laughing about the events of the summer, we will be in time. Soon I'll be describing for Eamon the way I wept all over the Canadian immigration officer, and he'll be telling me that he'd taken his pent-up emotion to the stage of the Reading Festival, where he'd made an off-color remark about another performer who'd subsequently tried to punch him in the face. In some way, we're even grateful for the months of lost faith, rejection, and poor personal hygiene—time apart has made us more self-aware, more communicative, and more certain that we are for each other.

My family is not quite so convinced.

After a brief visit to my folks' house, I come to find out that my mother—who has never approved of any boyfriend, let alone one who seemingly drove me, weeping, across time zones—had sat Eamon down at one end of the kitchen table. There, she brushes her hair violently out of her face and gives him a speech of some fist shaking and thunder. She tells him she'd never liked him. She warned him that she was watching him. She alludes to "assassins." ("I *know people* who could get rid of you.") She threatens to "put a price on his bald head" if and when he hurts me again. (My mother's story speaks of a different version of events. According to her, she got in

Eamon's face—so their noses were "literally just one inch apart"—and spoke sharply and quietly in her attempts to intimidate him. To hear her tell it, she also added: "Walk away from my daughter. Leave her now. She was a shell of a person after you hurt her last summer.")

Back in New York, when I hear about the incident and am overwhelmed by a deep pang of protective love for Eamon, I assure him I'll call home and discuss things with my mother. But an hour later I still haven't picked up the phone. Excuses are forming on my tongue. My mind gropes for ways around the confrontation. "You have to understand . . . ," I say. "It's just the way my family is. . . ." "No matter what I might say or how much I'd like things to be different . . ." "Where she comes from . . ." "The way she grew up . . ." At that moment, my guilt surpasses even my love. That right there is *the wall.*

29

"You have to understand," I tell Alice. "It's a thing in my family. Mothers always hate their daughters' partners."

As of March, I've been giving a lot of thought to the various blights and root rots that afflict my family tree. This, in no small part, is thanks to Alyssa. My dear friend is continuing in her Satir studies and has become enthusiastically involved in an empowerment exercise called "family reconstruction."

These reconstructions, which were developed by Virginia Satir, sound a bit like therapeutic theater. Alyssa describes a process in which a person acts as the quibbling director in the off-Broadway play of her life. First, a participant selects an actor to play her in the production. Next, she casts the roles of her parents and grandparents, as well as any great- and great-great-grandparents she might have information about. Once the cast is assembled, she then "sculpts" the actors into positions that best depict their disposition and history.

"What do you mean?" I ask her. "Like, 'Dad always was a spacey, self-obsessed bastard; why don't we show him in this scene with his head up his own fat, dimpled ass?'"

She laughs. "Sort of."

Once cast, characters get to write their own speaking lines. In the last act, the actors describe the thoughts that their body language brings to mind. ("Bent over at this angle, life feels rather unstable," Dad says. "I feel like I could lose everything at a moment's notice.")

It seems like an exercise in public humiliation, but the more Alyssa tells me about it, the more I see the logic.

"The stories we tell ourselves about our families are often wrong," she says by phone one dark night. "But these false versions persist for years—even generations—because the impressions we form in childhood are just too awesomely vivid."

Satir's followers, including Barbara Jo Brothers, say the ideas we form in early childhood—when we are completely dependent on our moms and dads for survival—often cause us to continue to see our parents as almighty Old Testament gods, even as we grow up and become adults ourselves. These "strange, unreal conclusions" are "simplistic," "drawn from the immature mind of a child." And Satir herself believed the best way to let go of them is to literally "watch" our mothers and fathers growing up in their respective families. By participating in a family reconstruction, we can truly see and experience a world in which our reproachful "gods" are human.

At the end of a reconstruction, Alyssa claims, a person can experience and appreciate subtleties that she couldn't understand as a kid. She will know why her parents had always lived, thought, and (maybe) screwed her up the way they did. If she has a pervasive and hidden desire to change one of her parents, she'll come to recognize it. And what's more, she'll realize she was the one who needs to change. The ultimate goal of a reconstruction is to bond with your family and embrace your roots, as opposed to denying or opposing them. Allegedly, this causes a dramatic shift in a person's identity. Only then can she finally be complete.

I'm not quite ready to enroll in another group therapy session (after SAP, I'm not sure I thrive in a group context). So, as much as Alyssa urges me to fly out to Boulder and participate in a reconstruction, I decide to try a similar exercise on my own.

I start asking about various ancestors. This is a challenging task given what often seems like an implicit familywide gag order. I manage to squeeze a few facts out of my mother, and even more from Jo-Jo, her youngest sister.

One snowy afternoon I find myself in Alice's office revealing my findings to her one by one, like human teeth strung on a wire— grotesque artifacts from my family's past.

"It's true after all," I say. "I think I might come from a family of man haters. My mom's despised every man my sister and I have ever dated. And her mother actively tried to break up some of her daughters' marriages."

"How does it make you feel to know this?" Alice asks.

"Traumatized. Fucked up. A little relieved . . . At least, less inclined to take it personally."

"What else did you find out when you went climbing your family tree?"

"Well, I asked about how my mom's family had handled their anger."

"And?"

I tell her my mother claimed everyone screamed bloody murder. They shouted if the toast burned. They cursed and wailed if they wanted the butter dish passed. My aunt said my grandmother was the one quickest to combust. The way Jo-Jo saw it, my grandfather was the obsequious one. He was the one who always seemed to be bowing down and bucking up. If he was ever cruel to his children, it might have been because his anger was displaced; it was easier than aiming the arrows at my *nonna*.

"So those were your mother's blueprints," Alice says.

I nod and feel my face twitch as it undergoes a funny shift of expression.

"I know that probably puts your own family in perspective, but how does it make you *feel*?"

"Sad for her," I say. "It gives me a little more compassion." But there's another emotion I'm not ready to acknowledge. A far less generous voice demands to know why she would clone that dynamic, using my dad, my sister, and me.

30

That March, Eamon and I decide to move to Paris for the summer. It's an incidental decision, fueled by so many flukes and fortuities that I find it difficult to explain to friends and colleagues who receive the news with mystified eyes.

Suffice to say, Eamon needs to be near Britain for work, rent in London is too expensive, and I stumble across a classified ad advertising a cheap-as-chips house share at the far end of the Bobigny metro line in a village the self-proclaimed-artist owner refers to as "the Bronx of Paris."

Are we *un petit excité*? *Oui.* For two weeks, François Hardy lives on our turntable. Eamon pores over an *Eyewitness* guide to the city while I pace around parroting phrases from a CD entitled *Fodor's French for Travelers.*

Pouvez-vous répéter cela, s'il vous plaît? I ask the dripping coffeepot.

Je ne comprends pas, I say to the error message on my laptop's screen.

For people of two different nationalities, France feels like a place where we can begin to build our life on an even footing.

Even my parents seem exhilarated by our plan when we tell them. "I think Paris is just the thing," my mother tells me by phone. "You're both young. You can both write from anywhere. I think it's exactly what you ought to be doing."

We feel like we've been handed the keys to a sweepstakes Cadillac. We're high on possibility, stupid in love, and glutted with freedom. Never in *mille* years do we imagine what's coming next.

———

It's a twist straight out of the pages of Richard Yates. I wake up one snow-bright morning with the sensation that something is—not wrong exactly, not yet different—but *changing* in some irrefutable way. In the bathroom mirror my skin seems to breathe like the leaves of a young, hearty plant. My reflection seems somehow riper on top and squishier in the middle. On the subway I feel warmer than the morning crush seems to justify. I tire easily, and all day long my head buzzes with a headache.

Later, it occurs to me to duck into the nearest dismal Duane Reade. I wander the aisle marked FEMININE PRODUCTS mildly disoriented before eventually taking my place in line behind a testy, exhaustion-crippled mother whose shopping basket (I couldn't help but notice) is filled with baby wipes, aspirin, and Nicorette.

As we wait, the toddler gripping her leg turns to face me. I smile in turn and she lets out a deadpan, ear-puncturing scream.

After the clerk rings me up, I carry my plastic bag protectively around the corner and across the snow-sludgy street. Back in my apartment, two decisive pink lines appear on a succession of three home-pregnancy sticks. It comes as no real surprise to me when the contraceptive sponge I've been using goes off the market later that month.

———

I've never really allowed myself to want a family of my own.

I have few memories of playing house as a girl. As a kid, I never knew how to relate to my baby doll with the balled fists and blank-blue, blinking eyes. Her helplessness always made me feel futile. Her tender expression only made me feel lonely. By age eight I had convinced myself that I'd never be any good at mothering. I believed I was too inherently selfish, difficult, and demanding for the job.

To my recollection, no one has ever disputed these points. Growing up, I had ached to play the Virgin Mary in our church Christmas pageant, but on the night of the performance my family had laughed and poked fun at the terribly "unmaternal" way they'd felt I'd slung the Savior into his manger.

As I'd neared high school, I'd added a short temper to my list of feminine faults. I lacked patience. How could I not be the kind of mother who yelled at a daughter when she dropped a glass; laughed if she awoke with nightmares; scolded her if she skinned a knee? I could not love people in the way that they needed to be loved. Even after *Smashed* transformed me from fiery fighter to docile good girl, I'd carried into my late twenties the belief that I was too defective to spawn. There was too much crazy in my pedigree to pass on my damaged genes.

Only in the past few months had I allowed myself to imagine a life that might include kids of my own. Only recently had I begun to—occasionally—steal slantwise glances into passing strollers. One recent afternoon, I had allowed myself a smile as I passed a mother walking hand in hand with her pint-size daughter.

It still seems like an ambitious dream, but if Eamon and I could create the relationship we wanted, it seems equally likely that our family could be whatever we want it to be. I only hope we'll be able to see our children for who they are and give them the respect that we give each other. I pray we won't blindly emulate or do the opposite of what our parents had done. Just maybe, we can be a family unto itself, something we might spend the rest of our lives redefining together.

Eamon is nervously preparing for a solo gig, so I decide not to tell him the news until later that night. Anyone who sees his spooked eyes and knuckle-cracking hands can tell he has enough on his mind.

For the rest of the afternoon, I leave him alone in the apartment to practice and rework his set list.

Later, in a shadowy bar, I hold my breath while he tunes his guitar and tells his stories to a drunkenly distracted crowd.

The revelation doesn't break free from my lips until after he's accepted his pay in dog-eared twenties and we've walked home through frozen drizzle beneath a big-bellied moon.

We're curled in our bed's warm jumble of down covers when I finally came out with it.

I'm only a month pregnant, and yet I'm anxiously aware of some change in myself. Emotions—goaded by hormones—feel more difficult to contain. Earlier that night tears had been quick to spring to my eyes as I'd watched Eamon sing across the bar's dark, echoey room. Never had affection welled more powerfully inside of me. Never had I felt so sentimental. Never had my gratitude been so complete.

Yet, even as he cups my ears, smoothes my hair, and touches his forehead to mine, nerves are with me too. No confrontation seems bigger than this. Here is a man who makes me look forward to each and every day, and yet, as I pull back and search his tired, contented green eyes, there's still the outside chance that this whole scene can be dashed by just two words:

I'm pregnant.

Words can't express my relief when I see his mouth curl into a bird-in-mouth smile. My Eamon, eyes twinkling, sits upright, squeezes the wind from me, kisses my stammering mouth, and whispers, "Excellent."

The next morning, Eamon wakes me with a heaping breakfast of coffee, red grapefruit, smoky bacon, tomatoes, and buttery eggs on a hot, crusty roll. We spend the morning in bed with the paper, collaborating on the crossword puzzle, getting stumped on number seven down ("Wake at dawn?") and laughing when we discover the apropos answer ("morning mourning").

We discuss if and how it might be feasible to have a baby in Paris, and by the time we reached the bottom of the coffeepot it seems possible, it really does, in spite of the language barrier and all that soft cheese. "The French love babies," Eamon assures me. Plus, there's always the American Hospital in the 7th arrondissement, and—look right there on the hospital's Web page—all the laboring women in the maternal unit looked pampered, relaxed, happy, and sufficiently anesthetized.

Later that afternoon I walk the eight blocks to Fourteenth Street to confirm my pregnancy with a doctor. Eamon's offered to come along, but, even as I appreciate his support, I think I could benefit from a couple of hours of thinking things through on my own.

I approach Union Square, tucking my chin deeper into the folds of my scarf and butting my head against the wind. I think: *This is no time to be impulsive.* I need to know that I'm acting deliberately and making fully conscious decisions. I don't want to be one of the passive-aggressive mothers I often come across in the pages of Alice Miller: "The humiliated grown daughter, if she has no other means of ridding herself of her burden, will revenge herself upon her own children." I can't stand to be the kind of woman who unconsciously expects a child to be what her own mother wasn't: a person who will be fully focused on her; who'll acknowledge and accommodate the full gamut of her feelings; who'll love her unconditionally—never deserting or mistreating her—no matter how emotional, demanding, self-interested, or time-consuming she got. It was a parent's job to protect a child and not vice versa.

As I walk through the greenmarket, I'm especially attuned to the families that I pass. I notice the newborn dozing in a linen sling against her mother's chest, the howling imp whose mouth is stained with the chocolate half of a black-and-white cookie, the pudgy tot stumping around the rows of lettuce and leeks and pushing a forlorn doll in a flimsy toy stroller.

No, I need to know with 100 percent certainty that I won't use a kid to work out any unresolved emotions from my childhood. To this end, it seems especially important that I find some balance between aggression and passivity. I don't want my issues to blind me to my child's own emotions, the way, in the past, they've made me stupid to those of Eamon and my sister.

31

My first trip to the doctor is brief. A nurse and I peer over a hospital-grade pregnancy test, watching a strip of color appear in its plastic window. "See there?" she asks me. "One of them's faint, but there are definitely two lines. Congratulations, looks here like you're going to be a mom."

On the way home I feel tender and exposed, as if anyone who looks at me can read my mind or see straight into the flurry of my soul. I stop in a pharmacy and fill a prescription for prenatal vitamins and then drop into a dark Lotto shop on the avenue. The clerk there has a pudgy, shaved head that he wears like an army helmet and a face that says he is all business. He eyes me strangely when I buy a twelve-dollar cigar, as if he senses my interest in it is only symbolic.

Back at my apartment building, I hear the *ooh-wee-ooh*s of a sixties girl group from the hallway. As I turn the key in the door, Eamon jumps up from where he's sitting hunched over a cup of cold black coffee.

"How was it?" he asks. "What did they say?"

When the words stick in my throat, I produce the stogie from the pocket of my winter coat and watch his face run from perplexity to joy as it dawns on him what the fusty thing means.

What shows on my face? I am cautiously giddy, but I also feel a strong clutch of panic. Am I good enough for the job? In touch enough with my emotions? I want to be the kind of mother I've read about in the pages of Virginia Satir: someone who expresses her own humanness and acknowledges the humanness in her child. But what if I turn out the opposite? What if, in spite of myself, I end up being the kind of mom who bottles up her feelings because she thinks they undermine her authority and comes out, as Satir says, "looking phony to her children?"

Eamon seems to sense me spinning my wheels. He moves closer and puts his arms around me.

"*Baby, I love you,*" the record says. "*Baby, I love you.*"

———

In the weeks that follow I begin to think that impending parenthood's wreaking havoc on Eamon's nerves too. He's acting freakishly out of character. To begin with, he spends all day out alone on the city streets, presumably on some mystery mission. He leaves just before noon and returns at nightfall with aching arches, tension headaches, and only hazy descriptions of the places he's been.

"I was just walking around the Upper East Side," he says, with a terror-stricken look on his face. Or he'll say, "I was in Midtown, when it suddenly occurred to me to take the subway downtown to the Bowery." As if this ought to clarify everything.

Around the apartment he is nervous and withholding, giggling or making cryptic notes to himself on small scraps of paper. When he's not in a complicated state of distraction, I catch him sneaking glances of great emotion and magnitude. I once awake in the middle of the night to find him watching me with a soft, private smile.

I don't press him to explain. The way I see it, he's obviously working through his own emotions about becoming a dad. Instead, I smooth his brow and assure him that I have his back. "I'm always here if you need me," I say. "We're a team. There's nothing we can't figure out together."

It occurs to me that he might be waiting for pregnancy to change me: to turn me into a moody, carping, sugar-craving cliché. One morning over breakfast, he randomly sputters, "I got you some chocolates!" And I watch him produce an outrageously expensive box of Richart bonbons, oblivious to his gift's strange timing.

As it turns out, Eamon isn't unraveling. On the contrary, he's been ring hunting, requesting my father's permission, and otherwise preparing to propose.

It all becomes clear on the night of April 7. We're standing outside the Dias y Flores Community Garden, between Avenues A and B. Although it's the tail end of winter, the lot is still manicured and alive. Looking between the iron bars of the fence, we can almost make out the thoughtful arrangement of dogwoods, the sleeping viburnum, the prized juniper, the dormant rosebushes, and the frozen yew tree.

We're standing on the same piece of sidewalk where two years before we'd had our first kiss. But for as much as the place has significance to us, we've never actually been inside. Eamon has obviously made arrangements to get in with the help of the owner of a nearby herb shop—a man with purple dreadlocks and taut suede pants who is presently rattling the door and frowning, trying every key on his cluttered key chain.

With each failed attempt, Eamon's face clouds with despair.

I take his cold hand in mine and give it a squeeze. "It was a nice thought," I say. I tell him it's enough just to be there, taking the same nighttime walk we'd taken as spellbound strangers.

It's just after sundown and the neighborhood is loose and lazy, as if it's storing up its energy for later. A piebald cat sniffs and rasps against a row of bruised garbage cans. A swaggering young couple scarfed in matching kaffiyahs slowly walks their bicycles down the sidewalk toward the avenue.

"I have a garden you can use," the man offers, after he's exhausted every key on his chain. "My place is just over there." He points to a brick tenement on the opposite side of the street.

Eamon nods mysteriously. We follow the dreaded man across the road, through his graffiti-tagged front door, and down a long, shadowed hallway lit weakly by a quivering fluorescent light.

He opens a door on a studio apartment filled with the sound of running water. Violet bulbs glow in the overhead fixtures. Against one wall, half a dozen bonsai trees are arranged in a way that brings to mind a miniature-scale national forest. The place is wonderful, balmy, outlandish. In a long aquarium a prehistoric-looking lizard sleeps on a blanched piece of driftwood. There's even an indoor waterfall trickling into a basin of speckled Japanese pebbles.

"Garden's out back," the man tells us before he turns to leave. "Stay as long as you need. When you're done, the door'll lock behind you." It's an astonishing act of trust and generosity.

When it's just the two of us, Eamon opens the sliding glass door and we step out into dusk's silvery light. The sweet stranger's "garden" is actually a cement patio—a dumping ground for fleeting interests and appliances on the mend. There's an empty clothesline, a dismantled bicycle, broken ceramics, a moldy birdbath, a rusted child's trampoline.

Eamon gives me a soft look and takes my hand. "In case you're still wondering what this is all about, I brought you out here because I've been wanting to ask you . . ." As he crouches down to one knee, I clench my breath. My happiness is irrepressible. My head breaks into ringing. Here's my match, my partner, not just someone to live with but someone I don't want to live without.

The moment—though it hasn't gone according to Eamon's plan— is perfect. Standing in that rusted-out patio, I'm reminded of what I admire about both him and the city where we fell in love. With each, the next adventure is always around the corner (or, more accurately, through a storefront, around a garden, down a long, hidden alley). I think, *As long as I have both Eamon and the city, there will always be strange insights and fresh discoveries. I'll never know where any given day might take me.*

Later, it will also occur to me that Eamon found the chink in the armor of my stoicism. Every day he reminds me of the function of human emotion. We wouldn't be (and hadn't been) possible as a couple without admissions of feeling. Our confessions reawakened us to each other. Our outpourings—whether they were smitten or sore—reaffirmed our humanity. It was with Eamon's help that I'd eventually come to see that even arguments can be a celebration of life and an attempt to take in all its sensations.

He barely gets a simple, silver ring out of his pocket before I lilt my *Yes!* I love him. It's as fixed and as certain as any law of physics—as long as we're both here, it will always remain.

32

We barely have three days to enjoy the thrill of engagement before Eamon has to fly back to Britain to prepare for a tour.

Before he leaves he shares the news of our engagement with his parents, who call to tell me how glad they are that I'm joining their family. I also call mine, who have known the news since Eamon asked my father for his permission. To the story of the proposal, my mom and dad don't respond with much but a stony "if you're happy we're happy" and a marginally offensive speech about the importance of prenuptial agreements.

As for the news that we're expecting, Eamon and I agree to stay true to tradition (and superstition). We're going to wait until the thirteenth week of pregnancy to let that lynx out of the bag.

During our time apart, our schedules turn stressful. Our to-do lists multiply by the day. Eamon is researching French marriage laws and trying to find an obstetrician in Paris. I am (in no particular order): putting my feet into doctors' stirrups; presenting my arm to various blood-work technicians; hiring movers; flying to a Midwestern university to read to an (enthusiastic) audience of (fourteen) college freshman; listening to remedial French language CDs; hunting for an off-price wedding dress; trying to finish the first draft of my anger book; and packing up the contents of our apartment to be placed in a storage unit just off the Brooklyn-Queens Expressway.

I sit on my naked hardwood floor and edit pages of my book atop cardboard boxes labeled LINENS or KITCHENWARE.

I tape French conjugation tables to the bathroom mirror on the off chance that they might permeate my memory whenever I brush my teeth.

I see a horrible ob-gyn in Murray Hill—an aspiring author who tries to badger me for the number of a literary agent while she still has the speculum in me.

To combat the stress of the move, I also agree to see Alice two times a week. But to be honest, our sessions only find me twitchy and distracted by all the other things I might be doing with the hour.

Because I'm going to discontinue therapy when I get to Paris, Alice spends our final weeks together working overtime to give me some closure.

"So," she says one day in the midst of a recap. "You first came to see me for help getting over your ex. You needed to do this in order to work on your book—a book that just, incidentally, happened to be about anger. Together, we figured out you weren't deeply angry with your ex, you were angry with your family. On an emotional level that wasn't even conscious until now; you still feel what you felt as a child: that your mother sees you only as an extension of herself; that your father admires you for what you can do as opposed to loving you for who you are; that your feelings are not as valid as your parents' emotions; and that you can't express even the simplest feelings—anger, pain, discomfort—and still have a place in your family."

I don't nod, but I don't correct her either.

"We also know that your instinct to protect your parents, especially your mom, runs so deep that you learned very early in life to make scapegoats of other people. That way, when the emotions really start to poison you, you can release them without confronting your parents, risking their abandonment, or lessening your ability to survive in your family."

Alice is certainly upping her ante. Since our breakthrough we've been circling these topics from a safe distance, as though in a holding pattern. But as our time together draws to an end she's going in for a hard landing.

"Once we pinpointed the feelings you'd never allowed yourself to acknowledge, your concentration for your work returned and—this part still blows me away—your ex became a real life-partner. So what happens next?"

I'm not sure what she means and say so.

"I mean, are you going to try to challenge your family? Tell them what you'd like to change about the way you interact with each other? Will you confront them before you leave for Paris?"

Hell to the no. A hot wave of horror sweeps over me. I tell Alice that I can't imagine ever wanting to do that. As a matter of fact, I believe I say it would take something "almost catastrophic" to make me want to take my family to task. I say a big showdown won't accomplish anything. I don't need one to make me feel better. I'm getting on fine. I'm in the kind of denial I'd been in back in September, when I first came to see her.

Alice tuts softly. "Remember that the opposite of anger and depression isn't the absence of feeling. It's the ability to experience spontaneous emotions."

Right. In that case, I am spontaneously okay, copacetic, simpatico. My family is imperfect. Big deal. Aren't most families? That's life. Everything's cool. It's manageable.

Or at least it is until the brokers arrive.

33

The first ones show up at ten in the morning, firing their digital cameras and using their cell phones in walkie-talkie mode. As the days go by, they multiply. Even now they tangle together in memory like the rat kings of folklore; they take on the shape of a diseased vermin with thirty-five heads, all of them squeaking and clawing for one commission.

There's the slimeball from RentFinders, the dirtbag from CityLiving, the rude woman from a brokerage firm called something cheap and condescending like Rents For Cents.

"Yes, that's fine," I'd told the superintendent's wife when she said prospective tenants would be coming to tour my apartment.

What she hadn't mentioned was that the owners had listed my apartment with half a dozen brokerage firms in the city. Every fifteen minutes a new batch of voyeurs leans on my buzzer or tries to unlock the door with a key they've procured and waltz in while I'm taking a shower.

This is not okay, I think. *It really isn't.* Not when I've repeatedly asked the brokers to show up only during the pre-agreed hours. *I work from home,* I think, working myself into a lather. *They're standing in my place of business. I'm trying to meet a deadline.* And *still* they're descending on me as early as 7:00 in the morning and as late as 10:00 at night: tracking mud into my bedroom; giving strange men a guided tour of the cupboard where I keep tampons; and trying to convince a gaggle of college-age girls that they can transform my 1.5-bedroom apartment into a place that can comfortably sleep six.

I've never experienced anything like it in the seven years I've lived in New York. The disruption is constant. Their attitude is entitled, their demeanor invasive. I have over three weeks left on my rent and my place feels more public than the Port Authority Bus Terminal.

I lose my mind after a real-estate broker lies over the intercom (claiming he's a UPS deliveryman) and turns up at my door (it is seven o'clock in the morning) and tries to nudge past me (I am standing in my nightgown) to take photos of my bedroom for his company's Web site.

I feel faint. It's the kind of first-trimester exhaustion that can't be underestimated by people who haven't experienced a pregnancy. I have hormones in overkill and a budding mother-bird instinct that will stop at nothing—not eviction, not assault, not even arrest—to get the sordid vulture away from my home.

My blood rockets. It surges up my spine and rings a boxing bell in my brain. I shove my finger in the offending broker's face, ordering him to look at his wrist and tell me the *fucking time*! Can he in fact *tell time*? I ask him with a hiss. Evidently *not*. Because there is no way, *no fucking way*, that a time-telling member of a civilized society would look at the face of his goddamn Swatch and think, *Hey now, this looks like an appropriate fucking hour to intrude on a stranger in their fucking home!*

I slam the door in his face with a roar and lower myself, trembling, to sit on a moving box.

I think about what I've read about healing aggravation, specifically the woman with a persistent fear of invasion whose house becomes overrun by insects.

I don't relax after he's gone. I simply can't catch my breath. I pace. I replay the confrontation in my head, imagining scenarios in which I respond in a way that's scarier, swearier, even more cutting.

As the day goes on, my worst fear becomes a self-fulfilling prophecy: I can't come close to regaining my composure. I'm lit up, wound up, fed up, bent so far out of shape I'm surprised I don't slip a vertebral disk.

What's more, I'm shivering like a fiend.

I make it a point to tell the next two prospective renters about the building's magnificent rodent problem, describing in lurid detail the scratching sounds the dirty creatures make in the walls; the way I've seen them gnaw off one whole quarter of a wrapped loaf of bread; the way the super, refusing to call an exterminator, once recommended that I either get a cat or keep a bucket of water on hand so I could drown the ones I catch in glue traps.

On top of it, I refuse to let any of the visitors use my bathroom.

When one Realtor tries to move my papers, I order her to get the fuck out at once.

You'd never believe that I was a person who has a hard time establishing boundaries. I'm not just setting limits, I'm building goddamn blockades. By lunchtime I'm a lunatic, flashing the finger at brokers when their backs are turned. I'm sneezing the word "asshole" into my shirtsleeve.

———

Word gets out that I'm being uncooperative. At 5:30 P.M. I open the door on another broker. As he stands there tapping a ballpoint pen against his palm, flashing his fuck-you smile, polluting the hallway with the stink of self-tanner and deodorant body spray, I maliciously note his frosted hair and cheap-suited swagger; his bloated, date-rapist face. He's alone. There are no potential renters in tow.

I begin to tell him that he isn't allowed to tour the apartment after 5:00—or, for that matter, before noon—when he lurches forward, pushes the door open with one hand, and backs me into my narrow entrance hall.

I can't believe it. He's bulldozed his way in. I feel a cold bolt of panic as I watch the front door slam closed behind him.

I starfish myself, splaying my arms and legs between the walls, trying to prevent him from coming any farther inside. "What do you think you're doing?" I ask, hating the shaky quality in my voice. "Did you hear me invite you in? What are you doing in my house?"

He actually says, *Look, bitch*: "Look, bitch, my colleagues and I have a right to show this apartment."

"*Excuse* me?" I wheeze. "You and your *colleagues*"—here an eye roll; it's too polite a word for such blatantly rude people—"have no right to barge in at all hours of the day and night! You have no right to lie about who you are at the front door! You definitely don't have the right to muscle your way in and try to intimidate me!" All bets are off. Any shred of civility goes right out the window. "Back up!" I tell him. "Back the fuck up and get out before I call the police!"

"The *police*." He spits the word nastily, narrowing his eyes.

"Yes, the police! You slimy bastard! You evil fucking cretin! If you don't leave right now I'm going for my phone."

His laugh is taunting.

"You don't believe me?" I ask him. "I'm warning you, get out immediately or I'm calling the cops."

For a moment we gape at each other. He makes no move for the door. In fact, he's looking over my shoulder in the direction of the living room, as if thinking he might test his luck and move deeper inside.

I lift one hand as if to slap him, but instead I bring it down against the closet door to the right of his head. I do it two and three times, and each slam produces a magnificent sound. The walls rattle. My voice soars to the ceiling, where it seems to break open, shatter, and cascade back down over our heads. "*Get out!*" I shriek. "*Get the fuck out this second!*"

"Whoa," the idiot says. The whites of his rounded eyes show. He flashes his palms in concession, as if miming the number ten. He takes one, two, three slow steps backward before he turns and runs like a spooked kid.

34

I decide to move out immediately. My hormones are surging. I am not weepy-variety pregnant. No, I am claw-your-eyes, fit-you-for-a-headlock, poised-for-prison–type pregnant. I'm afraid I'll be arrested for assault if I stay in New York one week longer than I have to. As the days pass the feelings brought on by the brokers become more potent but also less specific. My warpath is widening to encompass just about everything I lay my flashing eyes on.

I feel myself swinging too far to the opposite end of the spectrum. I've found my self-defensive instinct, but I suspect I've sacrificed too much of my empathy in the process.

When I see my reflection in the window of Alice's office, I see an equal-opportunity misanthrope. I've spent the past week showering everyone who crossed me with the same exuberant hatred and saying "fuck you" to a city that returned the sentiment.

"You'll find hormones definitely make it harder to squelch your emotions," Alice says.

We're engaged in our final session, and I want her to feel confident that she's taught me to have a healthy, responsible relationship with anger. To that end, I elect not to tell her that I kicked the grill of a cab that had nearly hit me on the way to her office. The livid driver had subsequently slammed his cab into "park," tumbled out into traffic, and tried to run after me.

"My sister's really into the old wives' tales," I tell her. "She seems to think all this aggression is a sign that the baby's a boy."

"So you decided to tell your family the news after all?"

I tell her pregnancy was exhausting enough without the added work of keeping it secret. I say it had all come out while I was asking if I could come stay at their house until I leave for Paris.

"Were they happy for you? Supportive?"

"Supportive enough. My dad was too stunned to say much beyond, 'Great. Surprising, but great.' My mom told me, 'It's as good a time as ever—you have the resources to have a baby.' Part of me wishes there were other things they'd said. But they did their best. It is what it is."

"What do you wish they'd said?"

"Just that they thought we'd make good parents. Something along those lines."

"Do *you* think you'll make good parents?"

"I do. And I suppose that's all that matters."

"So you're saying your self-worth doesn't depend on your family's approval?"

"Not anymore. Not in this case."

She gives me a prolonged look, as if to gauge whether or not I am bluffing.

I try my hardest not to squirm self-consciously.

"Well, that's good," she says brightly. "That sounds like progress."

We return to the subject of anger. I confess I feel ashamed, even depressed, whenever I think about my confrontation with the broker who forced his way into my house.

"I should have handled it in a more professional way," I say between biting my bottom lip. "I could have done it better. I should have asked for his card, taken his name, reported him to his supervisor."

"Listen to what you're saying," Alice says. "You've finally allowed yourself to express a spontaneous emotion and now you're being a perfectionist about it. I can practically see your wheels spinning. You think you haven't done anger *well enough*. You want to bring Little Miss Perfect into it. I know you're rewording, over and over, what you wish you had said to this jerk."

She isn't wrong. For days I've been rewriting the scene in my imagination. I've been obsessing over it. I keep trying to think of something else I might have said—a better way I might have staged my threats, a more articulate way I might have formed my insults. This compulsive self-editing is the same reason I made such slow progress on my anger book for so long. When it comes to emotion, I am still too selective and stingy about it.

"I think you handled the situation beautifully," Alice says. "You were a single woman, home alone. You were scared. You were defending yourself." When I don't respond, she pauses and confirms, "You didn't hit him, right?"

"No, I didn't hit *him*. But I did smack the closet door between us."

On this last count, Alice looks unconcerned. "You're certain you don't want to stay in your apartment until the end of your lease?" she asks. "You're paying for it. You have every right to be there."

I tell her I can't stand the constant disruption. I say I'm on a tight deadline and I'm dangerously behind. I think leaving for my folks' house is the only chance I stand to get some work done.

It's retrogression. I'm retreating, for a second time, to the house I grew up in an effort to elude my own rage. I can't yet see the connection, but this is exactly how my journey began when I'd made a quick exit from Brighton.

In retrospect, I wonder if Alice picks up on the pattern. If she knows what's coming, she doesn't warn me. When the hour is up, we exchange good-byes, and she lets me dash off toward the moment of discovery. Maybe she thinks it's time. Perhaps she believes I am ready.

I like to think she knew what I couldn't yet see: With every attempt to evade anger I'm coming closer to confronting it. Every time I try to distance myself from the feeling, I circle back to its original source.

35

The day of the move, four men from Long Island City come to help me unscrew the legs from my armchairs, pack my drum kit into garment boxes, and trick my fat, frowsy sofa through my building's narrow doorways and sharp-cornered halls. They're the same movers I've used every time I've ever changed apartments, and they've seen me through every transition since I was twenty-three.

"Paris!" remarks my favorite mover in the bunch—a young, Italian bud named Mike. He has exaggerated shoulders, a tiny-tapered waist, and the bounding friendliness of a golden retriever.

"I remember all those years ago," Mike says. "When we moved you out of that dive of a walk-up on the Upper East Side."

"Six years ago. It was Seventy-eighth Street," I say, laughing. "Remember there was a stair missing and everything? You and the guys spent the whole day trying to maneuver around a big hole in the floor?"

"And look at you now, a soon-to-be-married Parisian woman. Jeez Louise, time flies."

Brokers continue to drift in the door while boxes go out it.

"Hey, where's your mom today?" Mike asks with a playful smile.

No one who's met her ever fails to remember her. During one of my moves she spent the day teasing and goading him on, accusing him and his buddies of dragging their feet in an effort to charge me double.

"She decided to cut you some slack," I say. "It's just my dad along this time."

Dad came down to the city to give me a lift to Boston. It was generous—a terrific help—but for reasons I hadn't anticipated, and couldn't at the time digest, I feel more overwhelmed with him in tow.

He drifts aimlessly between rooms and repeatedly checks the face of his wristwatch, and I am intricately attuned to his moods, almost to the point of distraction. I can tell from the smallest gestures that he's bored with the wait, annoyed by my temperamental Internet connection, and concerned that we might hit rush-hour traffic on the Merritt Parkway.

Even though there's nothing I can do to fix any of those problems, I feel myself begin to take his cues personally. As the day goes on, my neck stiffens. A tension headache blooms between the inner corners of my eyes. It gets worse when my father tells me two separate brokers mistook him for my building's super—a mistake that clearly hurt his feelings. It's been years since he lost his job, and I can see that the comment made him feel even further away from the corporate world he once knew and still loved.

It's noon when Mike and his men have the whole of my miscellany piled into their dent-dimpled truck.

As my dad and I set out to follow them to my storage space in Brooklyn, I notice a pair of brokers mulling around the mailboxes and speaking into their cell phones with loud, brassy voices. I am thinking how glad I am that I won't have to deal with their rude intrusions again when one of them turns and shouts to my father, "Hey, man! Are you the super?"

My father doesn't slow his pace, but I know him well enough

to know that inside he withers. In a stung voice he fires back, "No, are you?"

My brain breaks. All the tension I've been carrying around for the past four hours has found a new target, and I'm going to pin that broker to the wall.

"Who do you think you are?" I demand. "You, with your little mortician's suit and your smug, fucking face?! Do you think you're entitled to speak to people with that kind of condescension?!"

"I didn't know!" It isn't until I hear the quiver in his voice that I realize how young he actually is. He must be fresh out of college. "I thought he was the super! How am I supposed to know he's not the super?!"

"*How are you supposed to know?*" I ape. "Wow, you're, like, the *Olympic gold medalist* of retards. Fuck you and everyone like you. I hope you get buried in that cheap fucking suit."

———

In the car, I avoid my father's gaze, turning on talk radio and hoping he picks up on the unspoken message. I don't want to talk about it. Discussing it will mean reliving it, and I am suicidally ashamed already.

I don't recognize myself. If I've ever had a tentative sense of who I am to begin with, I am now completely displaced. I want more than anything to regain some semblance of self-control. I need to distance myself from the past four minutes, to make it clear to my father and myself that—although I'd been ready to make the broker digest his own teeth—it's no reflection of the kind of person I am inside of our family.

All the way across the Manhattan Bridge, I'm aware of my father holding his breath. I sense the wrong emotion emanating from him. He isn't horrified. Good lord, he seems grateful. Admiring, even. "Did you see that Realtor's face?!" he asks later at the storage facility, when he can't seem to take my silence on the subject anymore.

"It wasn't funny, Dad. I was in the wrong. It really wasn't nice."

We're watching Mike and his gang stack everything I own into a room no bigger than a regulation-size parking space. My head buzzes. My eyes feel recessed in their sockets. My arms, which are limp from lifting boxes, hang heavily at my sides. Even exhaustion hasn't drained the ill temper from me. I worry it's poised to jump, flealike, to the next source of discomfort or aggravation.

"It's just—'little mortician's suit!' Good God! He was speechless! I'll tell you, Koren, you know just how to size people up and hit them where it hurts!"

"That's not exactly an admirable quality, Dad," I say through gritted molars.

I might have another reason to fear anger: I'm too good at it.

36

I expect to be punished every day of my life. I live my life like a character in a Greek tragedy, waiting for fate to exact its revenge on me.

Growing up Catholic, I learned to believe that it was possible to be saintly and perpetually calm—impervious to human itches like agitation. Even as I got older and the religion loosened its choke hold, that idea remained like the faint impressions of fingers around my throat.

I aim, always, to be sweet. If I fail at being sweet, I settle for bland, and when blandness eludes me—when some hot vim of fury bites through—I collapse at the center, crippled by contrition and a leaden feeling that I will be made to pay for my rage later. In my teenage and college years, booze helped me play out this cycle. Alcohol both blunted strong emotion and punished me slantwise for feeling, in the form of a blackout, a date rape, a hangover. In my midtwenties, I'd found Buddhism. Like the priests of my youth, the monks whose books I read also seemed to tell me that I would pay for my outbursts—only retribution wouldn't come at the gates of Saint Peter; bad karma might make itself known immediately.

So I'm not wholly surprised when we break for a truck-stop pee and I see a small tinge in my underwear. It's not blood. Not really. More like blood's insinuative. I take it as a warning that I need to take a breath, slow my pulse, and try to stop being so snappy with my father, who seems to be piggybacking some anger himself.

The whole ride, he'd been gunning the accelerator until the speedometer shot to the eighty-five mark, forgoing his blinker as he weaved through traffic, slamming his brakes, and flashing his high beams at whoever had the misfortune of slowing his course. At one point, I'd even woken up from a catnap to find him honking and mouthing death threats to a driver in the lane beside him.

"Stop it!" I'd screamed, making a fist around the inner door handle on my side and hanging on for dear life. I was struck, again, by that new protective feeling—that tenderness for my pregnant body. "It's like you're *deliberately* trying to kill us in a five-car pileup!" I'd thought it felt disrespectful, like he hadn't cared a mite that I was exhausted and pregnant.

Evidently, I was not the only one who felt disrespected. "Stop *picking* at me!" he'd bellowed back as he jostled the car into gear and begrudgingly slowed down. We are too much alike. From our family blueprints, he is the one I've modeled myself after.

Moments after this exchange, we each made a flustered, disyllabic apology. We spent the next hour nursing our self-pity and scowling at the wet scenery, each of us stewing in feelings of martyrdom. *We are blame-accepting receptacles,* I think to myself. *Pandering to other people's feelings has always enabled us to ride out our own.*

———

"So, you're already wearing baggy blouses?" my mother asks, leaning in to give me an arrival hug.

My parents' dogs bark wildly and circle our ankles.

My sister's German shepherd rears up onto his hind legs and clobbers me in a terrifying imitation of my mother's embrace. I wrestle the demonic beast to the floor and say something about how I'm going to be in France until my third trimester at the very least. I'd wanted to pack clothes that I can grow into.

"Show us your belly," my mother says. "Let's see what you've got."

Reluctantly, I lift my shirt over my navel.

"Pssh, you've got nothing," my mother says.

"Nothing," mimics my sister, who is home with Riley for the summer while her husband is on another tour of Iraq.

I let my blouse fall in mild defeat.

In a far-off recess of my mind, I'm still preoccupied with what I saw at the rest stop. I'm not worried, not yet—I'd read in *What to Expect When You're Expecting* that spotting occurs in a quarter of all pregnancies—but I do make it a point to pour myself a big tumbler of water and climb the stairs to my childhood bedroom with the intention of putting my feet up.

I stretch out in bed with my feet on a pillow, trying to corral my brain into some peaceful pasture. I can't get there. I am still annoyed by the length of the ride, which had been made longer by the fact that my father had stopped off at the supermarket and a liquor store.

It's after 9:00. I ache to put on my pajamas and go to sleep at a geriatric hour, but there's still a late dinner to be had. From the sound of it, my dad is already halfway through a bottle of wine while he sautés something that hisses back from the stove. I can hear him shout something to someone who is too far from him to hear.

I get up and close my bedroom door. Every sensation is raising my hackles. *What's wrong with me? Why does the old quilt on my bed feel so oppressive? Why do the familiar smells (potpourri, Dove soap, wet fur) burn in my nostrils? How can I possibly be enraged by little more than the sound of my parents' dogs barking?*

———

Later, at least two different voices screech "Koren! Dinner!" (To which I respond, "Yes! I hear you! *I'm coming!* Sweet Jesus, stop yelling!")

At the dinner table, serving dishes pass from hand to hand. There's bok choy, mashed potatoes made fancy with wasabi paste, and salmon (ditto with a miso glaze; in his forced retirement Dad's gotten into fusion cooking).

The latter is on special request from my sister. Prior to her pregnancy, she'd claimed, "If it's fish it's not my dish," but after giving birth to Riley she's been craving it morning, noon, and night.

I can tell that my sister and I make our parents feel uneasy, a consequence that pregnant women and new mothers will inflict on their loved ones. My parents are beginning to see us as strangers who act in atypical ways. We wear third-finger rings, eat oddities, trade off being sentimental and hormonal, litter our childhood bathroom with prenatal vitamins, and use phrases like "lactation expert." Overnight we've become unpredictable to the people who share our DNA. My father, in particular, doesn't seem to recognize us. I watch him spoon a pink portion onto my plate, saying, "You're eating meat and your sister is begging for seafood. This family's lost all sense of order."

———

"I don't think Dad's very pleased I'm pregnant," I tell my sister later that night. "It's nothing he says, exactly. I could just feel it all day in the way he looked at me."

My whole body aches from the move's strenuosities. Bed is beckoning. But my sister's been home for a bleak week already and is subsequently yearning for girl talk, so I recline on my bedroom carpet and shimmy my pounding feet up a wall, while we chatter on into the early morning.

My relationship with my sister has improved in recent months. Alice has helped me see that I've often treated my sister the way the hurt kid in me felt my mother had treated me. I can now see that there'd been times when I'd closed my ears to her feelings or, worse, reacted to them with shock and indignation, panic and aversion. Without even realizing it, I'd expected her to react to the world in the same ways that I did. Instead of accepting her as she was, I'd seen her as an extension of myself (the same way I'd felt my mother had always seen me). I'd inadvertently made her feel that she had to be exactly like me in order for us to feel close. This weakness was like a blind spot; simply knowing it was there seemed to reduce my chance of another major collision.

By the time I arrive at my parents' house, my sister and I have become as close as girlfriends. It is rare that we go a single day without speaking by phone, and we can fill hours with our talk about new loves, old grudges (save whatever ones we might have had for our parents or each other), dreams, desires, insecurities, ideologies, and our widely spaced childhoods.

"It's not that Dad's not happy you're pregnant," my sister says. "I just think he forgets. He didn't see me for the first time until I was six months' knocked-up. I was so big then that it couldn't slip his mind."

She's lolling on my bed in the prone position, flipping through a pile of pregnancy books. "Ooh," she coos. "I forgot to ask you, is your sense of smell, like, *crazy*? When I was pregnant, I couldn't stand the smell of dishwashing liquid, or raw onion, or fabric softener sheets. How big are your boobs? I swear I was already up a cup size when I was as pregnant as you are now. Look, it says here that your baby's essential body parts are accounted for by now. His eyes are fully formed. He has tiny earlobes. He weighs just a fraction of an ounce."

As my sister reads aloud, I'm aware of a sharp, quick pang in the northwestern hemisphere of my uterus, somewhere around Mongolia. I don't know whether it's denial or exhaustion that makes me disregard the feeling at the time. My sister has moved on to her old maternity folders and pregnancy journals. She's shuffling papers, looking for a better food-safety list than the one I'd received from my doctor.

The day has been difficult, and my sister is talking old wives' tales around the time I nod off. How's my skin? she asks me. Pimples mean I'm having a girl. Excessive leg hair is a sign it's a boy. Sleep pulls me under with the force of a riptide, and I don't even hear her kill my bedside light.

37

The next morning is the day before my mother's birthday, and my sister and I set out on a desperate hunt for a last-minute gift.

I watch my sandy-haired sibling push a cart at an obliviously slow speed down the aisles of a bargain basement store, stopping every few feet to scrutinize a porcelain vase or a sequined photo frame. It's in moments like these when I love her without restraint. She's twenty-three and becomes self-possessed only when she feels alone and unwatched by anyone in our family.

Riley is riding high, her car seat fastened to the cart's child-size basket. She sleeps, cocooned in fleece and stoppered at the mouth with a pacifier in the shape of a butterfly. Women of all ages pause to covet and coo over her as we pass through the clearance shoe aisle; they admire the newborn's wee hands and good show of serenity. Two gum-smacking teenagers want to know whether Riley is a boy or a girl. My sister spurns the gender-specific colors—pink, violet, coral—and dresses her baby exclusively in neutered creams. An older woman remarks on Riley's cherubic good looks and asks, rather intrusively, if my sister has a husband.

Like all errands we undertake with Riley, this one is an overlong mission. By the time my sister and I settle on an antiquish-looking tea set, I'm lightheaded and reeling with a woozy suspicion. I gather my strength. We still need to hit up the grocery store for ingredients. I'm planning three tiers of birthday carrot cake glazed with candied pecans and a marmalade cream cheese.

———

Back at home, there's blood in my underwear again. And this time, it's more decisive. The gore has lost its wavering. Gone is its initial hesitation.

I confide in my sister.

I shimmy my feet up a wall and try, with hush meditation, to lull my body back to ease.

When that doesn't work, I open my wallet with grievous decisiveness, remove my health insurance card, and phone the nurses' hotline printed on its backside.

Without thinking, I tell the RN who answers the line, "I'm bleeding."

She responds with a question. "From the head?"

"No," I say. "Sorry, I'm bleeding as in spotting. I'm nine weeks pregnant and I've had a rough week."

Down the hall, my sister is talking loudly on her cell phone with her sister-in-law. It is no consolation when I overhear her say, "Did you spot during any of your pregnancies? No, I didn't either."

When my father appears in the doorway to ask what's going on, I feel my temper rear up, pitch, and kick out. "Nothing," I shout, cupping my palm over the phone. "Don't talk to me. Don't *you* talk to me!" I am irrational, bristling, frightened, convinced it won't matter to him anyway. He looks shocked by my tone, the anger that's come as a surprise to us both. Until now, I've had no idea how furious I am by what seems like, at least from my warped perspective, his lack of support.

No matter what I've told Alice, I haven't come close to accepting my family's limitations, because I still won't allow myself to really feel and grieve them.

This exchange with my father ought to be the first indication of what will happen next. Before the weekend is out, I'll plow headlong into the wall at ninety miles per hour. I'll make a mess of myself in my attempts to persuade my family to my side. I'll hurt and bewilder them with my efforts to convince them that emotion can bring people together instead of driving them apart, that we can still function as a family when we share what we're feeling and each person can experience his or her own reaction.

But as I finally try to confront my fear of anger, I'll be missing the point. I can't prevent something that's already occurred.

Ten minutes later my sister and I are in the car on the way to the only hospital she knows how to get to. We don't have much to talk about. We haven't fully absorbed the idea of an emergency.

As we drive my father's car past the ghoulish woods and darkened houses of my hometown, I'm choking back a torrent of tears and my sister is clawing the dashboard to reach her ringing cell phone. The moment she flips it open I can make out my mother's ear-piercing hysteria on the line's other end.

"I'm on my way home from work," I hear her say. "I'll meet you at Marlborough Hospital."

"But we're on our way to Emerson," my sister says while she angles the car around a turn.

My mother begins to shout in broiling disbelief. "Emerson Hospital?! That's twice the distance! You know how to get to Marlborough! *You know!* Don't you remember?! You've been there!"

"Fine!" My sister yields. "We'll go to Marlborough, then!"

She grazes the CD changer in a sulky jab for the blinker, and the car suddenly fills with the weathered voice of a folk album Eamon had loaned my dad. "Easy to forget the things we need," the singer, Martha Scanlan, mewls. "Easy to stumble around mostly blind."

In England, it's 2:00 A.M., the bad news hour, and I pray I'll leave the hospital with bed-rest orders alone. I hope there'll be no urgent need for urgent calls.

———

My mother is already waiting in the emergency room when we arrive, wearing the red polo shirt her department store mandates as uniform. After I fill out my insurance forms and have a name tag braceleted to my wrist, I take the seat my mother and sister have saved for me between them.

The ward is busy with Friday night suicide attempts. We hear paramedics shout out their varied genres. "Sleeping pills!" they call. "Exsanguination!" "Carbon monoxide poisoning!"

Behind a glass booth, the intake nurse tells me to wait right where I am; she'll be ready for me shortly.

"I'm before you," a man turns and snarls at me. His face has a rawboned severity. Some ultimatum shines in his eyes.

"Yes, I'm aware of that. And thank you, sir," I shoot back at high volume. Then I turn to my sister, muttering, "I mean, I'm just sitting here, quietly waiting my turn, aren't I? What the hell? Really, what an asshole."

This gets my mother going on one of her snarling, cross-armed dressing-downs. "I want to warn you against this kind of . . ." She stops to choose the right word. ". . . *unnecessary anger* when you're dealing with the hospital staff," she chides. "It's only going to make the situation more difficult for everyone involved."

I tell her I haven't breathed a word of dissent or criticism to anyone in blue hospital scrubs. I ask if she *really* means to tell me decorum is her primary concern at the moment. "What is this?" I ask her. "High tea at the Ritz? An afternoon at the races?

"Who did you come to the hospital to 'support'?" I demand brattily. "Me or the doctors? Me or the other people in the waiting room?" When she treats me like a disobedient child I never fail to turn into one.

"Can you even respect the fact that I'm frightened? Or are you more concerned about the way it reflects on you in a room full of absolute strangers?"

"You're frightened, fine," she says, with a harshness that contradicts her words. "But you shouldn't be fearful."

"What are you talking about?!" My voices cuts through the hush like a gunshot, and a man who is bleeding profusely from the hand rubbernecks to watch our dysfunction. "'Frightened' and 'fearful' are synonymous! As far as the English language is concerned, they mean the same fucking thing! Besides, who are you to tell me which emotions are acceptable for me to feel?"

My sister jumps in to take our mother's defense. "What Mom means is—"

I hate the way this happens anytime I disagree with my mother. A bystander interjects like her interpreter, as though we speak different tongues altogether.

I decide I don't need to hear any more. "I *know* what she means!" I tell my sister. As far as I'm concerned, if there is any difference whatsoever between those two near equivalent terms, it's that "frightened" means *afraid* while "fearful" means *showing* that I am afraid.

I tell my mother that I've gone most of my life denying my emotions for the sake of etiquette and diplomacy. But I won't do it tonight. Tonight I'm entitled to wear everything—grief, fury, panic—on my oft-referenced sleeve.

I'm distracted for a moment by the intake nurse who beckons for the man who reproached me. Through the booth's glass partition, I can hear him describe his symptoms to her ("voices that won't go away") and what's brought them on ("PCP and mescaline").

My mother examines my profile as though waiting for some further reaction. "So, I hear you're blaming your father," she says, in a voice that seems to come not from her throat but from her spleen. "For what? Not babying you? Not lifting every moving box? So you're pregnant, so what!? You're not fragile unless your pregnancy's fragile!"

My sister chimes in to say, "It's wrong of you to blame Dad. Blaming your miscarriage on somebody else, I just think that's bad karma."

It's all happening exactly the way my dream foretold: I'm begging my mother to acknowledge what I'm feeling or, at the very least, give me the space to feel. My mom is visibly threatened and attempting to shut me up. And my sister is leaping violently to my mother's defense, either because she needs our parents' approval as much as I do or maybe, just maybe, because if I finally admit the truth about my childhood it might shatter the fictions she tells herself about hers.

I'm consumed by a lonely indignation. A stunned pessimism. I've never been more relieved than I am when the intake nurse calls my name. I leave my mom and sister puffing their cheeks and debating what the hell my problem is.

————

The intake nurse is a carelessly glamorous woman, all humane blue eyes and ponytailed black hair. She has an air of competence and compassion. There's no bad news on her face as she listens to my ailments. No foredoom in the way she scribbles in my chart.

"Is this your first pregnancy?" she asks, while she nooses a blood pressure monitor around my arm.

I tell her, between breath-squelching tears, that it is.

I can't contain my trembling fidgets. I quiver and shudder, vibrating like someone's put a quarter in my chair. I scan her desk for something to focus on when tears well up and blur my vision. Now that I'm emoting, I'm mortified. I'm still so uncomfortable in anguish apparent.

The nurse looks me deeply in the eyes. "I know this is upsetting," she says, with a maternal squeeze of my hand. "But we don't know anything yet. Nothing's definitive. The best thing you can do is breathe deep, stay calm, and help your body relax."

————

I lie for two hours on a hospital cot while a courier drives my blood work to the obstetricians' lab at UMass Memorial. The room has a morgue chill. The wall is decorated with heart defibrillators and instructions for disposing of hazardous waste. As I wait I remember all the times in the past when I've compared the process of writing a book to birthing a baby. Even the word is the same. You "deliver" a manuscript the same way you would a baby. Maybe I've been stupid to think I could bring a baby into the world when I still can't seem to finish my book.

The intake nurse reenters to ask me if I want her to send in my family.

"I know this might sound funny, but I'd kind of prefer if you didn't. It's easier to stay calm here, alone."

The woman gives me an honest, uncalculating look. "Oh, honey," she says. "Are you having a hard time at home?"

What is it that shows on my face? What in particular compels the pretty woman to embrace me in a tender, heart-to-heart hug? I feel like a traitor leaning on this woman the way other people might lean on their family. But I want access to her optimism. As it stands, she's the only one who's told me that these things sometimes happen and my pregnancy could still be okay.

After we disentwine, she agrees to let me hole up on my own for a short while longer. I lie, side facing and naked beneath my hospital gown. I hold my lower belly (where I'm still nowhere close to showing) with my free hand, the one that isn't anchored to an IV tube.

Allow me just one more moment like that. Alone I can be still pregnant and stupidly optimistic. It is only in the writing of this that I can commune with the part of me who was, as my sister said, accruing lungs, eyelids, knee joints, and the sweet genesis of little fingers and toes. I can still propose all the bargains to the God of my youth, a thug I'm not convinced I believe in but still manage to fear and loathe in my most private moments.

Beneath the partition I catch a glimpse of the doctors as they slalom by in their green rubber clogs. Phones sing. Ambulances whoop as they usher in the drunk, the gunshot, the heart-stopped, and the car-crunched. Under the ether of denial, I block out all emergencies, even my own. When I can't think of any Buddhist mantras to use in relaxation, I turn to baby names, going through each by letter. I curl, fetally, in an imitation of the person I'll never see on an ultrasound screen.

———

And then, all at once, I am sitting upright and telling my sister, in no uncertain terms, to please get the fuck out.

She's trotted in, arms laden with snacks she's pulled out of some vending machine, saying, "It finally occurred to me that I could ask them to come in. I thought it was going to be an issue? I thought I was going to have to persuade them. But then the nurse just brought me right back to see you. I couldn't believe how easy it was."

I watch her collapse into the doctor's wheeling chair and cross her blue-jeaned legs at the knees. She tucks her hands into the marsupial pouch of one of those oversize sweatshirts she favors and begins to hum a bar of something from the radio charts.

And it's cool, it really is. How can I fault the nurses? But my sister and I quickly renew the same fight I escaped upon intake. She accuses me, again, of slandering my parents. She says something about how tonight's neither the time nor the place for my mother and I to debate our disparate anger philosophies.

"No," I argue. "Communication means talking about the issues at hand in the moment that they need addressing."

I go on to ask her why she's here, in my room, to begin with. If she's just going to sit there in a scrappy, shit-stirring stance and argue on behalf of our parents, whom she is so assured I've upset with my grief. I tell her she's more than welcome to go home and lend them her support instead. Because as it stands, her presence isn't exactly what I'd call reassuring. She isn't quite a pep talk, a get-well basket of poppies and sunbeams. If anything, she's talking as though I've lost the baby already.

"Fine," she says, stuffing ridiculous articles—her cell phone, a tabloid, a package of crackers—into the bowels of her metallic handbag. "I'll leave. Mom went home. So will I."

"Good," I say. "Get out."

"I am."

"Fucking excellent. See ya."

But before she flings back the curtain and storms off into the blink and whir of accident and urgency, she turns and aims the spout of her water bottle at me. With the tone of authority she's acquired since becoming a mother, she shrieks, "You're so selfish! Pregnancy isn't about you! It's about your baby! You're going to learn that damn, fucking fast!"

She's one to talk, I think, as I watch her thundering exit. *Hadn't she called me throughout all of her trimesters in varying degrees of hysteria, panic, conniption, and tears? Wasn't she the one who'd gone around ranting at her belly when its kicking gained might? Hadn't it been my mother and I who had reminded her to lower her voice a few octaves because Riley, like some omnipotent presence, could hear every word she was saying?*

On top of that, I'm positive she's wrong. Pregnancy necessitates voicing one's needs.

A yoga teacher in one of the few prenatal classes I've attended is always droning on about how "in pregnancy, things are going to bother you a lot more than they ever have. Not only will you be more sensitive to sounds, tastes, and noises, but you may also be more affected by frivolous conflict. You'll have less patience for negative conversations." To that end, my classmates and I devoted long afternoons to chanting our throat chakras open. We sang in Sanskrit for practice, to enlarge our lungs so we would be better equipped to tell people when something felt wrong, when we found ourselves in discomfort or pain.

I think that's what I'm doing at long last: speaking up.

My only regret is that it's taken me years to remember how to get this furious. Who knew I was capable of this? *What a surprise*, I think. *What a waste.* My fury's like an Italian sports car, and before now I've never dared drive it at any speed over thirty.

———

In the end, my sister drifts back through my curtain after a lap around the parking lot. She's counted to ten. She's walked beneath a sallow gold moon. She tells me I'm right. She says she's here to support me. And she's sorry that she's been talking as though I've already miscarried. She hadn't meant to be so pessimistic.

We find ourselves drawn back to the subject of old wives' tales, in an effort to find some neutral conversation.

My sister asks me why I suspect I'm having a boy.

"But they aren't hairy!" she says when I proudly untangle my legs from the hospital blanket.

When I look down, I'm stunned to see she is right. My coarse coat had vanished. And come to think of it, the other symptoms of my pregnancy have started disappearing too. Somewhere over the course of the past two days, my breasts have lost their paunch tenderness. My face no longer burns with that pink, clammy flush. My thirst seems quenched for the first time in two months. For the whole of my pregnancy, I haven't been sated by anything less than a gallon of water a day; I've been drinking quantities better suited for a draft animal.

Seconds later the doctor comes in to perform one of those brief, invasive exams (feet in the stirrups, an abysmal draft, butt all the way off the edge of the table). She has a bland face and a flat way of delivering her words, her eyes watery behind her glasses. She removes her plastic gloves with a smack and informs me that my cervix is still closed. But there's still considerable worry when it comes to my blood test, which reveals a slightly low hCG.

"You're familiar with hCG?" the doctor asks me.

No, doc, not really. I'm tempted to tell her that the only informational reading my book-deal-grubbing gynecologist gave me was a quarter-size sheet of paper that advised me, "It is okay to have sex during pregnancy."

Although it sounds like a recreational drug, hCG stands for human chorionic gonadotropin, otherwise known as the pregnancy hormone. In most normal pregnancies, hCG levels double every two days or so. At nine weeks pregnant I should have around 220,000 milliliters of hCG in my system. But my tests show that I only have around 7,000—the amount a competent pregnancy has at the four-week mark.

"We'll have you come back in two days to repeat the blood test," the doctor tells me in parting. "We'll see then if your hCG has increased."

A different nurse comes in to hand me a clipboard filled with outpatient forms. As I scrawl my signature on a sequence of dotted lines, my sister speaks up to ask her, "Well, what happens if the hormones don't go up? Or if they stay the same? Or if they continue increasing, but at a really slow rate?"

While the doctor had been cryptic, this nurse is a whole different force to reckon with—callous and all too forthcoming. "That doesn't happen," she says with simpering condescension. "Either the hormones go up or they continue to fall. If they fall, that's generally the stamp of a miscarriage. If that's the case, next time you're back we'll perform a D and C. Dilation and curettage. We'll clean out your womb. It's an easy procedure. Just a little scrape and vacuum. It only takes about ten minutes."

Thanks, Florence Nightingale. Because, heaven knows, my concern is for my day planner.

38

Maybe I wake up crying. More likely, I never stopped. My dreams are embarrassing in their lack of subtlety. In one nightmare I give birth to a buzzard.

I can't remember the last time I experienced dread like this. Unbroken. Swell upon swell.

I've also never felt so helpless to the whims of my body. Whereas I've never fully trusted my emotions, I've almost always counted on my body to be the one thing I could govern in full. I've been its maestro and, occasionally, its czar. I decide on its rations and oversee its isometrics. I've fattened, nourished, sculpted, strengthened, or victimized it as I see fit. But a coup has taken place. Suddenly my body is making demands and issuing statements on a need-to-know basis.

I curl in bed, gazing hollowly at Riley's Fisher-Price cradle swing, which has taken up residence in my bedroom since my last visit home. It's such a clever and disconcerting device: six swing speeds, eight lullabies, four D batteries. So elaborate, and yet it's meant to be so maternal.

The rest of my family moves through the morning quickly, eating scattershot breakfasts in separate crannies of the house.

Company, welcome or otherwise, occasionally seeks me out. My dad cracks my door to see if I want to join him at something called a Synergy yoga class. He has his nonslip mat in his hand and is dressed in breathable fabrics with quick-dry technology. Somewhere over the course of the past year, he's gotten really into *vinyasa* and tai chi. He's started e-mailing me quotes from Gandhi. It makes sense that we've both gravitated to yoga. Bending over backward seems to come easily to us. Standing on our heads is second nature. We enjoy prostrating.

I tell him no thanks. I'm trying to stay off my feet.

My mom also checks in on me before she leaves for work. What with everything, I still haven't lettered her birthday card or wrapped her teapot.

"Happy birthday!" I tell her, trying to stretch my face into a look of enthusiasm.

She thanks me with an apprehensive look and asks me to keep her posted on what she's begun referring to as my "condition."

———

As for Eamon, he refuses to share my anguish. No, not yet. He wants to stay positive. Can we agree to stay positive? He needs confidence and wishful thinking.

Together, we turn to Internet research. We call each other every thirty minutes or so, whenever we unearth some new statistic. I phone and say, "Check this out. I found this Web site that says, 'Caution must be used in making too much of hCG numbers. A normal pregnancy may have low hCG levels and still result in a perfectly healthy baby.'" Eamon turns ebullient, saying, "Yes! Yes! I read that article too!" We agree that the results of an ultrasound would be much more reliable.

Abetting us, my sister helps me schedule an appointment for the following day at her local ob-gyn.

When I'd first burst into the study to tell her our plan, she was sitting in front of her laptop at my father's particleboard desk. R. was sleeping in an oscillating chair on the floor. A bisexual dating show played on the TV in the background. My sister claimed an ultrasound had been on her mind too. In her words, "it was deranged" that no doctor had checked for my baby's heartbeat.

By late afternoon I am having stabbing twinges. Blood, red as rage, spills into the toilet every time I rise from bed with profound dread to pee. It's around this time that my sister, who I've always known as a very vocal atheist, tells me all we could do is wait and, quote-unquote, "pray."

My shock is as shrill as a trumpet. My expression is one of self-conscious distress. *Where is this coming from? Who is she? Is this her secret self? Where is the woman who is always ranting about the lie of creationism and the right-wing Christian agenda?* As far as I know, her favorite sound bite is: "Religion is just a superstition. Or an OCD ritual. It's like compulsively washing your hands."

I feel disoriented. The world is severely unstable. It's my sister all right: her pixie haircut, her hooped earrings, her big Kewpie doll eyes. Earlier that morning I'd seen her reading a feminist blog with the headline "Why Glorifying Virginity Is Bad for Women." Her spur-of-the-moment Catholicism makes me think of her as some medium channeling a distant ghost from my past—my grandmother or my childhood parish priest, some lighter of candles and rubber of rosaries.

I take her advice, however, and try to pray the way I haven't since I was a kid, seeing as science isn't exactly on my side. I can't bear to read another statistic about how miscarriages happen in a quarter of all pregnancies, half of all first pregnancies. I can't stomach another doctor saying a woman shouldn't blame herself, as most are caused by chromosomal abnormalities.

Some months before I'd read a book about a woman who wrote long confessional letters to a god who seemed neighborly enough to listen. I drag my laptop into my bed and try through the cramps to compose a missive.

I won't bore you with that insipid, inarticulate document. I addressed it to "the Universe," which had become, in recent years, the only higher power I could wrap my resistant mind around. I typed loose apologies ("my wrongs are a legion"), misty contrition ("please don't let this be the way you punish me"), and to-the-point entreaties ("I need you" and "help me please").

Far more relevant to this story is the letter that followed as I continued to cramp, cry, and shed undeniable clots as the afternoon slowly died through my window. It's the better written note of the two. Perhaps because anger can be specific while faith can seem rather vague.

> *I only believe in you enough to fucking hate you all the way through, to the very tip of your mangy gray beard. It must have been all those years raised Catholic. Being raised hell-fearing and sign-of-the-cross-making made me too fucking scared to call you an asshole, a menace to society. You're all this and worse. Yes, you are. You are. You are. Guess what? The Sunday school teachers had it all wrong. You don't have the capacity to love anyone, handle shit. Ruler of heaven and Earth, my ass. You couldn't run a fucking bath. Tell your son he's equally incompetent, unhelpful, inadequate, inane. Chances are, you're no longer reading this letter, busy guy. You have billions of other morons to beleaguer, smite, or ignore.*

———

How strange it feels when I open this document again for the first time in months. Cut out the blasphemy, and at first it seems like just a typical—if colorful—letter of complaint. It references services unrendered. It refers to the account managers by name. But when I read it again, I get the feeling that even my cosmic anger is just my family anger, disguised behind a Sunday missal. I was looking skyward and saying to the heavens what I was still too scared to say to the people beyond my bedroom door: that I felt unheard and unhelped; that I felt eternally punished.

My sister comes in shortly after I've composed this complaint, standing by my bed in what looks at the time like a hypercritical posture.

What does she say to me? Nothing. She stares at her sneakers.

What do I say to her? That I don't want a D and C. I won't let anyone touch me with a sharp metal loop and a handheld vacuum. To punctuate this point, I throw the wadded-up wet tissue that I've been holding in my hand. The distance is good, the hang time impressive, and the snot rag lands directly in Riley's empty Fisher-Price swing. Swish. It's a basket. A clean three-pointer. *The Staph patient has a tendency to throw things.*

My sister is disproportionately livid. "Is that what you're gonna do?!" she shouts, with that tone of maternal contempt. "You're gonna throw things? You're gonna tear this room up?"

Destruction hadn't occurred to me. And a tossed tissue hardly constitutes an act of vandalism. I pick up the water bottle that's been resting empty on my bedside table.

"Yeah!" I shout, hurling the empty container to the opposite side of the room. "Maybe I am gonna tear the room up. That's exactly what I feel like doing."

The primordial anger has entered. It's steering me. Maybe because my sister inadvertently gave it permission. I don't recognize fury until she tells me I'm furious, just as, last fall, I hadn't realized I was sad until Hunter told me. I'm in survival mode. A new instinct is taking hold of me, something awesome and self-protective, wrestled from the meanest jungle beasts.

My sister storms out. I don't have much time alone before my mother enters like a one-woman replacement troop.

It's dusk by then. The pain in my lower half is constant and split-ting. I can't get to the end of the tears. Whenever Eamon's called to encourage me, I've cried.

When my mother, dressed again in her red polo shirt, perches awkwardly on the edge of my bed, I look into her guarded face and cry even more.

She says, "Before I had my miscarriage—the one between you and your sister—the doctor told me he hadn't seen anything at all on my ultrasound. No heartbeat. Not even a sac. I don't even think there was a baby in there to lose. Maybe yours is the same situation."

I wonder how this is supposed to be a comfort to me and quickly realize that it isn't. It has little to do with me. My mother isn't using her past to reassure me in the present. She's using my present situation to protect her from the disappointments in her past. If she can convince me that I'm not losing an actual baby, she can maintain that she didn't either.

How can Mom know that her speech—combined with the one she gave me about emotions at the hospital—are an explosive cocktail? They tap right into the two things that I've never mourned or said aloud about the way I grew up. For one, I've always felt as a child that I couldn't experience many feelings—sadness, anger, or the need for help—without making her feel insecure, as though she'd take it as a personal attack. And two, I've always had the sense that I'm not allowed to separate from her. She can't stand it when I dis-agree with her. Part of me thinks she still expects me to be as obedi-ent, passive, and adoring as I'd been as an infant. In the rare instances that I act otherwise, she is physically bothered. It seems to renew some sense of loneliness she must have felt as a child.

Sensing me seething, her spine goes straight. Her diction gets snippy. "You and Eamon are getting married this summer," she says, crossing her arms. "If you two really want a baby, you can try to have one."

What did that mean? *If* we *really* want to have a baby? Of course we actually, genuinely, and verily want a baby. And, more explicitly, we want this one.

"Look," I tell her. "Right now I'd just like someone to listen to how I'm feeling without moralizing. Barring that, I'd like the space to just experience it on my own. Even if you can't understand my feelings, maybe you could try to respect them. I've been taking care of the rest of you for the past two years—"

"That's not true," she tells me sharply.

Oh no? Haven't I played her operative and go-between when it comes to my sister? Wasn't I allowed a few emotions of my own? Was it too much to own my experience without her trumping them with stories from her past? I'm entitled to be as mad as a meat ax. Virginia Satir said, "[A]nger is not a vice; it is a respectable human emotion that can be used in an emergency." As far as I'm concerned, this is an emergency. I'm in pain. I'm sad. Given the situation, this seems acceptable. I'm allowed to worry a little about how the stress of all this will impact Eamon and me. The logical part of me knows we can handle it. But the scared kid in me still expects rejection to follow any change.

"So that's what this is about?" my mother clacks. "You can postpone your wedding if you're feeling uncertain about the marriage."

This one doesn't rate on the list of appropriate responses. This is the statement that sends expletives tumbling from the back of my metallic-tasting tongue. A year's worth of restraint is dissolving, releasing malevolence into my bloodstream, flooding my brain with abandon.

"Don't say one more fucking word," I tell her. "Say one more word about my wedding or my husband, and I guarantee this'll be the last time you see me in this house."

"Your emotions are just so much bigger than everyone else's!" she screams.

No matter how stoic I feel, no one in my family sees me that way. They have no insight into how many emotions I actually hold back. They only see the Spike 3–variety anger, the "impulsive" and "inappropriate" fury that comes hurling out of me when I can't stand to bite my tongue a single second more. This is our impasse. On one hand, I tend to freak out in some situations, bringing a depth of emotion to them that my family is at a loss to understand. On the other, they see *any* reaction as an overreaction. My miscarriage is confirmation of this. They would much rather I put on a resigned expression and pretend I'd never been pregnant.

"Your emotions are like a cyclone that sucks in everybody in its path. When you're angry, you're a danger to yourself and everyone around you."

For the first time in my life, I don't take that accusation to heart. I understand, for the first time, what the Buddhists meant when they used to tell me there were two types of criticism: fitting and unfitting. The person who makes fitting criticisms should be thanked and the person who makes unfitting ones should be staidly ignored.

The computer in me rears her head. "Why do you automatically equate anger with violence?" I ask my mother. "Do you realize that's awfully Darwinian? Some destruction is caused by anger, anger itself isn't destructive! Have you ever seen me physically strike out in anger? I've never thrown a punch, not even as a kid!" I say something about how if she feels threatened by hearing me raise my voice, it's the product of her own ignored wounds. I say more about how I'm sorry, but I won't let her past displace what's happening with me in the present.

This isn't fair, given that I'm not firmly rooted in the present either. I'm banging on about what my family "always does" versus what they "never do." I'm piggybacking twenty-eight years of unspeakable rage onto the way my family is handling the sad fact of my miscarriage. Just as my mother is using the circumstances as an excuse to make a case against emotion, I'm using the situation to make a case for it. Some part of me knows what I'm saying has very little to do with what's happening this instant. I'm addressing the mother of my earliest memories: a sulky twenty-eight-year-old (same as me), her mouth pinched in irritation, her dark hair rolled around tin-can-size rollers and held in place with a deep green bandanna. But I can't let the old, infantile anger go.

"Enough of this!" my mother says, throwing up her hands and making a move for the door. "Do me a favor and call your therapist. I think you need an objective third party."

———

I couldn't agree more. I claw through my wallet for Alice's number and, when an automated voice introduces me to her voice-mail box, I leave her a message saying it looks like I am having a miscarriage—an experience that is causing, shall we say, a considerable shit storm at home.

My dad comes in after I hang up the phone. He looks spent from his yoga class. I'm still sobbing as he comes into my room, sits on my bed, rubs my back with one big palm, and says my name over and over, in a tone that has an unmeant note of admonishment, a baritone that gently goads me to stop.

"At least you have your work," he says.

As far as I'm concerned, it's another response gone afield. It is the second time someone has said, with self-assured sympathy, the most infuriating thing they can say.

"Look," I tell him. "We're not talking about work tonight. We're not making any reference to my career." I tell him tonight is about my family, my new family, the one I'm building. It's about the portion of my life that is equally, if not more, important than my occupation. My mother has just struck what felt like two arteries to my anger, and my father inadvertently does the same. I'm bothered by the way it's always felt like his love depends on talents and achievements that fail me.

"Okay," he agrees. "But you can't just lay here and focus on the negative. Why don't you go watch TV? Why don't you go have some dinner? Have you eaten? I think you need to distract yourself. You can't just dwell on what's bothering you. That's why I go to the gym. That's why I'll lose myself in a computer game of solitaire. Sometimes I just want to forget about my problems."

Dad's denial sends another ripple of outrage through me. Avoidance, dispassion, silence. These are the family habits that he brings from his side. I've never met his mother, but my own has told me my grandmother dealt with emotion by hiding alone in her bedroom, eating sweets and draining wine coolers. I won't bury my head in the sand.

I trail him to the kitchen and choke down an omelet on toast. I sit alone at the head of the table, my legs bent at the knees and my heels on the edge of the chair. Jagged pangs fire through my abdomen, a sadistic mockery of labor contractions.

My mother's in the living room with my sister. I overhear her ask, "What happened to my birthday cake?"

I slip away from the table and resume my bedroom vigil. My phone rings. Its caller ID reads "ALICE."

"Koren," she said. "I called as soon as I got your message. I'm out to dinner with some friends. If you can believe this, I ducked into the bathroom. I'm talking to you from one of the stalls."

Has a more magnificent woman ever existed? I thank her wildly for taking time out of her Saturday night.

"I'm so sorry this is happening," she whispers. "And to think, in our final session you said you weren't going to confront your family during this visit unless a situation arose and required it."

Yes, how ironic. Have I mentioned I was miscarrying on my mother's birthday? It's as though my body is enacting some vengeance, with or without my conscious collaboration. "This sucks, Alice. I just want, in this one instance, to be monumentally upset about it without anyone telling me that my feelings are abnormal or undignified."

"Theirs is the behavior that sounds a little far left of normal," she says. "You wouldn't be human if you weren't feeling all these things right now. They're too lost in their own problems to be there with you, in the present. That's the devastating part—feeling like nobody sees you. But you're normal, Koren. And your anger is too. You can see it now, can't you? *You're normal.* You're alive, not dead the way you've sometimes been in your dreams. Isn't that some relief to know?"

It seems like a pitifully small consolation. Like free bus fare home from a rape clinic. I let Alice get back to her dinner party, promising to call her if anything more transpires.

"I'll be praying for you," Alice tells me before she hangs up. I resist the urge to tell her not to bother; she'll never get beyond the hold music; the universe has no operator manning its switchboard.

I feel defeated, resentful that I have to endure a miscarriage here, of all unlucky places, in a house where I can't confide in anyone, where I'm convinced I have to shape my face into the same mask I've worn since I was a kid: placid, detached, as doe-eyed and blinking as another goddamn doll in my mother's collection.

———

"Early American efforts to limit anger through child rearing were central pieces in the growing reproval of the emotion." It seems like years ago when I'd first read that passage by Carol and Peter Stearns. I remember the way the couple said that America's "anger-control effort" has always focused on quelling tempers that flare within the family's four walls. It's a statement that now bears personal significance given my own parent's admonishments about anger when I was a kid and my resulting adult aversion to the emotion.

Thinking back to *Anger*, I remember this brief timeline.

According to the Stearnses, parents first began to discipline kids against anger in the 1830s, when "restraint of anger became a fundamental part of good character training." For the first time in American history, moms and dads across the nation began to break up squabbles between siblings and to discourage children from the time-honored pastime of chasing and tormenting pets. Christians of the period wrote about parents' "sacred duty" to lead by example and stay mum on the subject of their own vexations. And Evangelical magazines preached about the lasting threat of a childhood outburst: The same temper "that smashes a childhood toy" can "kill a man when the child is grown."

When Darwin burst onto the scene, so did the idea that children have certain animal impulses, including anger and a fighting instinct. The Stearnses say, "Darwinian findings about the animal bases of human behavior, including elaborate inquiries into the evolutionary role of anger, helped alter the view of childish innocence in the mainstream literature." From the 1860s on, child-rearing manuals began to acknowledge that many kids—even those whose patient parents treated them kindly—often held their breath, raised their voices, and beat their tiny, clenched fists. While anger was still regarded as dangerous, Darwin also convinced Americans it was inevitable. Child-rearing experts began to accept the idea that tykes would always feel fury (it was an unavoidable, human instinct), but they advised parents to restrict kids' expressions of it.

Between 1900 and 1910, G. Stanley Hall began a large-scale research project on tantrums, and the Stearnses say the result was the subject's inclusion in child-rearing manuals. Prior to that, these handbooks looked more like 4-H manuals; they only told parents how to feed kids, exercise them, and stave off disease. Parenting experts began to focus their collective attention on a subject we now know as "childhood discipline." Hall and his supporters criticized parents who indulged young children's anger. Thinking back, I'm convinced my family's attitudes about anger stalled then, when the Stearnses also say, "Other [child-rearing experts], including several authors in *Parents* magazine, advised outright physical punishments for displays of anger, lest public tantrums embarrass parents and "reveal that a child is unduly spoiled."

The Stearnses argue that American attitudes toward anger grew conflicted at the late end of the nineteenth century. They say G. Stanley Hall denounced anger, particularly in children, as a threat to health, a sign of "weak will" and "decaying intellectual power." But Hall was also quoted as saying a "certain choleric vein gives zest and force to all acts." He must have sensed the contradiction, because he went on to write, "[H]aving strong passion held in check" creates the tension under which "the best work of the world is done. . . . There are those who have been stung and thus attempt greatness and find the sweetest joy. In the feeling of success they compensate for indignities they suffered in youth." The American Institute of Child Life also seemed mixed up about how to manage anger in children. The institute said a kid in the midst of a tantrum was no longer a child but rather "a creature under demonical possession" and suggested his fits would lead to "wars, rapine, and misery." However, it also urged parents not to stamp out their kids' anger altogether: "Anger is a great and diffused power in life, making it strenuous, giving zest to the struggle for power and rising to righteous indignation." Parents began to absorb an addendum: Fury could also be a motivator.

Somehow, this idea that anger can be beneficial if it is properly channeled disappeared in the 1960s and 1970s. Incidentally, my parents met and married during this time, and as they were preparing to start a family of their own, children's television shows began trying to depict anger without attaching judgment. Mr. Rogers asked questions like "This makes you feel angry, doesn't it?" And *Sesame Street* came up with a song that aimed to help kids articulate what anger felt like: *"I feel so angry that I want to roar / I wanna run home and slam the door / I don't want to see nobody no more when I get mad."* But both shows seemed to suggest that the emotion was a painful, disagreeable feeling, one that a kid should deal with alone and dispel as quickly as possible. According to the Stearnses, most of these attempts to teach children about anger taught kids that although some anger is unavoidable, it is generally bad and "cannot be turned to good." "The Mr. Rogers approach conveyed a strong sense that anger was a disagreeable feeling that did occur but that should be purged as quickly as possible and without result—a problem to be handled by the child himself until it went away because attempts to express anger against those who provoked it would clearly be inappropriate. The more tough-minded *Sesame Street* largely followed suit, certainly in urging that anger should be dissipated without action against the cause."

By the early 1980s, when I was born, the Stearnses say parents were advised to avoid tantrums by cajoling kids, separating dueling siblings, and "bribing them to minimize tension." This new approach was a return to the child-rearing advice of the mid-nineteenth century, before people began to think anger could be channeled for good. According to the Stearnses, "Anger demanded more care and loomed larger as a priority than it ever had before." And in an effort not to teach their kids to repress their anger, parents were quick to "assure their angry children that they knew how they felt." But they might have had ulterior motives: "After all, if the most common target of childish anger—the parents—constantly assured [their children] of their sympathy, it is clear that the real message was that anger should never lead to conflict."

When I'd first read this passage, I'd been shocked by how closely it mirrored my own experiences growing up. My anxious parents had never considered themselves overly strict or purposely insensitive. But the lesson I absorbed in times of distress was *buck up and hush up.* Even as a kid, their discomfort and panic in the face of anger (their own and others) had been obvious to me. In times of trouble, it had always been there in my father's averted gaze and my mother's narrowed eyes.

Now, over twenty years later, I lie in bed, letting my eyes unfocus on the same patch of ceiling I stared at as a kid, feeling just as outcast and forsaken as I ever have. I'm contorted at the waist, nursing a cramping pain and a grinding resentment. My door is closed on the family that cannot give me the kind of support I'm seeking. I'm convinced any confessions I make to them will be belittled, trumped, picked over, negated, treated like a joke, or used against me later.

———

The consummate fall of night. There's an electrical storm both outside and in. A low dread is grumbling in my pelvis, interrupted every so often by fulgurous pain. Nothing can eclipse it. Not lying on my side nor on my stomach, not taking full-lung-capacity breaths, not elevating my feet up a wall.

There's static in my ears and a tremor in my step as I cross the hall to my father's study. Inside, I find my sister in front of her laptop, sipping hot water with lemon and typing back and forth with her husband on an instant message screen. The computer makes a rhapsodic ringing sound every time a sentence is sent or received. "So much has changed since Vietnam," my mother often said of these techno-savvy exchanges. What does it mean to a person to own a Web cam? To emote into it? I suspect it's freedom, an alternate life, an uninhibiting agent, a younger generation's take on therapy.

I need help, I tell her, leaning against the doorknob. "I'm in really bad pain."

She stares at me blankly. Maybe hers is a look of fear, but it manifests as a mask of indifference. The computer chimes as more messages arrived on her screen.

When she doesn't respond, I turn back the way I came and inch the door closed behind me.

I reconsider. I decide I don't need medicine, advice, or human succor. What I really want is to be left alone.

I stumble into the bathroom and lock the door behind me. I adopt a concave stance, slightly doubled over at the waist, the way people are said to look after they've been punched in the gut or before they lose their dinner.

I rest my weight against the sink. I stare into the mirror, and I'm pale as a bone. My eyes are watery and my hair is nested in a vicious tangle that looks almost postcoital. I slide my pants to my slippers and collapse on the toilet. All at once, I feel a small, distinct sensation pass through my body. With sad, animal understanding, I hear a splash in the bowl.

———

Minutes later, I am sitting on the edge of my bed, staring at the phone that I hold in my hand and trying to decide who to call. A fuzziness swirls around my head. Competing emotions tug me this way and that. At the very least, the suspense is over.

After a brisk knuckle rap, my mother opens my door.

"It's gone," I tell her. "I lost the pregnancy."

"Where is it?!"

What did she mean, where is it?

"You flushed it?!" she screams. "No! Why would you do such a stupid thing?!"

What had she expected me to do, exactly? Fish around in the toilet? Put it in an old Hellman's jar for safekeeping?

"We needed to examine it!" she shrieks, in a voice shrill enough to draw my father and sister upstairs to our corner of the house.

"It was a complete miscarriage," I say.

I know what my body has just accomplished. I don't understand why she's yelling at me. My heart goes racing. Why is she attacking me mere moments after I've lost my pregnancy? I'd have rather miscarried in New York, on an airplane, alone in a Ramada Inn, pretty much anywhere where I might have grieved without being told to shut up about it.

When I scream as much back at her, a remarkable thing happens. Not only can I *feel* my throat, but I feel the blood curdle there with each spittle-flecked word. I feel my vocal cords shred and strain to deliver such a shrill tone and high volume. My senses are sharpened. I feel a reckless surge of relief.

I tell my mother I've taken her advice and called my therapist.

"Good. Glad to hear it," she says with acridity. "And what did she have to say?"

"Funny, she said this family is *dysfunctional.*"

I let the last word drip from my mouth like syrup. To anyone outside the Zailckas family, it might seem like a rather gentle insult. But in a family of avoiders, its directness booms like a thunderclap. The word hits a sore spot. Its effect is catastrophic.

My sister jolts forward with the intention to punch me. Her ringed fist is drawn up by her ear, her elbow aloft and waggling. "Shut the fuck up!" she screams, while she lurches in, chestily, for a shot. Maybe, with her husband in Iraq, she needs to believe she's spending the next four months in a sympathetic place. Or maybe she is piggybacking her anger too. Maybe, subconsciously, she is getting me back for times when her emotions had fallen on my deaf ears or moments when I'd stood tacitly back while my family picked on her.

My dad snatches her around the waist before she can connect. He ushers her out, and she continues to wail, "You're a *bitch*! I'm leaving tomorrow! I'm leaving all because of you!"

The moment feels just as chaotic as it is. Virginia Satir says change in families is a three-step process. In the first stage, everyone maintains the status quo, but in the second, one family member pushes beyond it into emotions she's been afraid to reveal either to herself or others. This is when the person in question lifts the lid on anger (this brings me back to SAP) and finds a way to express the underlying vulnerabilities of which she's always been ashamed. In the third step, a hopeful family is willing to do things a new way.

Satir says this lid lifting can create considerable anguish for the rest of the family. "Everyone involved," she writes, "may be flooded by irrational fears and a feeling of impending doom. These fears are similar to those he or she experienced as a baby when the removal of love was synonymous to death and when this extreme dependency on others for survival meant he or she was completely vulnerable."

I can't get over the timing of my sister's raised fist. I'm in such deep disbelief that all I can do is recap aloud to make sure I'm not hallucinating like the man at the hospital the night before. "Do you people understand that I just had a miscarriage?" I ask them. "That I just lost my pregnancy? Is this really the time to be screamed at? Is this really the moment she's choosing to hit me?"

Silence. No one knows how to proceed. My father reenters the room, and I look from him to my mother and back again. She was raised in a house where nothing was communicated without fury attached to it; yelling was the only surefire way to be heard. He grew up precisely the opposite way, learning anger was a vice to be obliterated or indulged in private; he learned to turn anger inward, to be self-critical and self-punishing. I wonder if I can teach my own children some happy medium. How will I ever find it myself?

"Here's what's gonna happen. You're gonna take me to the emergency room," I say, snatching my father by the hand, in the manner of one schoolchild leading another. "We're going to the hospital. We're leaving right now. Where the fuck are my shoes?"

39

"Are you sure you're not thirsty?" the doctor asks. "Check out your bladder. It's the size of a pea."

I let my gaze wander to the instrument. It's seems cruel that I'm only getting my long-awaited ultrasound when my womb is as empty as a zero.

A black cavity glows on the screen. I know, of course, that the doctor is checking to make sure my miscarriage was complete. But I also wonder if she's televising it to aid in my reluctant acceptance, just as an open casket funeral might persuade mourners the dead aren't ever showing up for Thanksgiving again.

"Well, it looks like your body has done its job well," she says, flicking off the monitor.

"So I don't need a D and C?"

"No. We'll just draw a little more blood. You don't even have to stick around for the results."

It's the same hospital as the night before but a different room, a far more personable doctor. Her face is soft and built for laughter, with glimmering eyes and a big, wry mouth. Even her New England accent is a comfort ("We'll just drah a little mowa blood"). It's the dialect of other people's mothers, of all the mahs I had known in my youth.

I change back into my clothes and wait for the nurse to return with my outpatient papers. Medical supplies gleam on the surfaces around me. Jars of cotton swabs, canisters of tongue depressors, boxes of plastic gloves in sizes labeled "small" through "large." *Vain attempts*, I think, *to order a world with no meaning or design.*

Tears rock my chest. For the first time I feel like I've truly acknowledged the depth of my loss. I feel like I know real hate. *Anger, the product of a thwarted goal.* In a few days' time a home pregnancy test will revert back to negative.

I hate, indiscriminately, everyone who crosses my mind, including myself. I call myself a misanthrope, a wretch. I'm back to abusing my SAP-issued inner child for emoting. Even "wretch" is a word with special significance. My mother often called me one as a kid. My only love, my only empathy, is reserved for Eamon. I hate knowing that I will have to wreck his dogged hopefulness.

"Well! You've had a rough couple of days!" a brusque voice announces.

At the time, I'm weeping, both hands over my eyes like someone newly blind.

I look up with great regret to see the infuriating nurse from the night before. Plastic buttons dangle from her earlobes. Her sugary perfume reminds me of my sister's.

———

Back in the hospital's waiting room I find my father in the crash position, head between his knees. I'm not sure whether he's been crying or sleeping.

He rights himself when I lay a hand on his sloping shoulder. He looks disoriented as he opens his bloodshot eyes, like a man who's just returned from a war zone—a place where his survival was always in doubt.

I feel like I'm seeing him for the first time. He has no more solutions than I do. We stare at each other for a few moments, across our shared inadequacy.

"If you don't mind, I'd like to sleep at Dave and Jo-Jo's tonight."

My aunt Jo-Jo and uncle Dave live less than eight minutes from the hospital. They're notorious for their early bedtimes, lights out at eight, but I've called ahead from the examining room and they've assured me I'm welcome to stay.

I don't have the strength or the sanity to argue any further tonight. And I'm not yet prepared for the despair that might strike if I have to hold my crying niece in my arms so soon after a miscarriage; she's too close a reminder of what I've just lost. But more than anything, I need the space to talk openly, a place where people might give me carte blanche to grieve.

I need to mourn not only a baby, but also the fact that I've finally come face-to-face with the source of my anger. My family has never really loved me for the person I am, only as the competent robot I pretend to be. I've never really been accepted without fine print, in the absence of stipulations or strings.

If I don't come to terms with these lonely facts now, as an adult, they might eventually affect the way that I mother too. The legacy will continue. If I am to have any hope of one day being receptive to my children's emotions, I must first learn to be attuned to my own. I don't want my children to pick up my lifelong avoidance techniques. I don't want them to rely on drinking or other addictions to distance themselves from their emotions, to throw themselves into other people's feelings as a way of circumventing their own, or to be so entirely in their intellects and imaginations that they live their lives as though they're sleepwalking. I want the family Eamon and I build to be awake to all life's joys and present for its sorrows. I can't stand to make a child go through life as blind, deaf, and dumb as Plato's self-eating beast, being no more in touch with the world than she'd been at, well, my pregnancy's ninth week.

40

The roads are empty, which means Dad and I don't have to bicker about his loose interpretation of speed limits and stop signs. The clock on the dashboard reads 2:00 A.M. It's a surreal hour, other-worldly and tender. The windshield wipers flop at a slack, sleepy pace.

"I don't think your sister tried to hit you," Dad says while we hang a right onto Dave and Jo-Jo's street.

I'm floored. "Don't you remember holding her back?"

"I held her back?"

Maybe his memory hasn't registered what he didn't want to see.

"I didn't see it," he says, shaking his head with heartbreaking certainty.

When we pull into the driveway, my aunt and uncle are waiting for me. They stand in the headlights, each with an arm around the other's waist, dressed in woolly slippers and plaid flannel pants.

It's time to go. I thank my dad for taking me to the hospital. I tell him that all I'd wanted tonight was someone to confide my feelings in. I lost something that meant a lot to me.

"It meant a lot to all of us," he says with a tremor of emotion. "I don't know what's gotten into the two of them. Your mother's got a little bit of your grandmother in her. And your sister's just been acting a little wacko ever since Tom deployed."

"Don't do that," I say, leaning across a cup holder to give him a hug. "We speak for one another far too much in this family. When it comes to me, you only ever have to worry about what's going on between the two of us."

A half smile appears on his tuckered-out face.

I feel renewed and embarrassed; sentimental talks still do that to me.

We exchange "I love you's" and I watch him reverse his sedan into the shadowy road, and then I walk to the porch to embrace my aunt and uncle beneath a moth-besieged light.

———

I change into a pair of my aunt's spare pajamas and join them on the sofa for a mug of milky tea.

My uncle sits on the carpet, letting my aunt stroke his head with long, gentle, manicured motions. The affection that passes between them is hypnotic. I often experience this kind of culture shock when I visit them at home. My uncle, now legally blind, has a degenerative eye disease called retinitis pigmentosa. He and my aunt have been a couple ever since they were fifteen-year-old kids, long before his vision showed any problem. In all those years together, they've developed an intricate conversational shorthand. They laugh conspiratorially, massage each other's shoulders and feet, and quote one-liners I can't seem to place. For reasons no one's ever figured out, they've embraced the name Joey as a term of endearment. It's what they call each other, almost exclusively.

"Gosh, Joey, I can't rememba the last time we stayed up this late," my aunt says, exaggerating her New England accent for effect. She's sensitive and nonconfrontational, what my uncle always calls "as gentle as a pussy cat," but she is a comedic talent too. Visits with the two of them always feel like improv theater.

"I know, Joey," my uncle agrees with a smile. "We didn't stay up this late when the Sox won the Series."

Despite the hour, they stay awake and talk with me, loaning me a pair of wool socks and asking, without a hint of embarrassment, whether I have enough maxi pads. My aunt tells me hero stories about some of her female friends. One who'd had her first baby after eight consecutive miscarriages. Another whose doctor had prescribed a year's worth of prenatal vitamins before he gave her the okay to go ahead and conceive. It happens to one of four pregnancies, don't forget. I am slight in frame, she says. Plus, I've been under a holy heap of stress. "Just goes to show, the impact that stress can have on your body."

Jo-Jo isn't holding me to blame. Although I admit that's how I take it at first because my mind is already moving in that direction. Even harder than standing up to confrontation is staving off the urge to turn anger on myself. Miscarriage lends itself particularly well to this vice; I was the one who had carried the baby; therefore, the implied misstep is mine.

But I feel less rattled in that house, less combative. The decor reflects its owners to a T. The room itself seems to take me into its arms. My eye dances over the chipper wallpaper, musical knick-knacks, and curios from Nantucket. Everything is dusted and well ordered, as much for the sake of my aunt's neat freakishness as for my uncle's visual impairment.

"Maybe we're just not talkers?" I wonder aloud. "Is that it? Do I not come from talk stock? Are we all just really tragic communicators?"

"Look," Dave says. "The thing about our family is: They love to live in the past. Just can't let go of a grudge. Use the past as justification for everything."

As much as I want to distance myself from this tendency, I can't escape the fact that I've spent the last two years reliving experiences that were over and done with. In my writing, I've reanimated them. They bring tears to my eyes and a shortness to my breath, and riddle me with indigestion and heartburn. I stare into my mug.

"Speaking of the past!" my aunt says, jumping up from the sofa and bounding to the kitchen with a happy stride. She returns with something written on a small sheet of notepaper. "I found the real names of the first immigrants on your mother's side. Now you can pull their records if you want to."

I thank her, and our small private party begins to break up. Jo-Jo and Dave wander to bed arm in arm, and I descend the stairs to the basement guest room. It's 8:00 A.M. in England, and time to wake Eamon.

———

"I'm so sorry," I tell him, listening to his muffled tears.

"But our plans," he says.

I tell him this doesn't do a thing to our plans. I'm still marrying him in a few months' time, exactly as we've envisioned. We'll still see the *mairie* on the hill, the foie gras on baguettes, the rings from the goldsmith in Gloucestershire. Our folks will still be there to act as our witnesses. And it will still be one of the luckiest, scariest, and most vivid days of our lives.

"But our baby," he says.

"You're my baby," I tell him. "We're already so fortunate. In each other, we already have so much more than many people ever get."

"But what you went through last night. All of it."

Never mind that, I say. It happened because I was ready for it to happen. It happened because I finally had the wherewithal to handle it. Don't put too much stock in the rage. Conflict's healthy. It helps us move stuff around. Anger can only harm us if it solidifies in one spot and blisters there for years. What happened last night isn't going to stay with me that long. I'm not going to let the past define who I am and how I make choices. Forget the eccentricities and imperfections of family. I'm conscious of them now, which means I won't perpetuate them, won't pass them down. Ignore the pedigree. That emotional lineage ends here, with me.

"You're a strong woman," he says. "That's one of the reasons why I love you."

I say, "You've done your part to help me realize it. That's one of countless reasons why I love you."

Eamon and I agree we want to be together as soon as my airline will allow. Two weeks is too long to wait. He's bound, contractually, to an upcoming solo tour. But we agree that I'll go along. We will have to console each other between the loading in and out of equipment, between long drives through the Midlands, rest-stop sandwiches, sound checks, and nights spent in Travelodges or on friends' long-suffering futons.

"You ought to check with a doctor and make sure it's safe to fly," Jo-Jo says over coffee the next morning. I've changed into a blouse she's found in my size. It's one of her castoffs from the seventies, a flowered polyester in periwinkle with a pointed collar and tubular sleeves. I'm dressed like the ninth member of the Brady Bunch, as if to punctuate the family utopia just beyond my reach.

I call the ob-gyn I've scheduled my Monday morning ultrasound with. Unfortunately, the phone lines are attended by an answering service, which means it's no small feat to get a doctor on the line. I explain to the virago who answers that I need to change my appointment from an ultrasound to a pelvic exam.

She gives an aggrieved sigh and says, "Matters of appointment are not in my domain."

"Well, look, ma'am, I've just had a miscarriage," I confide. "I'm leaving the country, and I'm trying to find out if it's a danger to fly."

"Well, *ma'am*," she echoes while she chews on something, "perhaps you have me confused with a doctor. It's not in my domain to diagnose, advise, or otherwise give medical advice."

"Look, lady," I snap. "I'm really very sorry to interrupt your morning coffee break. But if it's not too much trouble, maybe you could, oh, I don't know, *page a doctor*?! Only if *that's* in the realm of your responsibilities, that is! Only if it's in your very limited domain to be any help to anyone at all!"

My aunt wanders off into the sunroom with widened eyes and a look of unease.

After a doctor calls me back and tells me that she can't change my preexisting appointment, Jo-Jo returns to the kitchen. "I think you have to be very careful with your anger. You've got a knack for it. You were horrible to that woman."

Dave, who's standing by, says, "You're not an angry person, Koren. I know that's not who you are."

41

"Big deal," Alice tells me later, in an improvised phone session. "So what if you yelled at an answering service? I've dealt with those people before. They're paid to be miserably rude."

As for the question of being an angry person, Alice says, "You can see now why you're so afraid of the emotion, can't you? Why you have this idea that if you get angry just once—even when it's justified, even when it's a matter of self-protection—you can never come back from it? Why you think it will become your identity?"

I'm talking on the phone in Jo-Jo and Dave's basement. On the walls around me are photos of my immediate family. My parents and I at my first ever book reading. My sister smiling self-consciously in her college cap and gown.

Yes, I tell Alice, I can see it. Anger is off-limits in my family because it taps into everyone's fear of inadequacy and imperfection. It breaks us apart. It spins our systems into chaos and brings everyone right back to the lonely childhood he or she doesn't want to face.

That was why my mother shrank to the size of a child in my dream. She's not the only one who turns as helpless as a kid in the face of strong emotion. Just as last night transformed her into the nine-year-old girl who, proudly revealing her report card to my grandmother, was punished for "bragging," it had also turned my sister into the little girl whose family laughed at her for using her stuffed animals to reenact the kinds of emotional heart-to-hearts she saw on the TV sitcoms she constantly replayed. In an eyeblink, I had morphed the little girl at the easel, finally screaming back at the mother who so often screamed at her for getting paint on her dresses and grass stains on her china-white tights.

Alice turns serious. "You can't try to change them, Koren. I mean it. They'll come to their own conclusions in their own time. Yours, like all families, operates on what's familiar. It has its coping mechanisms—old habits that give everyone a sense of equilibrium and make them feel they can survive. Going to the unknown is enormously scary. You, of all people, know that. It's taken you all year to build up the nerve to change the way you experience anger, and even then you didn't really have a choice in the matter. You embraced the idea of change only because it got too painful to keep bottling everything up. And you kept at it because, in your relationship with Eamon, you got a vision of what was possible. You saw there could be another way."

She asks me if I'd thought, even for a moment, about hitting my sister back.

The option never occurred to me, and I say so.

"You know," Alice says, "when you told me your dream last week, I thought maybe you really might be inclined to act violently under the circumstances. But I think now it was just a metaphor. What you saw was the fist of your family's anger. I think, maybe, you suspected what could happen by way of repercussion."

"So what about you?" she goes on to say. "Where are you in the process of dealing with your own grief?"

Upstairs, a clock chimes. I'm not sure what to say.

"Ah," Alice says. "That's what I thought. It's going to be a long process."

She tells me we can resume therapy, if I want. We can find some way to arrange phone sessions that accommodate the time difference in France.

I tell her I'll think about it. I tell her I don't want to schedule anything I'm not sure I can commit to in full. But a private certainty burns warm in my gut. I'm a student who senses the conclusion of her lesson. Alice has taught me where my anger comes from. Now it's my turn to decide when to part with it, to know when it is no longer useful.

———

We're getting ready for an afternoon walk when the phone rings. Dave is rooting in the cabinets for a thermos and Jo-Jo is modeling a series of jackets I can borrow to stave off the rain. My mother is on the other end of the line.

Jo-Jo says, "Koren's here, if you two want to speak."

There's a pause, during which I know my mom is asking whether I want to talk to her.

"Tell her yes, I want to talk to her," I say, making a reach for the phone.

"How are you feeling?" my mom asks me when I cup the receiver to my ear.

"Good," I tell her. "Or at least much better."

"Did you get some sleep?"

In truth, my eyes never closed for a second.

"Your sister and I have been talking," she says. "And we're both very confused as to what happened here last night."

"*Please*," I snarl. "Please speak only for yourself. Please don't call in the reinforcements of 'we.'" I tell her I share her confusion. But I want to speak to each of them individually when I get home.

"If that's what you want," she says, and hangs up the phone.

42

Later, Jo-Jo and Dave drop me off at home, and I go about the business of confronting my mom, while my dad looks on like a cage-match referee.

Mediators go against my one-on-one rule, but it's painfully clear that I'll never get my mother alone. I already fended off my sister when she appeared at my mother's side and began to defend the status quo. Seeing the venom in her face when she left the room, I lost my resolve. I tacitly allow my dad to stay. I remember what Alice said: You can't force people out of their comfort zones, and my family rarely seems comfortable unless my mom is protected.

If my anger had seemed explosive to my mother the night before, it was because I'd been keeping it a secret for too long. For as long as I could remember, I'd denied the things that were bothering me. I'd glossed over them. I'd discussed them with everyone but the sources of the trouble. And they had brought me to the edge.

"You're a danger to yourself and other people when you're angry!" my mother insists.

I counter that the only times in my life when I'd ever been self-harming were the times when I'd felt I had to keep my feelings to myself. There was only one person who'd approached last night's conversation with raised fists, and it wasn't me.

"You're right," she says. "You've never hit anyone."

So why again is my anger "dangerous"?

"You have to understand, when you throw a water bottle, it reminds me of when my father used to throw my brother up against a wall."

I feel my body steel itself in resistance. Some part of me is still terrified to really absorb the image, which would mean fully feeling the depth of her anguish. It occurs to me that my mother is not the formidable force in our family; it's her ancient suffering. My father won't leave me alone with her for fear I'll reignite it. My sister tried to clock me for the same reason.

I fight the temptation to argue that an empty water bottle is a fairly harmless projectile, and she hadn't even been in the room when I'd lobbed it. Instead, I tell her I'm very sorry that she experienced what was no small trauma. But it just doesn't have any bearing on my so-called violent tendencies.

"You don't understand what she's saying," my dad interjects.

"I do understand," I say. "It just disappoints me that we, as a family, can't be in the present. What transpired forty years ago overshadows what happened here last night."

"The worst part is that you're disappointed in me," my mother says shakily. "I've never really disappointed you before.

"I'm so sorry," she whispers, as she buries her face in my hair. "You know how I am. You know what my family was like. I'm sorry I yelled at you so much when you were growing up. It's my biggest regret. You'd break a glass and I'd scream at you. Maybe a broken water glass doesn't seem like such a big deal. But when you've grown up in a house where all your glasses are from the gas station . . ." Her voice dies out and then comes back with a vengeance. "You may say that we're quote-unquote dysfunctional. But you have this." With her index fingers, she draws a box in the air. Maybe it's a picture window or a TV screen.

"What does that mean?" I ask defensively, repeating the gesture.

"It means you grew up in a house. Your parents weren't divorced. You didn't have to move apartments every nine months."

I cut my losses. My mother has done the best she can to make a family from the blueprint that's been laid out for her. She is still as shocked and outraged as the nineteen-year-old girl my grandmother had pushed out of the house and told to go live on her own. She can't see through her own childhood to give me any closure about mine, and I can't see through mine to help her either.

———

"I just don't understand how a doctor can make a diagnosis without meeting any of us."

Later, my dad and I are talking as we sit in parallel armchairs, our gazes aimed at the TV. A chewing gum commercial flashes across the screen. In it, an angry woman uses her teeth to let the air out of her ex-boyfriend's car tires.

I tell him I'm bottomlessly sorry I said it. Alice isn't a doctor in the strictest terms, and we never talk pathology. I say that when I reached for the word "dysfunctional" I was trying to get at a disturbance in— what? Our communication, I guess. The system we have in place doesn't always work for me. A few family members shouldn't get to do all the emoting all the time while the remaining ones do the on-eggshell tiptoe. I can't continue behaving like a completely different person inside my family than I am outside. And I mean "can't" quite literally. As soon as Alice showed me my defense mechanisms, they stopped working for me.

Dad begins to sob, his big face slick with tears. This is his genuine identity, outside the roles and realm of family. Here's the man un-disguised, complex and storied. He nods meaningfully and calms enough to say, "I see so much change in you lately. You're so much more confident and assertive than you've ever been. And I think that is a productive talk you had earlier with your mother. There were miscommunications on both sides. I'm not sure either of you fully understood what the other was saying. But I still think it was productive, don't you?"

———

After I finish with my parents, it's time to confront the most hostile party.

I find my sister in her bedroom, folding baby clothes with brisk-gestured precision while Riley lies awake beneath a mobile of stars. I tickle the baby's feet with one index finger, aware of my sister giving me an admonitory look that seems to say, *Back away from the crib*.

"I think it's important that we talk," I tell her.

"I don't want to talk to you right now," she says, turning her back to me and starting in on a pile of booties. "I'm still really pissed off."

"It's okay that you're pissed off. That's what people do: They talk to each other when they're pissed off. You can tell me about it. You don't have to squirrel your feelings away and deal with them on your own. What if, just for a change, you get the sinker off your chest? What if we just hash it out so we can fully move on?"

She won't face me. She continues to ball Riley's booties into tight little knots.

I say, "I know this is hard. I know you're under a lot of stress in your own life right now—"

"Don't you *ever* fucking talk about my life!" she says with a wail.

"I'm sorry it scared you to see me upset. But I know you know how it feels—"

"*Lower your fucking voice!*" she yells, "Or better yet, *just leave*! Get out of my room! *Get out of this house!*"

"*I am!*" I shout back, feeling my pulse patter and my mouth grow tight. "Believe me, I'm going! My flight's tomorrow. I'd rather tear out my larynx than stay here."

Back in my room, I collapse against the closed door and gather my breath. Just at that moment my sister tries to ram it open from the other side. For a few seconds we struggle that way: me bracing the door shut with my small, stubborn weight and her elbowing in from the other side.

It will be months before I get wind of why my sister's reaction was so fierce on the night of my miscarriage. She'll tell my mother that, moments before I threw that water bottle, I'd proclaimed that her life was "worthless." I don't know how to account for our conflicting memories, except to say that—while I don't discount her emotion—I'm not sure she got the quote right, given how very far counter it runs to what I was feeling at the time: a hint of envy that she got to be the proud mother to a healthy daughter.

If anything, the word "worthless" mirrors the kinds of speeches my parents gave her shortly after she eloped. ("What is your degree *worth*?" they used to ask. "What's it worth if you're going to throw it away to go live on a military base?") Her outsize reaction seems a bit like the kind of retraumatization that I experienced in Brighton, back when Eamon was "the Lark."

———

I drive myself back to Dave and Jo-Jo's house. A wussy move, but it's the second time in two days that a conversation with my sister's abruptly veered toward smackdown, and thinking of the way her Cuban ex-boyfriend taught her how to street fight, I don't want an introduction to her repertoire. When I told my dad I wasn't all that comfortable sleeping at home, he offered in all earnestness to help push my bureau in front of my bedroom door to keep my sister out. "Do you hear what you're saying?" I'd asked him through my dropped jaw. "What's wrong with this picture?"

When I arrive, Jo-Jo and Dave are on their hands and knees in their sunroom, clanging the radiator with a yardstick.

"There he is! There he is!" my aunt shrieks. "Hit the lights! Start the siren!"

The industrial flashlight in my uncle's hand flashes a red-and-blue strobe light. It fills the room with a frantic whooping sound.

"We found our mouse!" my uncle shouts to me over the ear-splitting noise. "If we can't kill the bastard, we're gonna traumatize him! He ate all my breakfast bars! The little shit got into my cookies! We're gonna give him a heart attack if we can!"

"Oh! Ew!" my aunt shrieks. "Ew! Gross! He's under the entertainment center! There! There! Shine the flashlight on him!"

My fear of mice predates even my fear of anger, but something compels me to drop to the floor and glance under the TV stand. A mouse the size of a cocktail shrimp preens himself in a stark white halo of light. He's piddling and innocuous, like all phobias finally glanced at close-up.

SEVEN *Aftermath*

Do not be angry with the rain; it simply does not know how to fall upward.

—VLADIMIR NABOKOV

43

In the hours leading up to my flight, everyone's ignoring me, giving me either a cold shoulder or a wide berth, depending on what I choose to believe. My mom and my sister are particularly exclusive and aloof, spending most of that time together behind a closed bedroom door, laughing, cooing at Riley in bright, singsongy tones, and talking about things I can only guess at. "They've been supporting one another," my father tells me.

They do say good-bye. My sister, holding Riley over her shoulder (perhaps so she won't have to hug me), says "See you" in a strange helium-high voice. Her blue eyes seem both alarmed and vacant. My mother tells me with what seems like passive-aggressive timing that she hopes I "have a very special day," even if she "doesn't make it over to Paris" for my wedding.

My dad then gives me a lift to my last ob-gyn appointment, in which a doctor confirms that my pregnancy wasn't ectopic. There is another ultrasound. Another vial of blood gets taken away. Eventually a doctor with a fatherly Irish face gives me the go-ahead to fly.

Next thing I know, I'm strapped into a window seat, listening to the roar of the jet engines as I angle up and heave off in the direction of my story's beginning.

Do I feel better about everything that's happened? Not even close.

But there's nothing to be done. There's no immediate way to improve the situation with my family. I can only take some solace in the fact that, having done what I can to express myself honestly, I'm hurling toward something completely foreign. The next few months promise a home I've never seen, a language I don't yet know, a relationship that will continue to change and reveal itself.

I feel free to experience things with an open heart. I remember an interview I'd once read with Virginia Satir in which she said: "Do you know what makes it possible for me to trust the unknown? Because I've got eyes, ears, skin. I can talk, I can move, I can feel, and I can think. And that's not going to change when I go into a new context. . . . I can move anywhere. Why not? . . . I never have to say yes when I feel no. I never have to say no when I feel yes."

I felt confident that I'll be okay just as long as I remain firmly rooted in the present, in touch with my surroundings and aware of my emotions.

——

In the two weeks that follow I feel as raw as an oyster on a half shell. I recall it the way I remember early childhood memories: as snatches of images with little context. From today's vantage, I can't figure out what gives them their small, brilliant power. I can only remember with a kind of choppy chronology:

Lying on the bed in the guest bedroom in my future in-laws' house in the Cotswolds. Eamon is curled up beside me, my head on his shoulder and his legs entwined with mine, while a thunderstorm flashes silver through the window. "You've been so strong," he says. "I can't believe how strong you've been. It's all right if you want to go to pieces now."

Another night, I am standing on the seafront in Brighton, wearing a short, buttery dress that still bears the wrinkles of my suitcase. It's night. It's my birthday. My hair beats wildly against my face in the wind. I'm laughing for the first time in weeks as I tell Eamon about the way I'd come down to the pier to ride the Spinball Whizzer after our midnight argument. "It was a stupid fight," he says. "That's all. Just a stupid fight." In some ways it *was* just a fight (not the last word in our relationship, as I'd imagined in the morning that followed), but it was also the catalyst for what became a year of discovery.

Eamon's solo tour becomes our road trip for two. I go along, tracing our route in the *AA Road Atlas*, "PopMaster" playing on the radio in the background. I wade through the muddy expanses of outdoor music festivals. I work on my book in the graffitied dressing rooms of nightclubs. And every day, from the rolled-down window of our tenacious Ford, I watch the country reveal itself to me—accent by accent and city by village—like beautiful, green glass beads on a string.

It seems fitting that the idea of "home" is fluid during this emotional transition. Together, Eamon and I live like carnival geeks, or gypsies, or old-timey actors in a traveling theater troupe roving the countryside in a clapboard wagon. On the road, we're truly able to build our life together from scratch. There are no old behaviors, no bad habits. Neither of us has a favorite armchair, a fixed morning routine, or a designated side of the bed. Most nights we don't even *have* a bed. We make do with futons, couches, car seats, or bundles of bedsheets on a friend's living room floor.

It hardly matters that we don't have a permanent mailing address. If we have each other to confide in, we are home, and so home becomes the first sunny spring day in Glasgow, or the crypt room in London's Sir John Soane's Museum, where we duck inside to dodge an afternoon drizzle, or Old Wardour, the ruined castle in Wiltshire, where we stop the car to stretch our legs and rove the tragic, crumbling towers.

It's a lonely time too.

G. Stanley Hall once described "a well-poised lady, so sweet-tempered that everybody imposed on her." One day, at the age of twenty-three, this woman "had her first ebullition of temper and went about to her college mates telling them plainly what she thought of them, and went home rested and happy, full of the peace that passeth understanding." Although my situation resembles hers, I don't share this woman's contented serenity. I frequently cry in the beds of Travelodges, thinking about the weekend of my miscarriage. And the more I come to think of Eamon and my future in-laws as family, the more I'm aware of the unresolved problems in my natural-born one. I'm in contact with my father occasionally, my mother rarely, my sister not at all.

There's a point that summer when I attempt to reach my sister by e-mail:

I'd really like to make an effort to talk about these things. I know you're still upset, but because I hear this only via second and third sources, I have to piece together the hows and whys on my own. If I knew how things looked from your end, I might be better able to make it right. I really need you to try to articulate things. If you're pissed off at me, that's all right—just explain it to me. Conflict, I see now, is nothing to be scared of; it helps move stuff around. Please, let's talk or even fight this out if we have to so we can fully move on.

She doesn't write back for over a week, and, even then, all she has to say on the subject is: "Honestly, I really would rather not mention the whole thing again. I know you're hoping to talk everything out, but I would rather we just let it be."

I let it be. Or rather, I let *her* be. Whenever I think of the e-mail, the Beatles song tumbles sarcastically through my head: "She wants me to let it be?" I tell Eamon. "Fine. Think of me as Paul Fucking McCartney."

Another memory:

Eamon and I are weaving through a thatch-roofed village in Dorset, watching the hedgerows slide past the car's open window. We are taking in the rippling fields of cuckoo flower and bluebell, the sun-streaked forests of oak, the arched stone bridges, the streams lined with wood garlic flowering in snowy bursts. It's all preposterously picturesque. So beautiful it's almost harrowing. My eyes begin to fill and the scenery loses focus. These days, there's a limit to my happiness. There's a threshold that I cannot cross given the stony silence between me and my family.

In the same memory, I tell Eamon that I don't know if I have the nerve to write about my family, no matter how relevant it is to my book. "I know I can't speak about my anger honestly if I leave them out," I say. Which is more uncomfortable? More impossible? Taking it all back? Can I return to a world in which I assume whatever form they require of me? In which I cast my personal feelings aside and say whatever I needed to say in order to be accepted as a Zailckas? Or is it a lesser agony to plow onward? Defend the small territory that I've bloodied myself for?

Can I ever imagine myself acknowledging—on paper, in a most undeniable way—that even though I was materially provided for as a kid, I hadn't always felt emotionally supported? How to say that love has always felt conditional? That for as long as I can remember I've felt like I've had to compromise my feelings, my fabric, my very human nature, in order to prevent my ties from being cut, the earth from rumbling, my family home from buckling and falling away?

Maybe it's not admitting these things to a reader that frightens me. Maybe what scares me is acknowledging them in print to myself.

I tell him I've painted (or more accurately, *written*) myself into a corner. Loneliness awaits me at either juncture. I can be crawling and agreeable, aware that my family welcomes only the phony, stony me, or I can be obstinate, which will most likely result in my being iced out altogether.

Eamon reaches his left hand across the gearshift to squeeze my fingers. When he glances at me, his look is deep, warm, sad, filled with love. "I want you to know you can write about me," he says.

"And when I've made you angry—you can write about that too. I don't mind. It's important to you."

I feel awed by this gesture. Touched by the accuracy with which he sees straight through to the molten core of me. It doesn't make up for the essential loneliness of my revelation. But then, it shouldn't have to.

44

The time comes to move to Paris.

On an afternoon in late May, Eamon and I exit the Gare du Nord and stand, smoking and sweating, on the Boulevard de Strasbourg, taking in the scalloped red awnings of the tourist cafés, soaking up the pink flush of the afternoon light and listening to the traffic scream at the top of its lungs. We feel bullied by our suitcases. We are half deafened by the station's yak and blather. But, as we climb into a taxi, we are grinning too. Accordion music plays in our heads. We are quietly tickled when the pop-eyed driver calls us Monsieur and Madame.

Our excitement mounts as we pass along rue du Faubourg Saint-Martin, where we register *le petit* scooters, the carved wooden doors, the sapphire signs announcing the names of the boulevards. There are the *tabacs*, the *fleuristes*, the *boulangeries*! Dear God, so many *boulangeries*! Each beckoning like Henry Miller's bordellos. The windows: parading *pain polkas* like heavy, doughy *seins* and their pale gold *moules* like plump, naked haunches. Rolling down the windows, and sniffing the smell of cooling baguettes, it dawns on me how much the phrase "bread baking" sounds like "lovemaking."

The city is electric. It's like New York, only less clenched and self-loathing. Paris seems like Manhattan's prettier, prouder, and sluttier older sister. It's more in love with its own voice and the curves of its own figure. It's New York if New York's pleasures weren't guilty.

We aren't staying in Paris proper. The cab keeps hurtling along the Avenue Jean Jaurès, past Le Pré-Saint-Gervais, through Pantin, until we arrive in a neighborhood of empty lots and industrial parks, where dogs bark behind barbed wire and morose *grandmères* drag shopping carts full of canned goods onto groaning city buses.

Dread flogs us as the cab pulls away, leaving us standing with our suitcases at the door of a quiet warehouse. "Is this home?" we whisper. "Is it safe? Was this a terrible mistake?" We exchange reassuring words. We ring the bell twice but there is no answer.

Just when our misgivings are turning into full-fledged panic, the lock clamors and the door swings open on Leon in all his bumbling, aging, beatniked glory. He's like a hip grizzly bear—and I wanted to hug him, even if he might bite.

As we're saying our *bonjours*, Leon wipes his hands on his barrel chest and claws his long, salt-and-pepper hair out of his face. He has dark, woolly eyebrows, full lips that end in a sarcastic curl, and glittering eyes that hint at younger days as a lothario. Some spill has occurred, soaking one corner of his black T-shirt. His jeans end at bare feet and hairy toes.

Leon's English, as he puts it, is "no good." So in the time that we share his house, he'll speak primarily to Eamon, who has enough French in his arsenal to keep up with Leon's boisterous rants and profanities. (One of Leon's favorite speeches begins: "Americans are stupid the way the French are stupid, but the British? The British are the ass.")

In the times when Leon is feeling loose and generous he'll try to include me with the aid of pantomime. A pinkie finger raised and wagged indicates espresso. A wet, razzing sound and a flick of his wrist means "It is shit, *phufft*, it's no good." When Leon's drunk, he'll lock his eyes on mine and address me in aggressive, badgering French, as though he doesn't truly believe I don't understand him or thinks I might if only I really try. In three months, the only conversations we'll ever manage in English will be about Henry Miller. More than once, Leon will tell me: "To truly understand our village you must read *Quiet Days in Clichy*. The people here are like that."

There is a lot of talk that summer about the differing natures of "the French," "the English," "the Belgian," "the Dutch," "the Chinese," New Yorkers, Parisians, the people in the village. It's not that our landlords are nationalists. Just the opposite. They are as transient as Eamon and me, and they've filled their home with subletters in order to finance their love of travel.

I call it their "house," but it's more like a compound: four small buildings huddled around a common outhouse and a small concrete courtyard, three of which they've converted from a factory, one of which used to be a church before they transformed it into a painting studio.

While we camp out in the main apartment, a Dutch girl named Marieke sublets a room on the far side of the courtyard. French Tibault sleeps in a loft above the reading nook and is often visited by Italian Riccarda. It seems like no coincidence that all of us have gravitated to this spot. Our village is Romainville—named for the Roma Gypsies who inhabited it—and we are accepted in the streets around town because we too are immigrants among outsiders.

Our landlady Anique is Belgian born, German raised, and French nationalized, and her side job as a flight attendant takes her to America weekly. She's a slight woman, a Dunhill smoker, a passionate speaker with a knack for languages, and the most generous woman this side of Mother Teresa.

Following a flight to the States, Anique's Lufthansa uniform is always washed and flapping on the clothesline on the terrace, and, for a few days, she wears an air of affable exhaustion—wandering the house in her bathrobe, chain-smoking through whatever cold she's picked up, hoarsely barking at Leon for forgetting something from the market. But as the week goes on, Anique gathers strength and becomes a whirlwind of sociability and artistic inspiration. It's not uncommon to see her still holding court among a group of poets, photographers, and painters at 3:00 A.M., singing along to Léo Ferré or crowing about something in French and then translating it into Italian or English for anyone who is listening from the other side of a language barrier.

It's Anique who first tunes me in to the differences between French and American expressions of anger. "You must get angry, Koren! You must! It is essential!" she says, as though my very life is hanging in the balance. "In France, if we are dissatisfied, we demonstrate! We are indignant! Maybe we are too quick to anger, but you Americans are too slow to it! You are dissatisfied in America, you blame yourselves instead of your government. You think the problem is yours alone. You become depressed! You become fat! You go *blaaah*." Here, she makes a catatonic face. While Leon's favorite speech is about Britain being the asshole of Europe, Anique is always referencing what she calls the "zombie people" that she sees during her frequent trips to Detroit—people she feels have anesthetized themselves instead of standing up to the U.S. government. I never find any sociological evidence to back up Anique's claim, only passages from French writers like Chamfort, who said that "[w]e should act more, think less, and stop watching ourselves live."

Although Alice is gone from my life, I don't stop thinking about her concept of blueprints. It's nice to live so intimately among Anique and Leon. Privately, they help me expand my ideas about what marriage can look like. As a couple, they are the life of the party. They are spectacular at living. They seem spectacular at loving.

If the mood strikes them, Anique and Leon also can argue like cats in a bag. After a couple of bottles of the South African wine Leon buys in bulk at the neighborhood Lidl, it's not uncommon to hear doors slam, saucers smash against walls, or the phrase *va t'empaler encule* ("go fuck yourself") ring out across the night. Their anger doesn't scare them, so it doesn't scare us. I, for one, am incredibly grateful to see firsthand what Alice has so often tried to convince me of: It's possible for a man and a woman to disagree and still adore and respect each other. "Quarrels in France strengthen a love affair, in America they end it," goes the quote from Ned Rorem, whose *Paris Diary* I devour during our months in Paris.

I realize how comfortable I've become with my emotions when I find out Anique thinks Eamon and I share the same kind of fire. "The two of you are just as crazy as we are!" Anique says one evening over dinner, giggling girlishly and grabbing my wrist.

A few nights earlier Eamon and I had had our most explosive fight since one year earlier in Brighton. It had begun with shattered glass. I'd make the mistake of closing—but not locking—a heavy window above our bathroom tub. (Our apartment was two blocks from the Canal de l'Ourcq and for weeks mosquitoes the size of hummingbirds had been making a slow family buffet of our faces.) Disastrously, the window's weight brought it crashing back open, where it shattered against the showerhead while Eamon was seated on the commode.

He'd been (rightfully) frightened. The shards were as long and sharp as kitchen knives, and everywhere. But, as soon as the danger passed, Eamon's fright erupted into outrage. He railed over my weeping apologies. He wouldn't let it go, not even after I swept up and accidentally cut myself on the glass. He wanted to know what was wrong with me. Did I not understand fucking physics? What kind of idiot did not understand that a window of that size could not simply *rest* in the frame?

When I'd cried that it was an accident, he'd said, "Big deal! Even accidents are somebody's fault! Aren't accidents still the result of *someone's* negligence? Isn't someone always clearly to blame?" When he wouldn't let up I'd finally started screaming about how he was a disdainful, snobby, audacious bully. I'd locked myself in the guest bedroom and hollered while he pounded on the door.

We'd kept the fight up for hours, until we collapsed in each other's arms in a state of teary exhaustion. The next morning, the incident was not too fresh to laugh about. We'd made eggs Benedict. We'd walked all the way to Jaurès—his arm around my waist and my head on his shoulder—and seen an English movie at the MK2.

———

I don't forget about healing aggravation. I am still learning how to be assertive—this, I figure, is the way around being aggressive—and I'm still not great at setting boundaries.

I think of the woman with the persistent fear of invasion, when I realize Anique and her friends come and go from our apartment at will. As the summer goes on, it's not uncommon to wake up on a Sunday morning and find a stranger sleeping in our downstairs guest room. Nor is it unusual for small objects—DVDs, juice glasses, paintings—to mysteriously disappear from our apartment and turn up in other parts of the house. Sometimes, I return from a trip into town to find an ashtray glutted with someone else's cigarettes and a carton of juice sitting out on the counter.

As the summer goes on, more intruders emerge. Of the creepy-crawly variety: Not only do we have mosquitoes, but also spiders the size of the palm of my hand and one fat, aristocratic-looking rat. There are also strange men who smell of desperation or violence: a gangster, maybe, followed by a homeless psychotic, his hair sweaty and his face lined with dirt. They turn up at the front door, saying things not even Eamon can understand. *Pardon!* We shout at the ones who try to shoulder inside. *C'est* ma *maison!* ("This is *my* house!") It's like the situation with the brokers is playing on. We usually slam the door, turn the lock, and watch from the roof as our uninvited guests walk reluctantly away. Privately I wonder if the universe is hell-bent on provoking me, as though training me to put my foot down.

———

One night, Eamon reveals a bit of news. We are standing in the kitchen, frying up a whole trout from our village market for dinner (the fish vendor guts the critters but leaves on the heads, so we have to decapitate them while they stare back accusingly).

He says his sister-in-law is pregnant.

It's no real surprise—it's been well known that she and his brother have been planning for a third—but the announcement still hits me like a bludgeon. My heart sinks. If I'd been holding something, it would have slipped through my fingers. I'm overcome by a feeling of injustice, my knees shaking. I need to know how pregnant she is. When the baby is due. I work out that she'd been pregnant when I was, and it makes me feel even more humiliated, more antagonized, more personally *wronged* by the fact of our miscarriage. My eyes fill. I don't know where to direct my anger, but I'm furious.

Eamon catches me in a hug before the force of the feeling brings me to the floor. I sob audibly. I cry so hard my skeleton rattles. "I know," Eamon says, rocking me. "I know. We'll have our time. Our time will come."

———

Here, I am forced to make an unsavory confession. During my time in Paris, I've come to hate pregnant women with a strength and viciousness that frightens me. I find myself glaring at their full, porcine bellies whenever I sit in a seat opposite them on the metro. I feel myself actively loathing their peachy glows, their self-contented fatigue, their proud belly buttons pushing up through the fabric of their shirts.

Sometimes I catch myself actively wishing them ill. I curse them with stretch marks, hemorrhoids, and varicose veins. I pray they have back labor. I hope their breasts fall to their kneecaps. I hope their children grow up to be criminals.

I tell no one about this anger—it's shocking and antisocial—but when Eamon is away playing music festivals, I spend long nights on the Internet reading miscarriage message boards. There, thread after thread is devoted to green-eyed fury.

"My best friend is pregnant and I want to break every glass in my house."

"Everyone expects me to pick up and move on. They keep saying 'God knows best.' Screw them. Screw God. There is no bright side to this."

"Yesterday was my due date and my husband actually asked me why I was upset. He doesn't understand me. He doesn't give a shit. I am completely alone."

"I spent the night on the beach alone with misoprostol in my hand

and a case of wine beside me. This, has been the most traumatic experience of my life."

   These forums are filled with women subverting their anger too.
They wonder aloud whether they've caused their own miscarriages. "Was it when I had an argument with my husband and was
overwhelmed by stress?" I identify with these women the most. "My
baby is dead," they write. "I killed my baby."

   I secretly count myself among the women who hold themselves
to blame. As I work on my book, I go back and review some homeopathy Web sites, looking up the ailments Staphysagria is purport-
edly used to treat. On one list, in between "cystitis" and "colic," are
the words "miscarriage due to anger."

45

As my wedding nears, I grow panicked to the point of distraction. I
can't sleep. I can't touch the baguettes Eamon spoons with canned
tuna, homemade mayo, and sliced green olives. It's not that I'm nervous about committing my life to Eamon or planning our tiny picnic
reception. I'm not even concerned about how I'm going to rally the
translator or pick up the *croquembouche traditionnel* from a patis-
serie in Les Lilas. (The baker can't speak English. I can't speak French.
We'd had to establish a bumbling common ground in rudimentary
Spanish.)

   I am terrified to see my parents for the first time since my miscarriage. They've agreed to come over for five days. During the first
night, they will meet my in-laws. During the second, they will join
us on our respective hen and stag nights. On the third day, they'll
help us cook, decorate, and prepare for the wedding. Finally, there
will be the ceremony, followed by a day to themselves in Paris, where
they can walk hand in hand along the Seine and celebrate their
wedding anniversary.

My sister isn't joining them. This causes me a considerable head full of steam. Her excuse (she didn't apply for Riley's passport) seems flimsy, preventable, and passive-aggressive. She's known for months that our wedding would be in Paris. Besides, doesn't the passport office offer expedited service?

I'm also hurt that she doesn't break the news to me herself. I have to hear it from my mother, who seems to be waiting, just *waiting*, for me to call it bullshit so she might use the opportunity to remind me that I'm hysterical and self-centered. During this time my family often hints that it was selfish of me to get married abroad. They have no patience for my reasons: Britain is Eamon's, America is mine, France belongs to both of us.

On the afternoon of their arrival, my father is sweating like a field hand. Mother is complaining of blisters. They are both ticked off that our apartment is so far from the closest metro station.

Eamon and I hug them tentatively, already feeling as though we've done something wrong. Maybe we should have met them at the airport after all? Even if it meant missing the deliveries of the white roses and crepe paper bells, the paper doilies and plastic champagne flutes, the paper luminaries to fill with tea candles and weigh down with kitty litter.

For the remainder of the day, the tension is palpable.

My mother unpacks a suitcase full of small gifts she's brought for me. There are more paper goods for the reception. There are baseball hats for Eamon and me to wear on our bachelor and bachelorette nights (one reads BRIDE, the other GROOM). There's a pajama set she had bought for me at the mall. She seems to thrust each one at me tersely, a preemptive look of hurt on her face, as though she's already decided that I don't like or appreciate them.

The more I thank her, the more closed off she seems to get. "Sure," she says stiffly in reply. "Don't mention it." She perches on the edge of our sofa with her arms crossed and her foot pumping at the end of her crossed legs.

Later, when I ask her if something is wrong, if I've offended her in some way, she snaps back that she's fine. "Not *everything* is about *you*," she adds. This last part makes Eamon laugh nervously. Her demeanor sets me on edge. It makes me despondent. It cocks me like a revolver.

Eamon and my mom get into an argument over the window in the guest bedroom (she takes offense when he asks her to keep it closed and locked); all four of us trudge to Montmartre to meet Eamon's family at the apartment they've rented there for the weekend.

The first part of the evening goes well enough. Eamon and I, along with his youngest brother, Steve, sit back and watch our parents interact. Our fathers get along like long-lost fraternity brothers. Our smiling mothers share a sofa and chat brightly over glasses of Vouvray. We then climb to the top tier of Sacré-Coeur (Paris's very own "wedding cake" basilica) and take snapshots of one another, a sea of tourists and glowing roofs in the background. From there, we have steak au poivre at Chartier, a cheap, roaring *cantine* near the Musée Grévin with soaring ceilings and a no-nonsense army of middle-age waiters.

But the night takes a turn. We take a painfully long walk to a bar near Notre Dame. My mother seems sulky and irritated by the lightning-fast pace with which my father is walking. And I feel myself growing annoyed with both of them. Later, when I go over the evening's photos, I'll see that old deadened quality in my eyes (the look of the computer). I still want to change them. I am thinking to myself, *Why can't we just try to celebrate? Why can't we ever seem to enjoy one another's company?*

———

Things get worse the next day at my hen party. While Eamon spends his last day of so-called freedom go-karting, boozing, and getting hazed by his brothers, I spend mine at the St. Ouen Flea Market with our mothers and my future sister-in-law, Rachel, who arrives that morning looking roundly and happily six months along.

When we stop for croque madames, my mother spends the entire lunch talking about babies, specifically Riley. Is she really trying to be hurtful? Probably not. But I still ache over my miscarriage and the family breakdown that surrounded it. Her timing seems cruel. As she quizzes Rachel all about when and how she introduced solid food to her kids, set a nap schedule, dealt with colic, and so on, I think to myself, *If a stranger happened upon our conversation right now, they might think it's a baby shower as opposed to a bridal shower.* I sit silently, biting my lips and fighting back tears, my fingers clenched clawlike against my thigh.

From Riley, the conversation naturally veers toward my sister.

My future mother-in-law makes some innocuous remark about how it's a shame that my sister isn't there to join us.

Rachel, who hasn't heard the story, asks why not.

And my mother, losing her chatty air, grows visibly defensive. She puts a fist to her mouth. Her spine straightens against her chair. She gives a combative speech about how my sister is not outlandish in her reluctance "to *cross an ocean* with a seven-month-old baby." At the end, she throws her paper napkin onto the table and announces at high volume, "Now, if you don't mind—that is, if no one else has any other questions about my youngest daughter—I'd prefer not to talk any more about her not being here."

The wind is gone from my sails. I want the rest of the day—no, the rest of the weekend—to be over as quickly as possible. I wish I could skip the ceremony and go straight to being married. I understand now why my sister eloped. I suddenly want to celebrate this rite with Eamon alone.

"Are you feeling broody?" Rachel asks later, as we walk around the Latin Quarter.

For a moment, I'm startled. Unacquainted with the British definition of "broody" ("wanting kids"), I assume she's asking me if I'm sulky and angry ("brooding") with my mother, who is walking somewhere behind us. "How do you mean?" I ask skittishly.

"Oh, I just mean to ask if you and Eamon are thinking you'd like to have a baby soon."

The question hits me in the underbelly, but it's still easier to talk about than my present relationship with my mom. With the one subject, I can tell Rachel the truth (Eamon and I have been pregnant already), but with the other I might have found it easier to feign hunky-dory. I might have even betrayed my feelings by defending my mother's demeanor, saying something about her sensitive nature.

———

How is it possible to feel protective of my mother and, at the same time, deeply furious with her? Later in the subway, she corners me while Rachel and my mother-in-law stand in line for metro tickets.

"What did you say to them?" she asks me, her face flushed from the crowd and the heat of the day.

"What do you mean, what did I say to them?"

"It's just the questions they were asking earlier. Did you tell them? Do they know about your miscarriage?"

I don't have time to ask her to elaborate. (Does she mean to ask if they know I've had one? If they know about the family apocalypse that accompanied it?) Rachel comes pushing her little belly through the turnstile and jaunts brightly toward us. "They know," I say cryptically, with narrowed eyes. I add cruelly, "*Everybody* knows."

Eating ice cream cones later on Île St.-Louis, the conversation finally turns to the wedding, with everyone giving me marriage advice. My mother claims the "itch" didn't just happen on the seventh year, but also on the fourteenth, the twenty-first, the twenty-eighth, and so on. Rachel claims the key to happily-ever-after is accepting that there will be times when Eamon and I will be closer than others: "You have to trust your relationship enough to give each other space from time to time. Like an accordion, you'll constantly be moving apart from one another and then coming back together."

I recount the story of our engagement for Rachel, because she's never heard it told before. When I'm finished, she turns and asks my mother, "Were you incredibly excited when you heard Eamon had proposed?"

My mother's face grows tight. She leans back on the stone wall where we're sitting above the Seine and dabs her mouth with her napkin. "To be incredibly honest, I had my reservations," she says. "As far as I was concerned, he didn't have a good track record. After last summer—"

I don't just interrupt, I combust. "We're not talking about any of that this weekend!" I shout, while I stare downward at my dusty, sandaled feet. Some shame still keeps me from making eye contact with her when I'm angry. "It's my wedding, and I'd like that one demand met."

When I look up, Rachel and my mother-in-law have both taken a sudden, embarrassed interest in the river beneath us.

My mother's mouth is open, although she seems to be having a hard time finding the breath to form words. She's gone directly from looking like she's ready to storm Versailles to looking like she's going to cry.

There. I've set a boundary. Only I don't feel empowered. I feel horrifically guilty.

Over dinner at the Pink Flamingo, a pizzeria where all the pies are named after "inspirational" hacks, I gaze at her over the black-and-white checkerboard table. I watch her pick over her slice of "Basquiat" and try to gauge how deeply she hates me.

After dinner, on the bank of Canal Saint-Martin, I feel tremendously wicked when she confesses, with considerable embarrassment, to not knowing how to pop the cork off a bottle of champagne. Under the blustering and blaming, she is naïve, as innocent as a kid. I watch Rachel teach her how, with the cheap bottle from a nearby grocery, and feel a flush of tenderness. Holding it as far away from her body as possible, my frightened mom shrieks when the cork cracks like a gunshot, sails upward in a high, wide arch, and plummets (to the irritation of a group of French teenagers) down into the black, glassy water.

Saying good-bye to the rest of the "hens," Mom and I take the metro home from Jaurès and then the bus from the Raymond Queneau station. On average, she drinks no more than three times a year, and after two glasses of bubbly she's as exposed and helpless as a little girl—just the way she had been in my dream.

"You hate me!" she sobs, as we grope our way along the dark, rank streets toward my apartment.

Beneath the light of the moon, bits of glass glimmer on the asphalt. From far off, probably the nearby rue de Noisy, comes the pumping baritone of a car stereo.

I take a deep, exasperated breath. "I don't hate you," I say, meaning it.

"Fine then, you're still mad at me! That's fine! Sometime down the line, you'll get over what happened the last time I saw you. You'll forgive me, and when that happens—"

I stop and turn to look at her. It's after midnight. I'm exhausted. Even though her voice has lost the shrill quality it's had all afternoon, she's still talking loud enough to wake the burly French neighbors. "Look, Mom," I say. "It's over, okay? It's fine. I forgive you. See?"

"No you don't!"

"Listen to me: I forgive you for that night! If you're still angry with me, that feeling's yours! *You* own it! Don't go pinning it on me!"

I'm not lying. It isn't the night of my miscarriage that I want to punish her for. I really want her to apologize for the years in my childhood when I'd never had a mother who was available to me—at least not when I was angry, frightened, disappointed, flailing, failing. I want her to understand that, even as a toddler, I'd revealed only what she expected of me and numbed out a part of myself because it jeopardized her comfort.

While I'm at it, I want her to say that she's sorry for making me feel like little more than a hand mirror casting her reflection. I want her to know that I've spent my whole life the same way I spent my hen night: monitoring her moods, accepting responsibility for them, letting her digs slide, allowing the weight of her criticisms to slowly accumulate until recently, when I managed to fly magnificently off the handle.

I know these are a child's demands, but I'd never been able to acknowledge them as a kid. Helpfulness. Compliance. Competence. Stoicism. These are the traits that always spared me from my mother's wrath when I was a little girl. The word "conscientious" appears again and again on my grade-school report cards. Even standing three feet tall in Stride Rite Mary Janes, the image I gave off was serious, meticulous, controlled, particular. But I was also lonely.

"I know I talk about Riley too much!" my mom wails. "But she's all I have! You've been here! We've hardly spoken in months!"

As I stand in the street, looking into my mother's bewildered face and feeling my synapses fire wildly, it occurs to me that my worst fear—the worry that if I get angry my mother will leave me—already happened twenty-five years ago. And whereas she used to hold me at a distance, I now hold her that way. She's trying to find a way to be meaningful to me, but she doesn't feel valued by me either. She doesn't really trust that I care about her, and the result has made her self-protective, even combative.

Virginia Satir believed all feelings (even fear, humiliation, anger, helplessness, and hopelessness) are the ready-made bases for our connection to all other human beings, and as long as I keep those emotions to myself I'll never know my mother on an equal footing (the very thing I wanted in that long-ago dream).

46

I wish I could say that relations with my mother improved instantly following that private revelation. But the next day was even more strained.

There's an incident with Eamon. Saying how happy he is to join our family, he leans forward to give her a hug and a kiss on the cheek. She does not, shall we say, return the sentiment. Instead, she pushes him away with the heel of her hand and says in the biting tone she tries to pass off as a joke: "Uh-uh. No. Sorry, Eamon. We're not that close. We don't have that kind of relationship."

Moments later, while we wait at the bus stop with my father (Mom has opted out of our rehearsal dinner, saying her stomach aches), Eamon paces the sidewalk. He is hunched and chain-smoking, flexing the fingers of his free hand and working his jaw.

"You don't really expect that kind of attitude from a grown woman!" he vents, not listening for an answer. "It's the night before our wedding. As of tomorrow, we will be in each other's lives forever. *Forever!* Does she realize that? Why would she make things more uncomfortable than they need to be?"

Passing headlights fan over us. I pull him off his circuitous course and squeeze him with all my might. But I don't apologize for her. I do not make excuses the way I might have once.

My father, on the other hand, grows nervous. His mouth turns sad. "Look," he says to Eamon. "You don't know her very well. She doesn't mean anything by it. She has Sicilian blood in her."

Standing there, in the approaching dusk amid the smother of exhaust from the rue de Noisy, I realize where my anger for my father comes from. When I was a child, his incessant business trips left me home alone with my mom. When I was a teenager, he'd blamed me for every argument that my mom and I ever had ("Look at how you've made your mother feel" was never far from his lips). As an adult, I couldn't speak to (or about) my mother honestly without him butting in to shield her like a human bunker.

I want to hold this against him, to make him understand how hopeless I felt growing up without an ally. But then, in an instant, when I glance back to my adult ally—Eamon, the man I've chosen as my life partner, the person I feel my own deep drive to protect—an image comes to me in a searing, black-and-white flash.

I see a photo of my mom and dad cutting the cake on their own wedding day. I see his giddy smile glittering through his beard. I remember her French braid draped over one shoulder of her peasant-sleeved dress. Less than a week after exchanging rings, they'd climbed into a blue VW bus with a broken heater and headed for my father's Michigan graduate school.

Something about seeing them helps me reframe the ideas (the blueprint) that I have about my dad. Time was, he hadn't had two nickels to rub together, but he had set out to protect my heartsick mother and lighten her load. Just as my uncle Dave, at sixteen, had vowed to make Jo-Jo's birthday a magical thing, every year, because her own parents (and my mother's) had been too poor, ignorant, and rejecting to acknowledge it with so much as a Sara Lee cake. All at once, the grudge that's spent years nipping at me is pushed aside by more overwhelming emotions: suffocating sorrow and love in a great, roaring gush. Some hurt of his own must have made my father understand my mother and devote his life to being her convoy.

———

On the morning of my wedding, I awake to thunderclouds. No raindrops have yet hit the windows, but there is a sticky closeness to the atmosphere and a dusky gray fog hanging around. It's 4:45 A.M. Filled with anxious energy, I can't seem to go back to sleep. I wrap myself in one of Anique's infinite number of waffle spa robes and walk with light steps downstairs to the kitchen to busy my hands preparing a few more trays of hors d'oeuvres.

Grabbing the large slab cutting board, I set to work slicing Bosc pears, setting them with domino-size hunks of Roquefort and binding them in ribbons of prosciutto.

I'm marrying my heart's greatest pleasure, the one true miracle of my life so far. I think of all his quirks and peculiarities, the things I never want to live without: Eamon laughing to himself while he reads the newspaper; Eamon in the morning, still wet from the shower, always giving me a hug before he starts his day. I am grateful for the way he'd woken me up, brought me back to life and back to the present.

Like Bulgakov's Margarita, I find it impossible to return to the way I had been (detached, sedated) before he dropped into my life. How ironic it is that *The Master and Margarita* was the first book we had ever read together, discussing it in letters long before we ever met face-to-face. I had been on a plane to Texas, bucking in turbulence, when I'd come to the part where Margarita—emboldened by love and made wicked by decades of bottled-up grief—smashes out half the windows in Moscow. Tears had slid down my face. I'd been both thankful and fearful, suspecting even then that I'd met my match and we might just liberate each other. What a strange coincidence that Eamon, like Ivan, had been asking himself how long he should go on writing his several poems (or songs, as it were) a year. We believed in each other. In bringing emotion into each other's lives, we brought spontaneity and, in turn, inspiration.

My parents wake up a little later, eager to help me.

My father offers to go pick up a dozen fresh baguettes for the reception.

My mother helps me tie my grandmother's deco broach into the bouquet we make from two dozen bunches of plain white roses. There's still static between us, something left over from the night of my hen party. I am guarded and clumsy around her. I brace for impact, like I'm waiting for the next confrontation.

It happens in the upstairs bedroom, which is lofted and connected to the kitchen by a precarious wooden ladder. I am up there, fully dressed in the designer sample I had found at a charity bridal boutique in New York. Its chiffon is ripe for makeup stains and its train is in a puddle behind me. I am fiddling in the mirror, noticing the way my left eye is red and irritated from a stray speck of eyeliner, and I am beginning to doubt the way I've decided to let my hair fall, in a wild mane of waves down my back.

With my dad still out buying bread, my mom scales the ladder for company. Seeing me fully dressed for the first time, she makes no comment at all. It's not the moment that you see in the movies, when the mother of the bride gasps approvingly.

As my mother remembers it, I was in a robe, not my dress. She also says she repeatedly told me how beautiful I looked at other points during the day. All I know is, in that moment, I was craving some approval that she would not give me. I knew her cues and was convinced that something about the way I looked was displeasing her. *Homeopathic Psychology* says: "With the Sweet Staphysagria . . . anger and resentment are repressed so completely they are no longer felt and their place is taken by a fear of displeasing the parents." At the heart of the matter, I nearly loved my mother *too* much and craved her approval too deeply. That neediness wasn't just alienating me from my emotions and preventing me from getting on with the rest of my life, it was also ruining my relationship with her.

"What?" I ask with exasperation. "What's wrong? Does this not look okay? It's getting late. I don't have time to change anything."

"Nothing's wrong," she says. "Everything looks fine. Looks good."

I grit my teeth. "Look," I say, my voice a little too harsh. "Can you not just stand there, saying nothing? You're making me nervous."

"Fine!" she trills, throwing up her hands. "I'll leave!" She turns with such fury that she twists an ankle, trips on the edge of her kitten-heeled shoe, and goes tumbling to the floor. A few more inches and she would have rolled headfirst down the top of the ladder and fallen the six feet to the kitchen.

She screams.

I scream.

I am irrationally furious. It's exactly like that time she smashed the crystal bowl and turned her hand into carpaccio. All my life, in the rare moments when I shouted or got angry with her, she immediately got sick or got injured.

"What's wrong with you?" I shout, while I take her arm and heave her up from the floor. "Don't you know how to walk in heels? What are you doing? Why did you do that?" I'm honestly expecting an answer.

"I don't know!" she shouts. "I slipped! I'm old!" As though she were not fifty but eighty.

———

Everything's a mess. It's 10:15 A.M. Anique has arranged for a cab to pick us up and take us up the hill to the *mairie* at 10:30 A.M. Eamon and I are getting married at 11:00, and my father, who left for the *boulangerie* over two hours ago, still hasn't come back with the bread.

"Where is he?" I bark at my mother, who is standing by the kitchen sink with her arms crossed, giving me a subtle version of the silent treatment.

In my head I am playing out various scenarios in which my father's been struck dead crossing the rue de Noisy, where there always seems to be gangsters flooring stolen cars or fourteen-year-old boys on motor bikes, popping wheelies and hollering *"putain!"* to every woman they pass on the street. Every abandonment fear plays out in my head. I wonder if I'm experiencing that old cliché: Maybe he's gone out for Gauloises and won't ever come back.

My head is swirling like a mechanical meat separator—all these thoughts flying around like revolting bits of gizzard and entrails—when I suddenly hear a loud smacking sound.

"What was that noise?" I ask aloud.

My mother shrugs her shoulders.

We check to make sure it wasn't the sound of my father knocking at the door. We nose around in the bedrooms to make sure a window hasn't blown open. We look in the bathroom to see if a bottle slipped off the countertop and shattered. Ten minutes later, when I've all but forgotten about the noise, I discover what caused it.

Instead of having a wedding cake, Eamon and I elected to buy a *croquembouche*—a tower of profiteroles that the French typically serve on special occasions such as weddings and baptisms. Like a traditional American wedding cake, it is topped with figurines of a miniature bride and groom. Unlike a traditional wedding cake, the whole thing is shellacked with gallons of caramelized sugar, which cements the whole soaring pyramid in place.

We had no idea how to store the strange, foreign confectionary until the afternoon of the wedding. So Eamon and I followed suggestions we had found on the Internet: We "wrapped it loosely in tinfoil and left it out on the counter."

Only we hadn't factored in the humidity. Even though it's the first of September, the weather is still muggy enough to have melted the caramelized sugar down to the thick, sticky consistency of honey. A landslide has occurred, causing the whole structure to sway, top-heavy, and break apart in the middle. This alone wouldn't be so ominously traumatic. But the cracking sound I heard earlier was the sound of the miniature bride's head snapping off at the neck. Where she once gazed adoringly at her husband, she now stands holding her bouquet against her virginal white dress: decapitated.

If it's an omen, it's not subtle. I pinch the bride's bitty head between my index finger and my thumb. I look into her black pinpoint eyes.

My mother is not so cruel as to laugh openly. Biting her lips and trying not to smile, she asks, "Maybe we can tape it back on?"

I erupt into hysterical tears, then hysterical laughter. Then I start crying again. At that very moment, there's the sound of a key in the lock, and my father humps in, breathless, sweating along his hairline and swinging a garbage-size bag filled with *pain de campagne*.

"Holy shit!" he says. "Holy shit, I got lost on the way home from the Atac! I couldn't figure out how to get back and no one that I asked spoke English!"

Atac is a supermarket. It's over three miles away from our house, at the end of a winding maze of unmarked streets and tiny alleyways. It's taken Eamon and I one whole month of living in Romainville to reliably figure out how to get there and back on foot. As a general rule, we try to limit our trips there to times when Leon is going too and Eamon can drive us all in his car. (Leon's license has been suspended after innumerable driving violations. So he can only sit in the passenger seat, covering his eyes with his big hairy hands and screaming at Eamon, "*S'il te plaît!* Please! Drive the car on the right, not the left! You are not in England anymore, you are in *France!*")

"Atac?!" I shout at Dad. "You went to Atac?! I thought you had gone to the bread shop around the corner! The one that's literally thirty paces away!"

Dad's face sinks as though he has no idea there is a *boulangerie* around the corner. As though we haven't waited directly in front of it every time we've taken the bus. As though I've never pointed it out to him or told him about the way the owner always says *bonjour, cuistot* ("hello, cook") whenever Eamon walks in, because his arms are usually laden with ingredients for soup—giant stalks of celery or bundles of leeks.

I say, "The taxi's going to be here any minute."

Dad flings the bread on the counter and takes off running to the closet for his suit bag.

"Don't worry," my mom says. "It will only take him two minutes. Men don't need more time than that to get ready. You'll see. He's very fast."

———

Barbara Jo Brothers, who has spent a good deal of time writing about Virginia Satir's family reconstructions, says the most powerful part of the process happens when the person exploring her family tree "gives a deep unconscious 'yes' to her roots." "In doing this, the Explorer becomes full," Brothers writes. "The Explorer completes the self. By saying yes to one's root system, rather than denying or opposing, increases self-esteem. . . . This involves a dramatic shift in one's self-identity."

Minutes later, as I sit in the passenger seat of the taxi, my bouquet in my lap and my dress hiked up between my knees, I turn to glance at the backseat and feel "yes" in a strong sudden swell. My mother, wearing too much lipstick, is pulling her hat away from her head with one finger and tucking her hair beneath the brim with another; the gesture looks haughty at first glance, but really it's self-conscious. My father, trying to look relaxed and unaffected, with one elbow rested on the open window, is actually bursting with a boyish excitement to count Eamon's brothers as kin. Yes, this is my family. Yes, we are bad at special occasions. Sure, we have our blemishes: Within the confines of our family, we're crude communicators; we don't always trust one another; we don't always trust ourselves. But every now and again there is comedy in our shortcomings. Our flaws make us human; our humanity means our days together are numbered; and the brevity of our time together is what makes it so very special.

Years earlier, back when I first began thinking I might like to write a book about anger, my friend and yoga teacher Rolf shared his philosophy on the subject. Whenever we spoke about what I was writing, he liked to say, "Koren, just remember, you can't blame the bear." This was shorthand for a longer conversation in which he'd asked me the rather disturbing question: "Would you be angry at a bear if it mauled you?" I'd responded by saying something like, I suppose I would be a bit pissed off if I ever came to and found a brown bear eating my entrails, but no, I don't know that I'd blame the bear in specific. Rolf had gone on to ask: "You wouldn't blame the bear because it's a wild animal, right? And that's what wild animals do. So why, for instance, would you blame your parents for failing you when you know all human beings are flawed?" Try as I did, I've never really found a decent retort. I know it's like expecting a grizzly to sit down over espresso and do my taxes, but I want my family to be a place of nourishment and support, unfailingly and always.

As we drive up the steep hill to the village's *mairie*, I don't just think of Rolf and his bear; my thoughts also drift back to the wall, the image I used when trying to describe to Alice how unreceptive and immovable my family felt to me. Like most riddles, the solution is subversively easy: Faced with a force I can't budge (my family), I have to alter my course. I owe an apology to the Buddhists. How right they were when they said, "If you want to change your life, simply change your perspective."

While it's normal to want my parents' acceptance, to still be striving for it as an adult is beyond futile. It's detrimental, childish. Once when a questioner came to Sri Nisargadatta Maharaj seeking advice about how to handle his difficult relationship with his mother, the Indian guru told him:

> *But, does love make you always happy? Is not the association of love with happiness a rather early infantile stage? When the beloved suffers, don't you suffer too?. . . You sought the love of your mother, because you loved her. She could not stop you. It is your complete ignorance of yourself that covered up your love and happiness and made you seek for what you had never lost.*

Constantly craving my family's approval made me furious. It made me blind to the present. It's made me miss out on life.

In all my reading of Satir, I've never truly registered a core theme: The only control a person has is over herself, her anger, her emotions, her love. I can't decide how my family relates to me, I can only control when and how I react. Now that I've finally allowed myself to experience all the abandonment and dejection I never really let myself feel as a kid, I can't hold them responsible for the way I handle my emotions as an adult. Satir wrote, "I own what comes out of me—my words, thoughts, body movement, my deeds. I might have been influenced by you, but I made the decision to act on that influence, so that part is my show completely." Why had I begun my "show"—my anger book—to begin with?

Not because I wanted to change Eamon or my sister or my

parents, but because I needed to change the way I related to them and other people. In reclaiming my anger I could reclaim my life and my humanity.

In Brighton, my fight with Eamon had snapped me awake. Before that I had been stumbling around in an eerie and detached mood much like the Vikings once described as "fey." Today, we know "fey" to mean effeminate, but in Lee Sandlin's article "Losing the War," which contains chilling descriptions of the phenomenon, he says the word meant "doomed" in Old Norse. Sandlin goes on to say it was a "transcendental despair" that came over some soldiers in battle—dread and acquiescence. American reporter Tom Lea describes a fey World War II soldier in the South Pacific's Battle of Peleliu, saying, "He seemed so quiet and empty and past all the small things a man could love or hate."

Incidentally, Sandlin says the Norse opposite of "fey" was *berserkergang* (from this we ultimately got "going berserk"). *Berserkergang*, which described a temporary insanity in Viking soldiers, was also a state I could relate to. In an article entitled "On Going Berserk," neurologist and psychiatrist Howard D. Fabing described berserk soldiers, saying:

> *This fury . . . occurred not only in the heat of battle, but also during laborious work. Men who were thus seized performed things which otherwise seemed impossible for human power. This condition . . . was connected to a great hotheadedness, which at last went over into a great rage, under which they howled as wild animals, bit the edge of their shields, and cut down everything they met without discriminating between friend or foe.*

———

In my earliest attempt to reconnect with my anger, I had flung it everywhere, attacking people wantonly and indiscriminately.

The remainder of my wedding is just as slapstick as the hours leading up to the ceremony. It's as clumsy as we are and, in that way, it's perfect.

At the *mairie*, Eamon and I sit together on a green silk love seat, tightly squeezing each other's hands. The translator, who has not even put on a dress shirt for the event—he stands in loose-fitting jeans and a moth-gouged green sweater—flounders terribly with every line. He even mispronounces the name of our village, reading Romainville phonetically (so it sounds like a small town of salad leaves) as opposed to the way the locals say it (with a an aitchy "r" and a silent "in," so, at least to English-hearing ears, it sounds like "Home-a-ville"). We cringe. The public servants, who had told Anique they were thrilled to officiate over their first English-speaking wedding, bite their lips and shoot the translator looks of annoyance.

Romainville's deputy mayor performs the ceremony. She's a regal-looking black woman with a shorn head and an easy, joyous smile, draped in a sash bearing the colors of the French flag. When it comes time to pledge our lives to each other and to vow to "raise our children with dignity and morality," Eamon says *oui* too softly for her liking.

"Louder please," she urges in sweet, teasing French. "You are happy, yes? Sing *oui* from the rooftops. Let them hear *oui* all the way down at Notre Dame."

And so Eamon shouts, "*Oui*," and I shout, "*Oui*," and our families do the same, until the word "yes" begins to take on a second, English-speaking meaning—until we sound like a group of people asserting our togetherness, referring to ourselves as "we."

Eamon and I exchange rings. I spend an awkward thirty seconds trying to get his onto his finger.

Then, at long last, it's time to kiss, to sign our marriage certificate, and to face our families as husband and wife.

While our families wait outside for us on the town hall's front steps, Eamon pulls me into a small room off the building's upstairs hallway.

"Let me just take a second to hug you," he says, cinching me tightly around the waist. He tells me how frightened he's been all morning, worrying that the translator wouldn't show up, and I tell him about the way my father got lost, the way my mother nearly fell down the stairs, the way the tiny bride was decapitated. He takes my temples in his hands and says, "Don't you worry. I'm going to look after this head all day. I won't let you lose it."

As we descend the steps hand in hand, our fathers are poised on the street with cameras. Eamon's brothers have party poppers in their hands. Anique and our mothers have bubble wands waiting at their puffed cheeks and pursed lips.

As we approach them, our picture-perfect wedding takes another turn toward French farce. The train of my dress gets caught under the doorstop and I am stuck dead in my tracks, while Eamon, who is still propelling forward, smacks his head directly against the other (closed) side of the glass double doors. That's how we enter the world as husband and wife: Eamon rubbing his lumped head, me holding both hands over my horrified mouth, and then both of us joining our families as they threaten to put the video footage on YouTube and laugh so hard they have to cross their legs.

———

I suspect, or at least I hope, that my life with Eamon will always be filled with the things of our wedding day: music, joking, and coincidences so bizarre they seem like magic. While we walk down the hill to the village park, Eamon's parents, who are British Columbian, are floored to find a Canadian loonie (a coin) in the street. Both of our families are shocked to discover that Eamon's aunt Helen was living in Jeddah, Saudi Arabia, at the exact time I was born there. The bus driver honks. The villagers wave from their cars. Even the sun momentarily tears through the clouds.

Anique has loaned us her art studio to use for our reception, so when we get back to the house, we all pile in there to dance, eat, and marvel at Leon's huge, swirling paintings.

Anique has laid a massive farm table with wild flowers, dripping candlesticks, and provincial tablecloths, while my mom and dad have helped heap it with plates of foie gras, cured sausages, smoked salmon; and Brie de Meaux, Chabichou du Poitou, and half a dozen other cheeses that we had bought during a *fromage*-happy spree. Eamon's precocious nine-year-old cousin shakes all the bottles of champagne in secret, so for the rest of the afternoon corks pop off them spontaneously. Bubbles fan out over the table and seethe lavishly onto the floor.

We watch Eamon's uncle, a translator for the UN in Geneva, as he bends over a cocktail napkin and writes a spur-of-the-moment poem for us.

Relationships begin in a flash
of the exotic
And develop over time with
healthy lashings of the erotic
Which preserve us
from becoming too neurotic
And comfort us in time
As we gently go sclerotic.

Eamon surprises me with a song he's written for me, and all of our family dances to it—everyone paired off and swaying, their arms draped around one another's necks. At the insistence of his brothers, Eamon wades through the crinoline of my dress and tries to take off my garter. (Eamon's prolonged fumbling there prompts his brother Josh to tease, "Crikey! I hope you're better with a bra!")

Together, Eamon and I cut our *croquembouche*. I say "cut," but, really, what we'd salvaged of it is wet and gooey enough to be ladled up with a spoon.

When we see an opening, we run off to the terrace to call Jo-Jo and Dave, who weren't able to make it, and to the bedroom, where Eamon helps me unhook the two dozen pea-size buttons that trail down the spine of my dress, so I can change into something that won't slow me down quite as much in the airport security line.

In a mad dash, we kiss our parents. We thank Anique (in addition to hosting our reception, she's also given us a series of black-white-and-very-French nudes she's shot with her friends, all of whom are pictured in various human knots bound with leather). Thirty minutes later we are at Charles de Gaulle, waiting to board a flight to the Basque coast for our honeymoon.

But wait. For all the day's joy, some unhappiness still eats at me like a bedsore. I call my sister twice from the airport, but she doesn't pick up the phone. At the sound of the beep, I tell the machine that I love her and am thinking of her.

47

Eamon spends the month of September recording a new album in Glasgow, while I spend it at my folks' house.

By the time I arrive, my sister is gone. Her husband is back from his tour of Iraq, and they're moving back down to North Carolina, where he is stationed at Camp Lejeune.

My parents' house bears only the smallest evidence of the six months my sister spent there with Riley. There are still stray, unmatched baby booties in the laundry room. On the back porch, a mobile that my father fashioned out of blank CDs, keys, and other household items still throws off rainbowed glints of light and swings forlornly in the breeze. I refuse to believe the timing is a coincidence (my sister has blown out of town not even two days before I arrive), but when I suggest as much my mom turns defensive. "You accuse her of giving you the silent treatment," she tells me. "But then, at your wedding, I saw you call your aunt and uncle, whereas you didn't call her."

My mother is still put out by most everything that happened in Paris, so I don't correct her.

I am back in her house, back on her turf, where she reigns supreme. Ever since I've come home, I've been listening to her tell me how she never wants to go back to Paris, which she's seen before anyway. The food there was too rich; the baguettes are too "binding"; the people there are kinder than she remembered from previous visits, but then they're still not exactly welcoming. She's realized she's a homebody, she tells me. She likes "her environment"—her dogs, her house, her routine. All the things, it's implied, that I dragged her away from.

"Something happened there," she says of Paris. She says it's something she can't quite put her finger on, but it had made her feel the way she had as child. She'd gone back to feeling self-conscious, shy, unhappy, uncertain, for which I wonder if she holds me accountable.

With the tension still thick at my parents' house, I spend multiple weekends driving down to Manhattan in a rented car and hunting for a new apartment. It's only the start of the housing collapse, and rents are still soaring. I look at apartments that are twice the price and half the square footage of the one I moved out of not more than five months earlier. I tour places with wires hanging out of the ceiling and dead cockroaches on the floor. In a fit of despair, I break down and call some of the brokers I had damned last spring.

Finally, I see an apartment on the top floor of a brownstone in a famously family-friendly section of Brooklyn. It's a Saturday morning, and there is sidewalk chalk on the front steps. The building's hallway smells like pancakes. I fall deeply and immediately in love with the place. Despite the blank walls and echoing rooms, it feels as though a happy family has lived there. Even the broker, a goofy kid fresh out of college, confesses, "When we went in there, I had an image of you sitting in the front window writing."

Later that afternoon I ring my parents' house to tell them that I've called off my search, signed the lease, and am on my way back to

Boston. My mother answers the phone. She seems pleased that I've finally found an apartment, but when I describe its neighborhood with the words "family friendly," I feel her voice change like a cold breeze blowing in. "Why does *that* matter?" she says in a tone that seems to suggest I've said something ridiculous. She seems irritated, impatient. She goes on to ask, harshly, "What? Are *you* looking to start a family?"

I try not to blame the bear. I try to stay present. I remind myself that I don't need her approval. With a calm, steady voice, I say, "Yes. We'd like to have kids in time."

She sighs in a way that says she's exasperated with me. "Ugh, Koren, how about you finish your book?"

It's too much. I'm rip-shit, even for all the work I've done to try to understand where digs like that come from and why they affect me. I try to say yes to my roots, to see my mother for the woman she is behind the starring role "Mom." During the drive home I try not to take out my frustrations on the accelerator. I bite my cheeks. I roll down the windows and let the autumn wind smack me hard across the face.

Somewhere around New Haven, it occurs to me that my anger, in this case, might actually be justified. Even if I hadn't grown up with the message that love was not forthcoming without achievement, I'd still be furious. The same could be said if someone unrelated to me had disrespected my desire to start a family. *Under any circumstances and from anyone's mouth, that's insensitive.*

When I get home that night, my mother is in the kitchen boiling water for tea. In a different lifetime, in an extremely foreign land, she'd set out to build a family entirely different from the one she'd grown up in. Now, on my purpled face, she sees the same emotion she despised in both herself and her parents. She sees the feeling she wielded guiltily when I was little ("I yelled at you too much, it is my biggest regret"). She sees the feeling she'd tried to outlaw as I'd grown up.

Right up until my grandmother died of a heart attack one year earlier, my mother had been dominated by the desire to be accepted and loved unconditionally by her, and also ashamed of her own needy rage. In trying to deny her fury for my Sicilian *nonna*, she had passed it on to her own daughters. Because of her own attempt to run from anger, she now stood face-to-face with it as she looked at me. "You can drive the devil out of your garden," said Heinrich Pestalozzi. "But you will find him again in the garden of your son."

Trembling, I stomp toward her. "You hurt my feelings today," I say. "I need you to know that. What you said earlier on the phone was insensitive. It wasn't nice."

"What did I say?" she asks, dropping the tea bag on the counter and putting her hands on her hips.

"What you said when I told you Eamon and I want kids. As far as I'm concerned, a career and a family are not mutually exclusive. And besides, I don't remember inviting you to give your opinion on the subject. When and how I finish my book is my business. So is when and why Eamon and I decide to have a baby. What happened last spring is still pretty fresh. It still hurts, okay? It's still awful. If you can't have any decency or any empathy, just keep your mouth closed." My pulse is clomping. My voice is loud in my ears and tears are dripping down my cheeks.

But instead of rearing up defensively, my mother surprises me. "Yes," she says calmly. "Okay, yes. I know what I said. I'm sorry."

I'm dumbstruck. I can't remember the last time she was so receptive. Is this really all it takes? Was confrontation always this easy? Virginia Satir says, "When someone takes a risk and reveals himself, the content of his revelation is usually frightening only to himself."

"Can I make a suggestion?" my mom asks.

I stare at her tongue-tied.

"I think from now on, when I hurt your feelings, you need to tell me immediately. Don't keep it to yourself," she says. "Don't wait until later. That only seems to make the matter worse."

"It's hard," I say. "I haven't always felt like you've been willing to listen."

"I feel the same way about you sometimes," she says. "You said some things in Paris that hurt me. I felt like they weren't acceptable. But, I held back saying anything because . . . I don't know. . . . It was your wedding. It was your time."

I lift my face and look into her deep brown eyes. "All right," I say. "From now on, we won't keep it to ourselves. We'll tell each other before it petrifies."

The question remains: How to strike a balance between my throat and my heart?

The challenge still plagues me two months later, when Eamon and I discover (to our cautious delight) that we're pregnant again.

I want to approach pregnancy differently than I had the last time. I want to be vocal enough to protect my body, my baby, but at the same time it seems important to have enough compassion for us both to live gently and stay calm.

"Pregnancy is exciting!" cheers a line in one of my pregnancy books. I can't relate. Mine is a time of endless self-questioning and immense terror.

To begin with, I worry that I will miscarry again. One Saturday morning, in my ninth week, I go to the bathroom and see spotting. A slow, animal wail escapes my mouth. My knees give out under me. I feel like my life is skipping like a record, like I'm cycling backward in time and reliving the same bullshit every six months. It doesn't matter what I do or how much progress I think I've made, things are always unraveling.

Shaking, I walk down the long hall to the bedroom, where Eamon is still stretched out in bed. "It's happening again," I say. "Oh god, Eamon. It's happening. It's happening."

But it's just a close call. Eamon and I spend the morning spooked and crying, but by late afternoon the bleeding has stopped. And

Monday morning finds us in my new ob's office, watching our baby's heart flicker, fireflylike, on an ultrasound screen.

After we've averted that disaster, new terrors claim me a few months later, when we see her—yes, *her*—elfin face and balled fists on the same device. "Oh, yes, our baby here is a girl," says the ultrasound technician, a round Russian woman whose eyes are rimmed in jet-black like Cleopatra. "Here is her flower, you see? Yes, it's beautiful. Little baby girl. So cute. So wonderful."

I spend many queasy and sleepless nights wondering if I can be a good mother to a daughter. Am I in touch enough with my own feelings not to squelch or feel threatened by hers? Can I help her to appreciate and, as Virginia Satir says, "develop" her emotional world?

I want to understand and, in doing so, free myself of the attitudes that have been passed down inadvertently through generations, so my daughter can in turn be free of the legacy of anger, repression, narcissism, self-sabotage, and abandonment. I want to have the presence of mind to see her not as a version of my grandmother, my mother, or myself, but rather for the person she inherently is and will be. I want her to be what Laurie Lee once called "a child of herself," a daughter, whose "life is already separate from mine, whose will already followed its own directions and who was always quickly correcting my woolly preconceptions of her by being something quite different."

One night toward the end of my third trimester I call Eamon, who is touring with his band Brakes back in England, and ask, "How can I do it? How can I be the kind of nurturing mother Virginia Satir writes about? How can I appreciate our kid's individual differences, tolerate her mistakes, and communicate openly when I've never seen that kind of family firsthand? It's like trying to rebuild an engine without knowing anything about cars."

Oddly enough, my mom calls the next day, just to tell me that she thinks I will make a good mother.

My eyes fill. Grabbing my huge, porcine belly, I reach for the closest chair and lower myself onto it, trying to get a sense of my bearings. The sentiment is completely unexpected. And even though I've long stopped needing or hoping she might affirm that for me, it touches me hugely.

"So what kind of mother are you going to be?" she asks me.

"What do you mean?"

"Oh, I mean, are you going to be the kind of strict mother who never lets her eat sugar? Or are you going to be the hippie mother who just lets her run around wild and without any rules? You know, what kind of mother are you going to be?"

I think for a moment, and then say, sniffling, "I'd like to be the mother who, no matter what, makes her kid feel seen for who she is, respected, and heard."

"Did *you* not feel respected and heard?"

"Not always. No."

"I'm sorry," she says, warmly, plainly, without anger or defense. I can't believe it. I realize I was half expecting her to say, *I'm sorry you feel that way.* Or *I'm sorry, but you had a roof over your head and food on the table, and two parents bound in holy matrimony.* Or *I'm sorry, but I was ten times saner than my mother before me, and I'd like to see you try to do things better.*

It occurs to me that, just as she's wanted me to strap a muzzle on my feelings, I haven't really wanted to experience hers. Most of my life I've avoided being honest with my mother for fear that it would ignite her own explosive emotions. I'm guilty of the exact same crimes I've charged her with. Yet, even as I've rejected her, I've loved her too. The fact that I've experienced both feelings simultaneously leaves room for the possibility that my mother loved me all along, even as she judged me. She might have spent years trying to change me, but she paid attention to me. If I was looking for proof that she cared, it was right there in her anxieties about me. Her nurturing instinct lay in her stringency. Like so many people in the world, her way of loving focused on training. Her affection had been there every time she said "don't."

"What's changed?" she asks me.

For the second time in ten minutes, I ask, "What do you mean?"

"Don't take this the wrong way, but you've always been my short-fused daughter. You know what I mean. But you're so calm lately. You seem different. So, what is it? Is it because of your book?"

Again, I'm taken aback. There's no precedent for this. My mother doesn't usually ask me such personal questions. I try to think of other times she's expressed a desire to know what I'm feeling and why, but come up short.

It occurs to me that she might be asking because she's not sure how to relate honestly to her anger either. For the first time, I realize that her attempts to raise unflappable children might have been born out of the distrust she had for her own emotions. *I don't want you to go through the things that I went through!* This had been her justification for some of her cruelest criticisms when I was a kid. I see, almost in a visual image, that every time my mother railed on me for crying, getting angry, expressing disappointment, she'd been trying to rescue me from her own family—a gang of shadows that was always with her, waiting to target any weakness or insecurity. As a girl, the only "emotion" language she heard was blaming. She'd never had anyone to tell her "I'm on your side. Talk to me. Let me help you."

I might have continued this legacy if I'd remained cut off from my emotions. If I don't stop looking for the validation I'd never had as a kid, I might later try to demand it of my children. As a mom, I want to respect and make room for my children's emotions, even if I can't always understand them. I want to do the same thing as a sister, as a daughter, as a wife.

In response to my mom's question, I tell her that once I found a little more compassion for myself—once I'd allowed myself the possibility of getting angry, not because it was always helpful, but because it was human—I started to feel less overwhelmed by the feeling. I'd also realized how much of my anger in the present was really deferred anger from the past. Once I disentwined the two, everyday aggravations seemed smaller and more manageable.

"I like what you just said about being in the present," she tells me. "Lately, I've been trying to do the same thing."

———

In late June, Eamon and I admit ourselves to St. Vincent's Hospital and emerge on an achingly clear summer evening with our daughter, Ayla—six pounds, eleven ounces of cherubic features and comedic expressions. Even shrunken, dented, and wrinkled, she has the compact energy of a coiled spring. She is bustling, lively, ready to assert her presence and be as near as possible to the world and its mysteries.

At the moment I write this, she is five months old and dribbling in her father's arms. Her blue eyes are widely fascinated. Her hands reach for any wonder within her grasp. Even on my breast, she hums to herself like a cartoon drunk and, as if pleased with her joke, flashes a teasing, gummy smile. Only fifteen pounds and she has all the energy of a nuclear reactor. Sometimes I watch her teach herself how to crawl—she inchworms across the floor on her stomach, head cocked in concentration, fingers fanned as she reaches for the object of her desperate desire—and remember an image I found in my anger research. A psychology professor named C. George Boeree wrote, "The problem is 'out there' and anger is the build-up of energy needed to solve it. Just try to hold back a baby from crawling, and see what you get."

Though it is not my daughter's job to give me anything, she has already given me motivation, a gift as heavy and dear as gold. For all her squeals and flailings, she's as helpless as a rock. Once or twice a night, I tiptoe into her room and check her sparrow's chest for signs of life and breath. Her every cry is a reminder that she is a creature who needs both my authority and my empathy, my voice and my heart.

Although I decide what she wears, where she goes, when she sleeps, and the like, she is still a full citizen of our burgeoning family. Still fresh from the womb, she sits hunched like an immigrant from the old country; she has her own reference points and still speaks her native tongue, but we have spent much time learning her language and getting used to her alien preferences.

She demands empathy, but then she also increases my compassion for my own mother. Whereas first I remembered my childhood as all easy, and then, later, as all difficult, my sweet girl reminds me of the small tender gestures in my own childhood. Ten times a day I find myself speaking to the little wriggler in the voice of my mother. When snatches of games or nursery rhymes come to me that way, as though by osmosis, I'm reminded that I knew affection and good intentions. My mother and my Italian *nonna* before her had loved me, and each other, in their own distinctive ways.

It has been four years since I first began working on this book—two years since the one-dimensional image that I had of my family collapsed like a stage backdrop that's lost its wooden supports. In that time, the dust has begun to settle. We are beginning to rise from the chaos.

Virginia Satir was right when she said that change is possible for everyone (even in the most stubborn of families). Even my mother, the technophobe, has learned how to text message. Most nights she dispatches a message around 8:00 P.M. Nothing major. Most are just small, thoughtful questions. "Does Eamon come home from his tour soon?" she wants to know. "Has Ayla's fever come down?" "How are you feeling?" Sometimes, instead of texting back, I'll call her, asking for some small piece of advice. Confessing that I don't quite know how to soothe my daughter in the days after a vaccine, my mother will tell me, "Of course you don't know how to make it better. No one does."

I visit my parents at home more often. It's important to them, and, in time, it will be important to my daughter. If ever she desires to see me not just as her mother but as somebody's daughter, it might help her to remember that big house standing mostly alone in the woods, to hear the coyotes howling out at night and smell the far-off burning of birch branches and dead maple leaves.

While being more forthcoming in my anger has helped me connect to my mother, my relationship with my sister remains careful and polite. She is a compassionate mother, a more dependable adult. Every day, she bears less resemblance to the schoolgirl whose white lies and avoidance angered me so deeply when she was in college. Though she still doesn't want to talk about events past, every five months or so she will drive the forty-five minutes to Brooklyn from her home in New Jersey, bringing with her big boxes of Riley's old baby clothes for her niece.

On days when I occasionally feel wounded and guarded (they still happen), we speak in awkward fits and uncomfortable starts (*less like sisters*, I think, *and more like work colleagues from different departments*). But on days when I'm attuned to the present, I can listen and love without terms and conditions.

It's impossible not to see the girl my sister once was in Riley. Twice, while I was pregnant, I babysat for her while my sister worked back-to-back shifts at her job as a police dispatcher. And on those nights, I did for Riley what I wished I could do for my sister: I held her when she howled; I rocked her when she missed her mom; I stroked her head and tried to comfort her with reassurances that I felt certain reached her, even though she didn't yet have the words to respond.

I've discovered that it's one thing to want your child to own her emotions and quite another to experience her dissent when it's focused hotly on you. Already, in my daughter I see the puckered brow of critique, the averted gaze of boredom, the purple-faced flash of rage. Even when I can't understand the source of her Didoian laments, I try to remember that she's entitled to them. Ours is already a relationship, and from time to time she's right to turn away from the face that hangs moonlike and doting over her expanding world's terrain.

Now and again I revisit some of the ideas this book first helped me uncover or rediscover, things like homeopathy, chakrology, psychology, prayer, meditation. I've come to see them as coping mechanisms, no one less ridiculous than any of the others. In my experience they were all equally valuable in the way they helped me access my emotions, and, along with them, my own inner remedy and blocked energy, my own inner Freud and inner guru—the voice that I research and write with, the person who wants to know the true nature of the world and herself, who sensed, from the very beginning, that emotion can be the glue that connects people just as often as the cleaver that tears them apart.

Hunter was right when he said facing my emotions and asserting myself would be a life's work. But it's not without reward and small, creeping signs of progress.

In all my scourings of Virginia Satir, it wasn't until the other day that I came across a segment I must have initially missed. It was a passage describing what change would look like. I couldn't help but reflect back on this book when I read that—instead of using facts and language to distance herself from her emotions—a reformed computer learns to put her intelligence to creative use. Nor could I help peeking into the room where my husband was strumming his guitar for our daughter, who was jumping maniacally in her toy bouncer. Both turned and chuckled when they caught sight of me. A changed placater, Satir had also written, "can transform her wish to please others into an ability to be tender and compassionate."

(reprinted with permission from Rachel Simmons)

This interview was conducted by Rachel Simmons, acclaimed author of *Odd Girl Out: The Hidden Culture of Aggression in Girls* and *The Curse of the Good Girl: Raising Authentic Girls with Courage and Confidence.*

RS: How would you define a healthy relationship to anger?
KZ: I think someone with a healthy relationship with anger accepts that it's a natural, normal, human emotion that's there to help her in an emergency. She expresses her anger directly and one-on-one with the person involved in the moment that the feeling arises. She doesn't go away and stew on the matter, doesn't put it in an e-mail, doesn't put it in an anonymous letter, doesn't seek revenge by ignoring or excluding the offending person, doesn't gossip, doesn't spread rumors or assemble a small army of other women or girls who share similar grievances with her foe.

As she's talking out the conflict, she resists the urge to blame or name-call. Instead, she focuses on expressing the deeper source of her fury (most often a feeling of fear or sorrow). Instead of saying things like, "You're insensitive" or "You only ever think about yourself," she opens up, speaks from the heart, and makes herself vulnerable. She says something like, "When you (fill in the blank), it makes me feel hurt and a little rejected."

Finally, she doesn't air her anger because she thinks she can change the other person or achieve some desired effect. She speaks up because her anger is genuine. She does it because she's human—not a saint, not a sinner, not a perfection-seeking robot—and all humans occasionally flip their lids. She speaks her anger because she knows it's essential to fight with the people she loves. Also, she's happiest when what she's saying aligns with what she truly feels.

RS: What advice do you have for girls and women who struggle with the Curse of the Good Girl and who have trouble accessing their anger?

KZ: I speak from experience when I say, if you're the type of person who grew up with the belief that anger was dangerous—or that anger and love are incompatible—it can be very difficult to be persuaded otherwise.

I think talking with a therapist works wonders. It's an incredible thing to open up to a counselor for the first time and reveal all the things that are driving you half crazy with rage. Inevitably, you discover that the world doesn't end. The therapist doesn't storm out in disgust. In fact, she empathizes with you. The conversation makes you feel closer to her and more in touch with the person you really are. Suddenly—maybe for the first time ever—you can picture yourself going and saying the exact same things to the people you're having conflicts with. Therapy becomes like a dress rehearsal or a training session for confrontations. Eventually, you find the self-confidence, language, and conviction to speak up in the moment, instead of waiting until a later date.

I also think talk therapy is great for the Good Girl simply because it requires her to tap into and acknowledge her emotions. Good girls are people-pleasers and we're often much better at reading other people's feelings than we are at recognizing and expressing our own.

RS: How can parents raise girls who feel authorized to express their anger?

KZ: Parents have various opinions on whether or not they ought to fight in front of their children. I, for one, think it's essential.

Over the course of writing *Fury*, I had a daughter of my own. Becoming a mom really makes you reflect on your own girlhood. It makes you acutely aware of which parenting patterns you do and don't want to repeat. I spent a lot of time reflecting and talking with my husband about how to handle anger in our home and how we want to approach it with our kids. As a mom, I always want my daughter to feel respected and heard. Likewise, I always want her to know that she can come to me when she's angry, hurting, in need of help, or just in need of a safe place to vent and it won't in any way diminish my love for her.

The only way I can really make that message clear is to be genuine, both in my relationship with her and with my husband. I want her to grow up in a household where she sees the full life cycle of an argument: how disagreements crop up, how my husband and I talk them out, and how conflict can even sometimes bring people closer together (this, as opposed to tearing them apart). If she grows up in a household that's as peaceful as a lotus flower, she'll never learn the language that she needs to weather conflicts with her friends, both at school and out there in the world at large.

(Reprinted with permission from newyorktimes.com)

I don't know where the idea originated that memoir writing is cathartic. For me, it's always felt like playing my own neurosurgeon, sans anesthesia. As a memoirist, you have to crack your head open and examine every uncomfortable thing in there. There's so much self-scrutiny involved, so much questioning. When I'm writing my stories, they rarely feel like emotions run wild.

Listening to music, on the other hand, is like venting my pent-up lunacy. I grew up in a family that despised displays of strong emotion, rage in particular. We stewed. We sulked. When arguments did occur, they were full-scale conniptions, and we regarded them as family failings. Afterward, we withdrew from one another and tried our best to strike the event from our memories.

Instead of baring my soul (or my teeth), I learned at an early age to fume in a far-off corner with a pair of headphones. A scathing lyric or furious riff became a stand-in for the anger I was too frightened or unwilling to talk out. In my adult life, I've come to regard this as a slightly destructive habit, a hindrance to true intimacy. But occasionally, a bad-natured song played at incredibly high volume still helps me to douse the flames.

Here's my Anger Playlist:

1. I Wanna Destroy You, The Soft Boys. I'm hard pressed to find a better soundtrack for revenge. The song sets itself up as a peace anthem; Robyn Hitchcock spits accusations like "They feed your pride with boredom / And they lead you on to war." But any moralizing is swiftly knocked aside by a base desire to settle the score. "And when I have destroyed you / I'll come picking at your bone / And you won't have a single atom left / To call your own." The lyrics aren't just menacing; they're audacious. Yet

313

there's something so exhilarating about the whirling guitars and Beach Boy-ish chorales that the tune ultimately begins to sound a little like falling in love. By the time the track ends, I'm never quite sure if I'm burning with rage or with relish. Have I just been threatened or wooed?

2. I Can't Stand to Stand Beside You, BrakesBrakesBrakes. Brakes is my husband Eamon Hamilton's indie rock band. He prefers the live version on *Rock Is Dodelijk*, but the first time I ever heard this song was on the band's debut album, *Give Blood*. Years before we met, I'd bought the CD for what many critics called its "hilarious rants." Like a good memoir, Brakes's lyrics had enough passion to seethe, but also enough self-awareness to poke fun at their own absurdity. Every so often, I listened to "I Can't Stand to Stand Beside You" while writing *Fury*. At the time, I thought it was a scathing assessment of a friendship turned sour. When Eamon and I later met and began dating I learned that he wrote it with himself in mind. With lines like "It's hard enough to see you when the lights are on," this will always be one of my favorite tales of furious self-loathing.

3. Gut Feeling/Slap Your Mammy, Devo. This song spells "resentment" to me. Maybe it's because the piano has a persistent, whining note of complaint. Or it could be because the introduction stretches all the way to the song's halfway mark, when the vocals finally flare impatiently, as if they can't bite their tongue a second longer. Whatever the reason, this is the sound of grudges compounding. When the moment of confrontation finally comes, the dissolution seems pretty final. Tell someone "You're rotten to the core," and you can be fairly certain he'll scratch you off his Christmas card list.

4. This Angry Silence, Television Personalities. Angry outbursts are often hasty, sloppy, childish—a lot like this song. The off-key quality to Dan Treacy's voice ought to be grating, but I find it endearingly human. Many of my family gatherings unfold the same way: with someone shouting, someone else threatening to leave, and the rest of us exercising the silent treatment.

5. Sam Hall, Johnny Cash. Scholars say the "Sam Hall" of this folk song was actually Jack Hall, a chimney sweep and criminal who was convicted of burglary and hanged in 1701 at Tyburn Tree. In Cash's version, the wrongfully accused Sam uses his dying breath to curse out his executioners and onlookers: "My name is Sam Hall and I hate you, one and all." I recommend playing this loudly on the days when it feels as though the world's conspiring against you.

6. 6'1", Liz Phair. Everyone's heard of "angry short man" syndrome, but as a "little" lady, I think petite women share the affliction. Like Liz, I'm 5 foot 2 and in denial about it. My short stature may have something to do with my tendency to shout when enraged. How else is anyone going to hear me way down here?

7. Been It, The Cardigans. In the psychologist Harriet Lerner's classic *Dance of Anger,* she writes about "the nice-lady syndrome," a designation she gives to women who throw themselves into mothering the adults around them, reading and accommodating everyone else's feelings and amassing a holy heap of resentment in the process. I think of the nice-lady syndrome every time I listen to Nina Persson sing "I've been your mother, I've been your father / Who could ask me for more?" The song now serves as a bit of a warning. I never want to attempt to rear anyone other than my kids.

8. No Children, The Mountain Goats. "You are coming down with me / Hand in unlovable hand." If there's a better song for embittered lovers, I've yet to find it. In my early to mid-twenties, a fear of confrontation made it difficult for me to end relationships in a mature or even quasi-sane way. Instead, I would hang on resentfully, praying that my doomed beau would end things first and spare me the displeasure. To add hindrance to hang-up, the men I chose were usually just as stoic as I was. Our relationships would chug on for months (or in some cases years). I still cringe when I think back on that time, but thanks to John Darnielle, I can also appreciate the black humor in this kind of shared martyrdom.

9. All You Need Is Hate, The Delgados. In the past few years, I've come around to the idea that anger is a natural, human emotion that can occasionally be a positive force for change. This tongue-in-cheek song reminds me of that. The message is deeply misanthropic, but layered over a happy-go-lucky sashay it begins to sound like "Kumbaya" to even the most cynical ear. To hear The Delgados tell it, hate is how they "broke the best indifference." And by the time they lilt "Build a different world, hate will help you find what you've been looking for," you wonder if they don't half believe it themselves.

10. Positively Fourth Street, Bob Dylan. "When I was down / You just stood there grinning." As far as angry ballads go, it doesn't get much better than this. My pal Jeff Klingman, a music journalist for *The L Magazine,* thinks "Positively Fourth Street" is almost so devastating that it doesn't seem mad. Therein, I think, lies its genius. Shrinks describe anger as a "secondary emotion." Beneath it, there's usually buckets of rain, buckets of tears.

Advice to You from You, Dear Reader

During the summer of 2007, just as I was wrestling with the personal wreckage that would eventually become *Fury*, I used my Web site to reach out to friends, readers, and fans of *Smashed*, asking them how they navigate their own stormy moods.

I suppose I was desperate for an intercession. I was looking for friends'—or, barring that, even strangers'—permission to honestly acknowledge and exorcise anger, which I'd always secretly believed was synonymous with cruddy morals, lack of feminine self-control, and nut-job tendencies.

I was dying to know what strategies other people use when expressing or repressing their rage. So, I essentially took a poll. My rather pathetic plea went like this:

I'm not convinced we know how to manage rage in this culture. For that matter, I'm not convinced that I personally do. I'm in the tail end of my twenties now, and I've devoted much of the past five years to yogic & Buddhist approaches. My own personal anger? I've tried to deal with it scrunch-eyed and pretzel-legged. I've meditated. I've chanted. I've spent tedious hours, silent and motionless. I've fingered mala beads alongside the barefooted, the robed-and-bald-headed, the vegan, the stoically patient and the relentlessly non-violent.

All of this to say, I've always bought, hook-line-and-sinker, that song and dance about not acting out in anger: "it's painful," "it's wasteful," "it's selfish," "it's the polar opposite of compassion and gratitude." I've subscribed to that fable about how unconscionably

mean people need sweetness most of all. But, seriously? All this
openhearted Thich-Nhat-Hanh logic is souring my shrunken soul.

So I ask you: What do you do with your anger? Do you scream
into your pillow? Stomp on empty soda cans? Box the nearest hard
object until your hand breaks and bleeds? Drop me a line. I'd really
love to know.

In return, I received an unexpected outpouring of responses. The coping
methods people described ranged from hilarious to profoundly helpful,
retro to revolutionary. Then and now, I find the need to share them, as a
kind of public service. A few common themes emerged, so I lumped
many of my readers' techniques into categories. Without further ado, I
present advice to you . . . from you:

The "Prolific" Angry

I smoke cigarettes and blog.

I like to write nasty, angry poetry when I'm mad. Or I just write
about the problem in general. Something about the act of processing the emotion into words on paper gives me a feeling of
satisfaction, revenge even. Relief. It gets the bad feeling out of me.

I play my drums. They help me let out a lot of pent-up rage.

If I'm angry at someone, I write them a letter. I never send it, but it
always feels better to write it down. If I'm mad at a situation, I
turn on the iPod to max volume and go into my studio and
paint/collage. Oh and I also smash up cars with steel bats. Kidding!

Studies show that drawing shapes continuously relieves aggression.

When I am angry or upset, that's when I break out the CDs and play
'em loud and sing. Often at midnight or 1 A.M. It's especially effective if I am angry with my neighbors, who bear the brunt of
listening to my singing. There is some "scientific" virtue to it. It
forces you to breathe, and the oxygen has a calming effect. Try it!

I pull weeds in the garden. It feels destructive, but in reality, it's
productive.

The "Fit" Angry

I run over the Williamsburg Bridge from my apartment in Green-
point to the Lower East Side. That seems to do it. I also play
angry music while I'm doing it.

I vent by putting my rage on a treadmill or elliptical machine. I set the resistance to the highest setting I can, and scream "out loud" in my head. Quite therapeutic.

Taking martial arts helps get anger out. You get to go to a respectable place and punch and kick things (and people) really hard and yell at the top of your lungs without seeming like a total lunatic. In fact, it makes you look rather sane and under control. It's fantastic.

Shadow boxing . . . but only if I'm in public.

I was told to turn my anger into something constructive, so I started working out when I'm angry. Lifting weights is the best because you feel like you have superhuman strength and I personally am more likely to push my limits when I'm running on a rush of adrenaline. I feel the way I would after throwing things, only this way I'm benefiting myself AND the breakable items in my house (or whoever they may be flying toward).

I take yoga. I breathe in, breathe out. I try to take thirty seconds or so, before I react. I pray.

Harry Truman said, "When in doubt, walk your dog. Even if you don't own a dog." It works for anger, too.

Exercise often works for me. It seems to drain or redirect blood going to my overtaxed little brain. Also, exercise alters my breathing, which is important too. So thirty bench presses will do wonders. Other times just writing a letter or a long e-mail (that you never send) helps too. (It helps pinpoint what you're angry about, as well.) Breaking things never works for me, since it means having to clean it up later. Also that gets expensive.

I have to do something physical. Much like hitting or punching, but without actually harming anyone. So I play racquetball—the physical exertion of slamming the tiny blue ball and following through with my backswing is better than any punching bag for me. My knuckles don't bruise after and I even like being surrounded by the white walls of the court. After a game, I am thoroughly exhausted—my adrenaline is racing so fast, leaving my mind so unfocused, I can't even think about what actually made me so stressed in the first place. So basically, I relieve stress by smacking the shit out of a small, blue ball that always bounces back for more.

When I'm angry I run. I run cross-country, and I have found that when I'm angry I can run much faster, much harder, much stronger. It just lets me kick some ass without actually kicking anyone's ass and hurting their feelings. Also I don't have to deal with the repercussions of expressing my anger at another human being. It seems that as women we are not allowed to express anger. If we express it regularly we are considered a bitch. If we express it on occasion, when it all builds up and we can't take it anymore, we are considered psycho. Men are allowed to let it go. This makes them "masculine" and more normal.

Punching bag. The sole reason I bought boxing gloves was so I would be able to beat the shit out of a punching bag when I needed to. This is a nonintrusive, pain-free way to deal with anger.

The "Frisky" Angry

When I am angry—depending on the level of anger—I hit my hanging punching bag, have barbaric sex with husband, or run until I can't feel whatever pissed me off anymore.

It might sound old-fashioned but there's nothing like some good old crying my eyes out to really clear my head and make me feel better! Sex helps too but I'd only suggest that to someone in a monogamous relationship. Otherwise it probably wouldn't be considered "healthy & responsible."

Projecting love through violence. I was once involved with a girl who taught me to harness my anger, and pull out the power attached to it. Anger is like a shot of adrenaline, but it also is a lost of control. If you can hold onto the shot of adrenaline and not lose control there is a power there. She was a bit of a freak, so she wanted me to use my anger to fuck her good and violently. She was right. It would shut the voices in my head off. It gave me a release. However, this requires another person. One who understands and is a bit of a freak.

The "Cleanly" Angry

When I'm angry I clean my house. It helps me work so much quicker, stops me from doing things I would regret later, and rewards me when I'm angry no more.

I shower. I know, it's strange. I also cry or simply talk out loud (very loud) to the person or thing I am angry with. I learned to do this years ago so my children wouldn't be scared of their psycho mother. It has worked well for me for over twenty years.

Anger Directed Inward

Control. Do nothing. Stuff it inside. Silently curse. Society demands this sometimes.

When I'm angry I scream silently, light a Marlboro, and watch the smoke curl. I also put on a really sad song and cry, or put on a really angry song and dance. I dance until I'm tired, but the pounding in my head stops. I dance until all the tension drains away.

I eat massive amounts of 45-cent croissants and drink a ridiculous amount of energy drinks. After an hour or so of doing that I have a lot more problems than being mad about something, but I'm sure its a lot healthier than hoarding all your rage in.

I bitch and cry then pop a Prozac. I also try to control my breathing to help me clam down.

I get silent. I keep to myself and never act on anger. I promised myself that when I was a child.

When I'm really upset I tend to get something pierced or tattooed. It lets me release all the bad energy I feel pent up inside when the pain is done.

Anger Directed Outward

I rip pieces of paper in half, then in half, then in half, then in half, etc. until I can't anymore. I also draw 3-D boxes over and over.

If I'm angry because of a phone call, I usually throw the phone. Probably not healthy, but it works. Putting my phone back together when pieces break (and they usually do) gives me a chance to calm down and decide what I can do about the reason why I'm angry and helps me to work through it.

I punch a wall. This way of dealing with anger I am pretty sure I was supposed to grow out of, but there it is. The reason this works? In bruising, breaking, or really hurting your hand the pain can distract your anger. This has to be done intentionally, though. If not the pain can act as a catalyst for greater rage.

The most constructive thing for me has been taking action in some form and standing up for myself. The more I try to ignore angry feelings because I "should" the worse I feel. Like if I am mad at someone, I have to tell them I am, or I will go insane. I used to never ever admit I was angry at someone, and it eventually turned inward.

I stomp around the house. Bonus points for shoes that add volume.

In the car, I yell. With the windows up though. I'm not brave enough to yell at unsuspecting people. Especially since I get obscene.

Maybe not creative, but I tend to make jokes about my anger. I'll be furious about something but I'll yell about it in a hilarious way that makes other people laugh, which in turn makes me laugh, and then suddenly I am able to see the absurdity of my original fit of rage.

Listening to Music Was Also a Very Popular Solution. Here Are Some of Your Anger Soundtracks

Playing music really loud and then singing to it even louder: Trapt, Linkin Park, Disturbed, Alien Ant Farm, Chevelle . . . the list goes on and on. Pretty much the lyrics that relate to me and my situation.

I listen to Hanson . . . seriously.

Usually when I get angry, it's when someone is doing something and I find that they're doing it so poorly (in my opinion) that I just yell at them how to do it correctly. In private, I like to blow off steam by listening to '80s hardcore bands (i.e., Black Flag) and just let the anger flow out of me along with the angry lyrics.

Loud music. Sometimes anger is not an impulse. It is not the quick reaction as something is happening. It can be a long march reaching your gates. On these occasions I find mind-clearing car rides to be the most affective. Windows down, CD player blaring the likes of Linkin Park's "one step closer," any song by Tool, Eminem's, "Kim." Understanding yourself is key with this. The idea is to give yourself a release before you boil over.

Angry music soundtrack: Unsane's compilation "Lambhouse" straddles the lines of brilliant/brutal with a precision that is ri-goddamn-diculous. Other notable steam-releasing choices: The Misfits's *Earth A.D.*, Poison Idea's *Feel the Darkness*, Slayer's

Reign in Blood, and Toxic Narcotic's *89–99*. When I'm at home I usually listen to jazz though—I can't be angry all the time.

And Finally, My Favorite Responses

I play Scrabble!

I eat red meat, chase my cat around the house, drink large beers at the Swinging Door Saloon, and play Irish folk songs on the jukebox . . . though not necessarily in that order.

I like to kick small trash cans across the room if I get frustrated at work. The fuller they are, the better. I also like to flip people off for no reason. Other than that, I'm pretty boring when it comes to that—I usually write or listen to music. Or if I'm really upset, I'll throw myself onto the floor (which sucks 'cause I have hardwoods) and cry and have a pity party that no one shows up to but me.

Me? I walk with my iPod and a long Russian coat. I mean, I walk using them, to a certain degree . . . not that they walk with me. If I was seeing those sorts of things I'm sure they'd call that "inward aggression," and then I'd be in deep trouble. But if I get mad at something not working or someone has irritated me or I can't untangle headphone wires or something falls out of the fridge or I trip on the stairs I usually act spontaneously with a fist thump and I always tend to use the phrase "For fuck's sake," even though I only ever use that in other situations when I'm watching football.

I visualize guns in my hands.

TIPS FOR TALKING ABOUT ANGER IN AN "EMOTIONLESS" OR "OVERLY EMOTIONAL" FAMILY

The more you can learn about your parents' backgrounds, the better your chance for understanding the way they raised you and your siblings. In the case of both the seemingly "unfeeling" family, as well as the professedly "volatile" one, parents were often unmothered or unfathered children themselves. It's quite possible that your grandparents mistrusted or misplaced their anger. In all likelihood, your mom and dad had their own share of repressed emotion and early childhood traumas.

Below are a list of questions you can use to kick-start conversation. Bear in mind, it's not uncommon for parents to have a lot of denial about their own troubled childhoods. There may be many details they claim they don't remember or say they aren't willing to share. Try your best to listen with compassion and withhold judgment. Also, remember to look at your parents' parenting as influenced by their generation and culture. A holy heap of factors influence the choices people make as parents.

Did you have a happy childhood?
Did you feel loved by your parents?
Did you feel you got enough attention growing up?
What did your parents teach you about emotions?
Did you feel your parents allowed you to express feelings like anger, fear, or disappointment? Were you encouraged to talk openly about these emotions?
As a kid, did you feel the adults in your life listened to you? Did you feel heard?
How were you disciplined when your parents were angry with you?

Were you encouraged as an individual and allowed to be different? Or did you feel as though you had to fit the family mold?

Were your mother or father particularly concerned about appearances or what other people thought?

What do you like about the way your parents raised you? What do you wish they'd done differently?

Do you think your parents' parenting techniques informed or otherwise influenced your own? If so, how?

PROLOGUE   *Giving Up the Ghost*

3   "A bad girl has never been born": Virginia Satir and Michele Baldwin, *Satir Step by Step: A Guide to Creating Change in Families* (Palo Alto, Calif.: Science and Behavior Books, 1984), p. 193.

ONE   *Incitement*

5   "Lost really has two disparate meanings": Rebecca Solnit, *A Field Guide to Getting Lost* (New York: Penguin, 2006), p. 22.
11   "Anger seems to listen to argument": Aristotle, *The Nicomachean Ethics*, translated by David Ross (Oxford: Oxford Unversity Press, 2009), p. 128.
13   "The typical episode of anger does not end abruptly": B. M. Fridhandler and J. R. Averill, "Temporal Dimensions of Anger: An Exploration of Time and Emotion" in J. R. Averill (ed.), *Anger and Aggression* (Berlin and Heidelberg: Springer-Verlag, 1982), p. 204. I originally came upon this quotation in William V. Harris's book *Restraining Rage: The Ideology of Anger Control in Classical Antiquity*.
13   "nice lady syndrome": Harriet Lerner, *The Dance of Anger: A Woman's Guide to Changing the Patterns of Intimate Relationships* (New York: Harper Paperbacks, 2005), pp. 6–7.
14   "ravaged by war and disease, or where there is continuous conflict": Geshe Kelsang Gyatso, *Introduction to Buddhism* (Glen Spey, N.Y.: Tharpa Publications, 2001), p. 33.
15   "Another powerful method for overcoming anger": Geshe Kelsang Gyatso, *How to Solve Our Human Problems* (Glen Spey, N.Y.: Tharpa Publications, 2007), p. 62.

TWO   *Anger Ignored*

17   "The weather today is an increasing trend toward denial.": Chuck Palahniuk, *Diary: A Novel* (New York: Doubleday, 2003), p. 7.
24   By nightfall, I've express ordered *Homeopathy: An A to Z Home Handbook*: Alan

Schmukler, *Homeopathy: An A to Z Home Handbook* (Woodbury, Minn.: Llewellyn Publications, 2006).

25 *We aren't shutting you out of the revel: Eros the Bittersweet* (Princeton, N.J.: Princeton University Press, 1986), pp. 18–19.

28 Christianity and Judaism take "a middle position on the subject of anger": Peter N. and Carol Zisowitz Stearns, *Anger: The Struggle for Emotional Control in America's History* (Chicago: University of Chicago Press, 1989), p. 21.

28 "justified anger . . . cruelty, impiety, and wrong": William Leslie Davidson, *Christian Ethics* (London: A. & C. Black, 1907), p. 80.

28 "A wrathful man stirs up discord": Proverbs, 15:18.

28 "Most hated to Allah is a person who is fiercely hostile and quarrelsome": HalalPak, "Anger Management" (www.halalpak.com/index.php?option=com_content&task=view&id=20&Itemid=35), 2007.

28 "Anger," the Buddha said, "is a poison": About.com, "The Basics: What the Buddha Taught" (www.buddhism.about.com/od/basicbuddhistteachings/The_Basics_What_the_Buddha_Taught.htm).

29 "[A]nger is everyone's": Geshe Kelsang Gyatso, *How to Solve Our Human Problems* (Glen Spey, N.Y.: Tharpa Publications, 2007), p. 59.

29 "anger is a negative phenomenological feeling state": Howard Kassinove, *Anger Disorders: Definition, Diagnosis, and Treatment* (Washington, D.C.: Taylor and Francis, 1995), p. 26.

29 "anger is the emotion into which most others tend to pass": G. Stanley Hall, *The American Journal of Psychology*, v. 26, p. 440.

29 "Often, there is no explicit definition of anger": Christa Reiser, *Reflections on Anger: Women and Men in a Changing Society* (Westport, Conn.: Praeger, 1999, 2001), p. 25.

29 "deluded mind that focuses on an animate or inanimate object": Geshe Kelsang Gyatso, *How to Solve Our Human Problems* (Glen Spey, N.Y.: Tharpa Publications, 2007), p. 21.

29 "Tonglen practice helps cultivate fearlessness": Pema Chodron, *Comfortable with Uncertainty: 108 Teachings on Cultivating Fearlessness and Compassion* (Boston: Shambhala, 2008), p. 83.

33 "In fact, men generally feel quite comfortable with anger": Celia Halas, as quoted in Carol Tavris, *Anger: The Misunderstood Emotion* (New York: Simon & Schuster, 1982), pp. 195–96.

33 "I've found that . . . the male is very blocked": Herb Goldberg, *The Hazards of Being Male: Surviving the Myth of Masculine Privilege* (Bel Air, Calif.: Nash Publishing, 1976), p. 28.

35 "Pollyannish and conventional": Robert G. Meyer and Sarah E. Deitsch, *The Clinician's Handbook: Integrated Diagnostics, Assessment, and Intervention in Adult and Adolescent Psychopathology*, 4th ed. (New York: Allyn & Bacon, 1995), p. 322.

35 "need to be liked," "unusual behavior," "dependent," "evaluative," "rejecting," "impulsive," "inappropriate," "poorly integrated": Terms from Alan F. Friedman, Richard Lewak, David S. Nichols, *Psychological Assessment with the MMPI-2* (Mahwah, N.J.: L. Erlbaum Associates, 2001), pp. 280–81.

36 His response gnawed a hole in my vitals ("A hole is being gnawed in [my] vitals") Anne Carson, *Eros the Bittersweet* (Princeton, N.J.: Princeton University Press, 1986), p. 32.

36 snatched the lungs right out of my chest: Ibid.

THREE *Anger Turned Inward*

43 "I will wear my heart upon my sleeve": William Shakespeare, *Othello* (New York: Simon & Schuster, 2004).

44 "When Anglo-Americans are angry": Carol Tavris, *Anger: The Misunderstood Emotion* (New York: Simon & Schuster, 1982), p. 66.

47 The word comes from Ifaluk: Anna Wierzbicka, *Semantics, Culture and Cognition: Universal Human Concepts in Culture-Specific Configurations* (New York: Oxford University Press, 1992), p. 147.

48 Linguists say *song* is less aggressive than anger: Anna Wierzbicka, paraphrasing Catherine Lutz, in Ibid.

50 Virginia Satir thought low self-esteem is contagious in families: Satir and Baldwin, p. 195.

50 "Often [two spouses struggling with low self-esteem] disregard [their] inner feelings": Ibid.

52 "the person whose poor self-image derives from a past": Pamela Nori, "Emotional Homeopathy," *alive* Magazine, Alive.com (www.alive.com/3712a1a2 .php?subject_bread_cramb=81), 2000.

52 "[most people who need Staphysagria] have a certain mellowness": Philip M. Bailey, MD, *Homeopathic Psychology: Personality Profiles of the Major Constitutional Remedies* (Berkeley, Calif.: North Atlantic Books, 1995), p. 321.

53 "a smoldering resentment": herbs2000.com, "Staphysagria," Herbs2000.com (www.herbs2000.com/homeopathy/staphysagria.htm), 2000–2010.

53 "the commonest cause of the [Staph patient's] resentment": Bailey, p. 321.

53 "After the remedy is taken": Bailey, p. 322.

53 "With the right homeopathic remedy": Randy W. Martin, "Homeopathy and Spirituality: The Hidden and Unspoken Power in Homeopathic Medicine," Shirley's Wellness Cafe (www.shirleys-wellness-cafe.com/homeopathy_randy.htm), 1996–2010.

56 sensations like "stupefying headache": ABC Homeopathy, "Staphysagria," Influenca Ltd. (www.abchomeopathy.com/r.php/Staph), 2001–2009.

57 "the assertion of an ought": Joseph de Rivera, as found in Tavris, *Anger*, p. 49.

58 "for most of Western history, it has been up to individuals": Ibid, p. 50.

60 "According to William Vernon Harris, *Anger* is the only book that attempts to chart American attitudes about anger over time": William V. Harris, *Restraining Rage: The Ideology of Anger Control in Classical Antiquity* (Cambridge, Mass.: Harvard University Press, 2004), p. 23.

60–61 there was even a Homeric appreciation for anger: Paraphrased from Stearns, *Anger*, p. 27.

62 "choose to be happy rather than right": Brenda Shoshanna, "How to Stop the Fighting in Your Relationship," SearchWarp.com (www.searchwarp.com/ swa30056.htm), 2005.

66 "detached," "noninvested," "less visible within our family structure": C. Black, "Effects of Family Alcoholism," in *Tōkyō-to Seishin Igaku Sōgō Kenkyūjo* (*Alcoholism in the Family*) (Tokyo: Psychiatric Research Institute of Tokyo in collaboration with Brunner Mazel, 1992), p. 275.

67 Satir claims years of playing the distractor: Satir and Baldwin, p. 200.

71 "Human beings seem willing to pay whatever price": Satir and Baldwin, p. 194.

74 the Lycopodium patient is "saddened in the morning": ABC Homeopathy, "Lyco-

podium Clavatum," Influenca Ltd. (www.abchomeopathy.com/r.php/Lyc), 2001–2009.

75   "deficient of ideas" . . . "can't bear to read anything she's written": From William Boericke, "Lycopodium clavatum, Club Moss," *Materia Medica* (1901), as found on Henriette's Herbal Homepage (www.henriettesherbal.com/eclectic-boericke/lycopodium.html) and Rxhomeo.com, "Lycopodium," Rxhomeo Inc. (www.rxhomeo.com/pharmacy/homeopathic.php?act=viewProd&productId=162).

76   I really feel "the pain and discomfort": Martin, "Homeopathy and Spirituality."

77   a dysfunctional communication process called "nominalization": Satir and Baldwin, p. 197.

78   "anal character": Sigmund Freud, "Character and Anal Eroticism" (1908b): Paraphrased from Seymour Fisher and Roger P. Greenberg, "the Scientific Credibility of Freud's Theory and Therapy (New York: Columbia Unviersity Press, 1985), p. 154.

78   the "aristocratic character": Wilhelm Reich, *Character Analysis* (New York: Farrar, Straus and Giroux, 1972), p. 194.

78   "unrelaxed, tense, joyless, and grim": Theodore Millon, Ph.D., D.Sc., and Seth Grossman, Psy.D., The Millon-Grossman Personality Domain Checklist (MG-PDC) (www.millon.net/instruments/MG_PDC.htm).

78   In the words of psychologist Theodore Millon: Theodore Millon, *Disorders of Personality: DSM-III: Axis II* (New York: John Wiley & Sons, 1981), as quoted in Claudia Naranjo, *Character and Neurosis: An Integrative View* (claudionaranjo.net/pdf_files/theory/character_neurosis_ch_1_english.pdf).

79   "It would be a mistake, however, to conceive of [the perfectionist] as a violent character": Naranjo, *Character and Neurosis*.

81   I might have heeded the warning: St. John of the Cross, *Dark Night of the Soul* (Alachua, Fla.: Bridge-Logos Publishers, 2007).

84   "where individual differences are appreciated, mistakes are tolerated, communication is open, and rules are flexible": Satir, *The New Peoplemaking*, p. 26.

87   Still exploring homeopathy: R. Dockx, G. Kokelenberg, *Kent's Comparative Repertory of the Homeopathic Materia Medica* (New Delhi: B. Jain Publishers, 2004). See also: ABC Homeopathy, "Natrum Muriaticum" (www.abchomeopathy.com/r.php/Nat-m) and Jennifer Wurges, "Natrum muriaticum," *Encyclopedia of Alternative Medicine* (2001) (findarticles.com/p/articles/mi_g2603/is_0005/ai_2603000544/).

88   "dislike[s] consolation or advice": "Natrium Muriaticum: Chloride of Sodium," Homeopathy and More (www.homeopathyandmore.com/forum/viewtopic.php?t=314), 2006.

89   *If I go to the butcher's house:* Alina Reyes, "The Butcher," in *The Butcher and Other Erotica* (New York: Grove Press, 1996), pp. 33–35.

92   "fetch up the spirits into the brain": Philosophers of Coimbra, from Robert Burton, *The Anatomy of Melancholy*, v. 1 New York Review of Books Classics (New York: The New York Review of Books, 2001) p. 422.

93   "denying one's own emotional reactions": Alice Miller, *The Drama of the Gifted Child: The Search for the True Self* (New York: Basic Books, 2008), p. 39.

93   "It is easy to notice": Ibid.

93   "A depression-prone person is distinguished by anger over the painful disturbances to his or her life": Walter Bonime, *Collaborative Psychoanalysis: Anxiety, Depression, Dreams and Personality Change* (Cranbury, N.J.: Associated University Presses, 1989), p. 162.

FOUR *Anger Intellectualized*

95   "When faced with life's needs and urges I used to begin by classifying": "Being Happy, Making Happy Is the Rhythm of Life," *I Am That: Dialogues of Sri Nisargadatta Maharaj* (anandavala.info/miscl/I_Am_That.pdf), pp. 278–79.

100 "Repressed and suppressed anger can thwart creativity and motivation": Beverley Engel, *Honor Your Anger: How Transforming Your Anger Style Can Change Your Life* (Hoboken, N.J.: John Wiley & Sons, 2004), p. 16.

104 *These people have all developed the art of not experiencing feelings:* Miller, pp. 9–10.

107 "ventilationist": From *The Century of the Self* (BBC documentary), directed by Adam Curtis, 2002.

108 Michael Murphy and Dick Price formed the Esalen Institute: www.esalen.org.

114 Charles L. Whitfield, who calls the inner child "the Child Within": Charles L. Whitfield, MD, *Healing the Child Within: Discovery and Recovery for Adult Children of Dysfunctional Families* (Deerfield Beach, Fla.: Health Communications, 1987), p. 1.

121 "Experience has taught us that we have only one enduring weapon": Miller, p. 1.

126 "Young hockey players": "Study Shows That Perfectionism and Parents Push Young Hockey Players to Anger." Article adapted by *Medical News Today*, Sept. 25, 2006, from original press release.

128 "strong on passion and commitment but low on intimate involvement": Robert Sternberg, *The Psychology of Love* (New Haven, Conn.: Yale University Press, 1989), p. 65.

129 Stearns, who coined the word "emotionology": Peter N. Stearns and Carol Z. Stearns, "Emotionology: Clarifying the History of Emotions and Emotional Standards," *The American Historical Review*, v. 90, no. 4 (October 1985), pp. 813–36.

129 "the view of *anger* as something that can be manipulated": Anna Wierzbicka, *Emotion across Languages and Cultures* (Cambridge, UK: Cambridge University Press, 1999), p. 31.

130 "English 'anger' includes an implicit negative evaluation": Cliff Goddard, "Anger in the Western Desert: A Case Study in the Cross-Cultural Semantics of Emotion," *Man*, v. 26, no. 2 (June 1991), pp. 265–79.

FIVE *Anger Displaced*

136 "anger is the acme of self-assertion": G. Stanley Hall, in a paper entitled "Anger as a Primary Emotion," given during the 1915 meeting of the American Psychopathological Association.

136 "Just let the words come out of this beautiful throat of yours": From the transcript entitled "Forgiving Parents," reprinted in Steve Andreas, *Virginia Satir: The Patterns of Her Magic* (Moab, Utah: Real People Press, 1999), p. 71.

137 "dull and monotonous": Marian F. Fatout, *Models for Change in Social Group Work* (Piscataway, N.J.: Aldine Transaction, 1992), p. 179.

137 as if lacking the air to maintain a "full, rich voice": Virginia Satir, *The New Peoplemaking* (Palo Alto, Calif.: Science and Behavior Books, 1988), p. 85.

139 "[Nonviolence] does not mean meek submission": Richard Attenborough, ed. *The Words of Gandhi* (New York: Newmarket Press, 1982), p. 134.

140 "compares anger to a crying baby": Thich Nhat Hanh, *Anger: Wisdom for Cooling the Flames* (New York: Riverhead Trade, 2002), p. 27.

141 "The grief process begins with a decision": Karyl McBride, *When Will I Ever Be Good Enough? Healing the Daughters of Narcissistic Mothers* (New York: Free Press, 2008), p. 143.

142 Lachesis is the poisonous venom of the bushmaster snake: Alan Schmukler, *Homeopathy: An A to Z Home Handbook* (Woodbury, Minn.: Llewellyn Publications, 2006), p. 19.

143 "a highly strung bow, taut with sexual energy": Herbs2000.com, "Lachesis" (www.herbs2000.com/homeopathy/lachesis.htm).

143 Psychological anthropologist Michelle Rosaldo wrote that *liget* represents a will to compete: Michelle Rosaldo, *Knowledge and Passion: Ilongot Notions of Self and Social Life* (Cambridge, UK: Cambridge University Press, 1980), p. 49.

147 In *Homeopathic Psychology*, I read about and relate to the "Sweet Staphysagria": Bailey, p. 323.

152 *A part of a healthy conscience is being able to confront consciencelessness:* Martha Stout, *The Sociopath Next Door* (New York: Broadway, 2006), p. 100.

153 *Once the Staphysagria's old, subconscious anger has been brought to the fore:* Bailey, p. 322.

156 "Girls often play the piano loudly": G. Stanley Hall, in a paper entitled "Anger As a Primary Emotion," given during the 1915 meeting of the American Psychopathological Association.

161 (*the Staphysagria patient often trembles when she is enraged*): See Vinton McCabe, *Practical Homeopathy: A Comprehensive Guide to Homeopathic Remedies and Their Acute Uses* (New York: St. Martin's Press, 2000) or D. D. Banerjee, "Staphysagria," *A Textbook of Homeopathic Pharmacy*, 2nd ed. (New Delhi: B. Jain Publishers, 2002), p. 361.

168 "Without free access to these facts": Miller, p. 43.

169 "There's this anthropologist, Robert Levy": Carol Tavris, *Anger: The Misunderstood Emotion* (New York: Simon & Schuster, 1982), p. 69.

169 "There's this pediatrician, Daniel G. Freedman": Ibid., p. 81

169 "the most hideous and frenzied of all the emotions": Seneca, "On Anger," *Seneca: Moral Essays*, v. 1, translated by John W. Basore (Cambridge, Mass.: Loeb Classical Library, 1928), p. 107.

SIX *Conniption*

173 "Let us picture anger": Seneca, "On Anger," *Seneca: Moral Essays*, p. 247.

180 "[r]epressed memories of the shy": Miller, p. 85.

182–83 "Alan Rappoport, writes, 'I define a relationship as an interpersonal interaction'": Alan Rappoport, "Co-Narcissism: How We Accommodate to Narcissistic Parents," *The Therapist*, 2005 (www.alanrappoport.com/pdf/Co-Narcissism%20 Article.pdf).

189 Virginia Satir thought that there will always be aspects of ourselves that we do not know: See Satir, *The New Peoplemaking*, p. 28: "I know there are aspects about myself that puzzle me, and aspects that I do not know. But as long as I am friendly and loving to myself, I can courageously and hopefully look for the solutions to the puzzles and for ways to find out more about me."

192 see our parents as almighty Old Testament gods: See Barbara Jo Brothers, ed., *Virginia Satir: Foundational Ideas* (Binghamton, N.Y.: Haworth Press, 1991), p. 108.

198 "The humiliated grown daughter . . . will revenge herself upon her own children": Miller, p. 74.

199–200 someone who expresses her own humanness: See Satir, *The New Peoplemaking*, p. 228: "Children have much more trust in humanness than they do in sainthood and perfection." Throughout the book, this is what Satir refers to as "humanness," of which "uniqueness" is a factor.

200 "looking phony": Ibid., p. 230.

236 Virginia Satir said, "[A]nger is not a vice": Satir, *The New Peoplemaking*, p. 122.

240 "restraint of anger became a fundamental part of good character training": Stearns and Stearns, *Anger*, pp. 72–73.

240 parents' "sacred duty": Flora H. Williams, "You and Your Children," as found in Stearns and Stearns, *Anger*, p. 72.

241 The same temper "that smashes a childhood toy" can "kill a man when the child is grown": R. Gordon Kelley, "Mother Was a Lady: Self and Society in Selected American Periodicals," as found in Stearns and Stearns, *Anger*, p. 72.

241 Hall and his supporters criticized parents: Stearns and Stearns, *Anger*, p. 73.

241 "Other [child-rearing experts]": Ibid, p. 74.

241 a sign of "weak will" and "decaying intellectual power": Ibid, p. 76.

241–42 a "certain choleric vein gives zest and force to all acts": G. Stanley Hall, as quoted in Stearns and Stearns, *Anger*, p. 76.

242 "a creature under demonical possession": Ibid.

242 Somehow, this idea that anger can be beneficial: Stearns and Stearns, *Anger*, p. 160.

242 Mr. Rogers asked questions like "This makes you feel angry, doesn't it?": Ibid.

242 it is generally bad and "cannot be turned to good": Ibid, p. 161.

243 "bribing them to minimize tension": Ibid.

243 "Anger demanded more care and loomed larger as a priority than it ever had before": Ibid, p. 162.

243 "assure their angry children that they knew how they felt": Ibid, p. 163.

246 Virginia Satir says change in families is a three-step process: Satir and Baldwin, *Satir Step by Step*, p. 209.

246 a hopeful family is willing to do things a new way: Ibid, p. 220.

SEVEN *Aftermath*

266 "Do you know what makes it possible for me to trust the unknown?": "Becoming More Fully Human with Virginia Satir," interview transcript from *Thinking Allowed, Conversations on the Leading Edge of Knowledge and Discovery*, with Jeffrey Mishlove (www.intuition.org/txt/satir2.htm).

273 "Quarrels in France": Ned Rorem, *The Paris Diary of Ned Rorem: With a Portrait of the Diarist by Robert Phelps* (New York: George Braziller, 1966), p. 34.

277 "miscarriage due to anger": See "Homeopathy and the Stages of Life: From Womb to Tomb," Healthy Life Essex (www.healthylifeessex.co.uk/pages/wellbeing/Homeopathy_and_Stages_of_life.html).

284 Virginia Satir believed all feelings (even fear, humiliation, anger, helplessness, and hopelessness) are the ready-made bases: Satir, *The New Peoplemaking*, pp. 232–33.

288 "With the Sweet Staphysagria . . . anger and resentment are repressed": *Homeopathic Psychology*, p. 323.

291 "gives a deep unconscious 'yes' to her roots": Brothers, p. 117.

293 *But, does love make you always happy?*: "Being Happy, Making Happy Is the Rhythm of Life," *I Am That: Dialogues of Sri Nisargadatta Maharaj* (anandavala.info/miscl/I_Am_That.pdf), p. 186.

293 Satir wrote, "I own what comes out of me": Satir, *The New Peoplemaking*, p.237.

294 in Lee Sandlin's article "Losing the War": Lee Sandlin, "Losing the War," *The New Kings of Nonfiction*, Ira Glass, ed. (New York: Riverhead, 2007), pp. 315–61.

301   Virginia Satir says, "When someone takes a risk": Satir and Baldwin, p. 217.
302   "Pregnancy is exciting!" cheers a line in one of my pregnancy books: Glade B. Curtis, *Your Pregnancy Week by Week*, 6th ed. (Cambridge, Mass.: Da Capo Press, 2007).
303   what Laurie Lee once called a "child of herself": Laurie Lee, *I Can't Stay Long* (London: Andre Deutsch, 1975), p. 78.
306   "The problem is 'out there' and anger is the build-up of energy needed to solve it": C. George Boeree, "General Psychology: Emotion," Psychology Department, Shippensburg University (webspace.ship.edu/cgboer/emotions.html).
307   Virginia Satir was right when she said that change is possible for everyone: Virginia Satir, John Banmen, Jane Gerber, and Maria Gomor, *The Satir Model: Family Therapy and Beyond* (Palo Alto, Calif.: Science and Behavior, 1991), p. 92.
309   It was a passage describing what change would look like: Virginia Satir, *Conjoint Family Therapy*, 3rd ed. (Palo Alto, Calif.: Science and Behavior, 1983), p. 256.
309   A changed placater, Satir had also written, "can transform her wish to please others": Satir and Baldwin, p. 201.

I can't imagine where I'd be without the loyal encouragement and unfailing wisdom of my editor, Molly Stern. Laura Tisdel's unsparing insight was invaluable, as were continued readings by my agent, Binky Urban. I owe my career as a writer to everyone Viking: Clare Ferraro; the publicity department, particularly Carolyn Coleburn, Sonya Cheuse, and Kate Lloyd; marketing; production and the art department that dreams up my books' striking covers. Thank you to John Pelosi and the rest of the legal department, as well as the copy editors and fact-checkers who authenticated four years' worth of research. Liz Van House and Kendra Harpster provided fresh perspectives that helped bring this book to completion. I'm grateful to the universities and communities that have welcomed me in the years since the publication of *Smashed*, and I'm indebted to Ken Eisenstein, Flip Porter, Beth White, and everyone at the American Program Bureau who helps make these visits possible. Thank you to Josie Freedman, Liz Farrell, and all at ICM; Web site designer Mary K. Elkins; childbirth educator Michele Reinbach; and midwife Maureen Reyson. Finally, my love goes out to everyone who lent me their help and stood by me through an emotional writing process: Mom and Dad, Tom and Nikki DiOrio, David and Joan Lehmann, the Hamilton tribe (David, Carol, Josh, Rachel, Ross, Rea, and Steve), Alyssa Fedele and the talented filmmakers at Collective Hunch, Devon Banks, Paulette Kouffman Sherman, Rolf Gates, Austin Carty, Matt/Max Heering, Brakes-BrakesBrakes (or Brakes in their native Britain), Tine Deturk, and the warmhearted village of Romainville, France.

AVAILABLE FROM PENGUIN

A *New York Times* Bestseller

Smashed

Story of a Drunken Girlhood

ISBN 978-0-14-303647-0

With one stiff sip of Southern Comfort at the age of fourteen, Koren Zailckas is initiated into the world of drinking. From then on, she will drink faithfully, fanatically. Eye-opening and utterly gripping, Zailckas's story is that of thousands of girls like her who are not alcoholics—yet—but who routinely use booze as a shortcut to courage and a stand-in for good judgment.

"Gripping. . . one of the best accounts of addiction, the college experience, or even what it means to be an average teenage girl in America." —Entertainment Weekly

PENGUIN
BOOKS